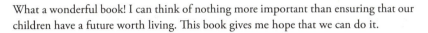
What a wonderful book! I can think of nothing more important than ensuring that our children have a future worth living. This book gives me hope that we can do it.

Dr Andrew Weil, integrative medicine pioneer, author of *Healthy Aging*

"Child Honoring, the book and the project, can bring us back to life. No initiative I know carries more galvanizing power of truth. It breaks open the heart and lets the light shine through, to ignite our deepest passions."

Joanna Macy, author of *World As Lover, World As Self*

A compelling and inspirational collection of essays on the ecology of the child and how societies can only advance by putting children and families front and centre of policy and program development. Our future depends on how we treat today's children.

Hon. Roy J. Romanow, O.C., P.C., Q.C. Senior Fellow in Public Policy, University of Saskatchewan Atkinson Economic Justice Fellow

Anyone who has ever watched a small child enraptured by Raffi knows his extraordinary power... We should listen to his ideas the way our children listen to his music.

Marianne Williamson, bestselling author of *A Return to Love*.

It is ancient wisdom to honor our parents. This book's impressive collaborators place a child in the midst of us, calling out for compassion and calling for our passionate response on behalf of the innocent. Truly to honor the child will change the world.

Paul W. Gooch, President & Professor of Philosophy, Victoria University in the University of Toronto

"Raffi Cavoukian's vision is a stunning wake-up call for all who care about the world our grandchildren will inherit...This book's exciting new approach to sustainability is an inspiration, for which we owe editors Cavoukian and Olfman great thanks."

Very Reverend Dr. Bill Phipps, Moderator of the
United Church of Canada 1997-2000.

This excellent book exposes the corporatocracy that challenges the very essence of good parenting by putting profits before children. It heralds a major shift in priorities for detoxing the womb environment and assuring that each child reaches its fullest potential as a human being.

Theo Colborn, PhD, co-author of *Our Stolen Future*,
president, The Endocrine Disruption Exchange (TEDX)

Child Honoring is a wonderful movement that calls to the hearts of all of us who see how different our world is from the one we want to give to our children. I recommend this book to parents, future parents, grandparents, and everyone who is committed to creating a world that reflects the values of the soul.

Gary Zukav, author of *The Seat of the Soul* and *The Dancing Wu Li Masters*

"'Honor your father and your mother' has become in Raffi's vision, 'honor your fathering and your mothering'. This is a serious book for conscious parenting and child-rearing that honors the souls of the young beings who come to rescue our planet. For taking responsibility for a soul, this book is an excellent guide."

Rabbi Zalman Schachter-Shalomi, author of *From Age-ing to Sage-ing*

Child Honoring provides a lens through which to view the deep interconnections between planetary sustainability and children's health in physical, emotional, intellectual and spiritual domains. As an Indigenous educator I am especially pleased to see our cultures recognized as sources of enduring, time-tested strategies for sustaining life.

Marlene Brant Castellano, Professor Emeritus of
Trent University (Indigenous Studies)

I read this and danced for joy. The writings that support the Covenant for Honoring Children illuminate its depth and clarity. This compassionate revolution reminds us why we are here, and gives us hope to "turn this world around!"

Debby Takikawa, producer/director of the film *What Babies Want*

Child Honoring offers a powerful primer for a better world. "Never in history has there been a revolution inspired by the growing child." Raffi's line in this book of eloquent moral voices sounds the revolution for our time: one to passionately embrace for activating glorious possibilities for our species and this planet.

David Loye, author of *The Healing of a Nation*,
founder of The Darwin Project and The Benjamin Franklin Press

This wonderful book articulates a vision that most humans will realize they believe in. Child Honouring calls on an instinct older than our species to protect our young! Beneath our official titles, positions and identities, we are really mothers and fathers, sisters and brothers, and each of us is somebody's child.

Severn Cullis-Suzuki, beluga grad, ecology advocate

Gandhi left us a "talisman of the last person", asking us to recall the face of the weakest and most vulnerable person we have known. In *Child Honouring,* Raffi Cavoukian and Sharna Olfman give us a "talisman of the last child" with which to reclaim our humanity. As Raffi points out, "the irreducible needs of all children can offer a unifying ethic by which the cultures of our interdependent world might reorder their priorities".

Vandana Shiva, pysicist, activist, author of *Earth Democracy and Water War*s

This great project, this extraordinary movement to honour the child, stands for our highest ambition, the work we can do, the best we can be. We must honour the child, and hold sacred the most defenseless among us. You have my full support.

Bruce Mau, designer, "Massive Change"

CHILD HONORING

How to Turn This World Around

CONTRIBUTING AUTHORS

Joan Almon, Ray Anderson, Mark Anielski, Lloyd Axworthy, Joel Bakan, Varda Burstyn, Fritjof Capra, Raffi Cavoukian, Ronald Colman, Heather Eaton, Riane Eisler, Matthew Fox, Mary Gordon, Stanley I. Greenspan, Barbara Kingsolver, David C. Korten, Philip J. Landrigan, Penelope Leach, Susan Linn, Graça Machel, Ron Miller, Sharna Olfman, Stuart G. Shanker, Sandra Steingraber, Paulo Wangoola, Lorna B. Williams

Edited by Raffi Cavoukian and Sharna Olfman

Foreword by the Dalai Lama

PRAEGER

Westport, Connecticut
London

Library of Congress Cataloging-in-Publication Data

Child honoring : how to turn this world around / edited by Raffi Cavoukian and Sharna Olfman.

  p. cm.
  Includes bibliographical references and index.
  ISBN 0–275–98981–X
  1. Children. 2. Children—Social conditions. I. Raffi. II. Olfman, Sharna.
HQ767.9.C44515 2006
305.23—dc22   2006002761

British Library Cataloguing in Publication Data is available.

Library of Congress Catalog Card Number: 2006002761
ISBN: 0–275–98981–X

First published in 2006

Praeger Publishers, 88 Post Road West, Westport, CT 06881
An imprint of Greenwood Publishing Group, Inc.
www.praeger.com

Printed in the United States of America

The paper used in this book complies with the
Permanent Paper Standard issued by the National
Information Standards Organization (Z39.48–1984).

10 9 8 7 6 5 4 3 2 1

The chlorine bleaching of pulp for paper produces toxic compounds that go into our air and water end up in human blood and breast milk. One way to reduce the output of dioxin, among the most lethal of these poisons, is to bleach paper with a process using hydrogen peroxide. Since toxic compounds most threaten the very young, we have a duty to use toxic-free manufacturing processes. As more and more pulp and paper mills and publishers turn to benign alternatives, as we work together to create the healthy world our children deserve, the costs of polluting technologies will no longer be hidden. Before long, sustainable means will become the moral standard for all our endeavors.

This book was made with recycled chlorine-free paper.
For more information, please visit www.chlorinefreeproducts.org.

To the beloved young people in my life,
to dear "Beluga grads" and their families,
to children of every nation, and the child in everyone.
And to all who are yet to come.
Raffi Cavoukian

For my dear children Adam and Gavriela
Sharna Olfman

Contents

Foreword

THE DALAI LAMA

I entirely agree with Raffi Cavoukian that children everywhere are like the seeds of the future of our world. By looking after them well, giving them a sound education, and instilling positive values in them, we will ensure a more harmonious, peaceful, and productive future for us all.

As I travel around the world, regularly seeing children's bright faces prompts the question, "How can we help them?" Often we pay attention only to providing them with or improving the physical facilities for health, education, employment, and so on. And yet, what I feel equally important is that as parents and guardians of children we should demonstrate the real worth of basic moral values such as love, compassion, and universal responsibility in our own way of life. Similarly, our schools, colleges, and other institutions have a duty to inculcate basic standards of behaviour, such as altruism and honesty, in children's minds from primary school to university level. If children are set a good example, they can be encouraged and inspired to follow it; then the hope we place in them will be well founded.

This question of a sense of values is particularly important because our lives become meaningless when we lose the values of justice and ethics. We all have an equal right to pursue happiness; no one wants pain and suffering. And yet justice and equality are uniquely human principles. We should not sacrifice these principles in the pursuit of power or material wealth. Instead, we should employ them in serving others' interests.

Everyone benefits if we put others before ourselves. I am convinced that steady efforts in this direction will bring about peace and stability in our societies. Since other people need happiness as much as we do, we should not exploit them for our selfish ends. If we try to be kind to others, we ourselves will enjoy happiness, while others benefit in turn. In the long run, this is how we can contribute to peace and security in society.

Many of the world's problems and conflicts arise because we have lost sight of the basic humanity that binds us all together as a human family. We tend to forget that despite the diversity of race, religion, ideology, and so forth, people are equal in their basic wish for peace and happiness. In this children have much to teach adults. They naturally recognize other children as being like themselves and easily befriend each other. This is a source of hope, but we must ensure that such natural good instincts are reinforced through education.

In 1959, when all was lost in Tibet and I had just arrived in India, Prime Minister Nehru assured me that the real way to serve the Tibetan cause was to give our children a proper education. Education is like a universal panacea, which is as appropriate elsewhere today as it was to the Tibetan community then.

Childhood and youth are a time of learning and training in preparation for life ahead. Although human beings are naturally intelligent, when we are young we have some freedom and flexibility of thought and action because we do not have many obligations. However, this natural freedom and intelligence will only become fruitful if they are given proper guidance and encouragement. Education is the foundation of all personal and social improvement and to make it available to others is one of the greatest gifts. To do so is truly to honour children.

December 14, 2005

Preface

SHARNA OLFMAN

In the Fall of 2004, I had the pleasure of meeting Raffi Cavoukian, the children's troubadour, through our mutual affiliation with the Council of Human Development (cochaired by Stanley Greenspan and Stuart Shanker). Known by millions of families throughout the world for his music, which speaks to the heart of childhood, Raffi is quickly gaining stature as a leading children's advocate, and as a systems thinker on the major issues that face humanity at a defining point in history. Through keen observation of and a sensitive connection to children, through his searching intellect and his evolving dialogue with educators, economists, ecologists, mental health professionals, policy makers, and spiritual leaders, Raffi has developed a new paradigm that he calls Child Honoring. It is visionary, eminently practical, and urgently needed.

In December, 2004, UNICEF released a document titled *Childhood Under Threat,* which states that the survival of more than half the world's children, numbering more than a billion, is now at risk. Twenty-nine thousand children are dying every day—mostly of preventable causes. More than three million are enmeshed in the sex trade. These statistics refer mainly to children living in third world countries. But children in wealthy nations are also suffering and record levels of mental illness, violence, and obesity provide ample testimony to our failure to meet their needs. For now, rich and poor nations differ dramatically in the ways that they fail children, but we will likely see these patterns merge in the fate of the *next* generation of children. Just prior to the 1992 Rio De Janeiro summit that led to the Kyoto Accord on climate change, half the world's Nobel laureates warned that we are on a collision course with nature, and many believe that we have only a generation in which to replenish and detoxify the earth. Meanwhile, industries continue to spew deadly toxins into our air, water, and soil. These toxins do not recognize national borders or socioeconomic status and can be found in human tissue, blood, and breastmilk halfway across the globe from their point of origin.

How do we restore our future? While many scholars and policy makers propose solutions that address the economic, political, ecological, or psychological dimensions of the problem, Raffi is offering a new approach that connects all of these, one that could turn our world into the global village we so urgently need to nurture and sustain future generations. He argues that we must make all vital decisions about ecological sustainability, the economy, national policy, and education, *through the lens of what best serves the needs of young children.* Children's exponential rate of development in the early years renders them exquisitely vulnerable to environmental influences. Their brains, bodies, and psychological integrity are easily derailed by exposure to physical or psychic trauma. Conversely, wholesome and loving environments enable children to fully actualize their human potential. An actualized person is imbued with unfettered curiosity, enthusiasm, initiative, and a growing sense of kinship with and respect for other living creatures. She is grounded in her family, her community, and connected to the natural order, and at the same time able to express herself and place her own personal stamp on the world. Her thinking is aligned with emotional and bodily experience, and infused with artistry, imagination, and soulfulness. Healthy children grow into adults who have the will, wisdom, and creativity to harness new and emerging technologies of humane and ecologically sustainable design.

Raffi's invitation to coedit *Child Honoring: How to Turn This World Around* has been a life-changing event for me. Our work together has helped me to see that the health and integrity of America's children are systemically linked to the well-being of children the world over. His vision resonates deeply with my experiences and beliefs as a developmental psychologist, clinician, and mother. Some of our finest thinkers, scholars, and policy makers contribute to this anthology, a book that is one piece of Raffi's much larger effort to launch a worldwide Child Honoring movement.

Acknowledgments

The subject of this book, Child Honoring, draws great inspiration from Nelson Mandela and the Dalai Lama, two towering figures of courage in action on the human stage. I shall always be grateful for their shining devotion to truth and compassion.

Three decades ago, Deborah Pike, a most compassionate kindergarten teacher to whom I was married, taught me the greatest lesson I've ever learned: how to "see" a young child, how to recognize the dignity of the very young. I'm very grateful to all those since who have taught me about the wondrous ways of the child, and about the child in all of us. Ongoing conversations with leaders in a number of disciplines—in children's environmental health, education, pediatrics, personal healing, quantum physics, ecology, and economics—tilled the ground from which Child Honoring emerged and emboldened me to guide its growth with confidence.

Among the early supporters of Child Honoring were Philip Landrigan, Riane Eisler, David Loye, Fran and David Korten, Fraser Mustard, Bill McDonough, Stuart Shanker, and Stanley Greenspan, to whom I wish to express gratitude for many stirring conversations. In recent years, I have had the good fortune to learn from several of this book's contributors, whose generosity both fed my imagination and comforted me. Among the many friends who have enriched my understanding of the vision, my thanks to Carol Douglas,

Theo Colborn, Bill Phipps, Carolyn Pogue, Claire Garrison, Coro Strandberg, Donna Morton, Eve Savory, Frances Picherack, Joanne Enns, Paul Ryan, Gabor Maté, Jill Swartz, Ken Dangerfield, Georgina Montgomery, Jacquie Brownridge, Nancy Fischer, Deirdre Rowland, Rinchen Dharlo, Bruce Mau, Lynn Goldman, Roger Brown, Michael Lerner, Sharyle Patton, and Susan Master. (My apologies to those whose inclusion here space does not permit.)

I wish to acknowledge my Troubadour Music colleagues Bert Simpson, Caterina Geuer, and Judi Wilson for being a constant source of ideas and support, both to me personally and to the conceptual development of the vision.

I would also like to thank members of the Child Honoring Advisory Council who helped me see the various facets of the Child Honoring crystal: Fritjof Capra, Carol Douglas, Riane Eisler, Stanley Greenspan, Budd Hall, Judith Hall, Fran Korten, David Korten, Philip Landrigan, Elise Miller, Fraser Mustard, Sharna Olfman, Rose van Rotterdam, Roslyn Kunin, Charles Pascal, Stuart Shanker, Joel Soloman, Lorna Williams; Mayne Island friends Terry Glavin, Tania Godoroja, Shanti and Don McDougall, Peter Mann, Helen and John O'Brian, Tony Pearse; my friends at the Social Venture Network, the Shad Valley program, the Business Alliance for Local Living Economies, the Positive Futures Network, the members of the Child Honoring task force at the University of Victoria; and to Victoria's Gordon Head family of schools for embracing the Covenant and Principles.

My heartfelt thanks to coeditor Sharna Olfman, whose work I highly respect, for so enthusiastically joining me on this project, and to Praeger acquisitions editor Debbie Carvalko for believing in it. (Thanks to Praeger for printing with chlorine-free paper.) Finally, my deep gratitude to the contributors of this anthology, without whom this book would not be possible.

—Raffi Cavoukian

Heartfelt thanks go to Raffi Cavoukian for inviting me to work with him on this book. This collaboration has widened my vision while at the same time resonating so fully with my own projects. It has been a great pleasure to work with Caterina Geuer, Bert Simpson, and Judi Wilson of Troubadour Music. I thank my friends and colleagues at Point Park University for their ongoing support. Deborah Carvalko, our acquisitions editor worked tirelessly on behalf of this project. My beloved children, Adam and Gavriela, and my parents, Bess and Mitchell Olfman, are my greatest source of inspiration to "turn this world around." I give special thanks to my husband, Daniel Burston, my closest friend and wisest colleague.

—Sharna Olfman

Introduction:
The Case for Child Honoring

Raffi Cavoukian

Across three decades, people and events have transformed a children's troubadour, singing life-affirming songs for the very young, into a global troubadour and advocate not only for children but also for a viable future we all might share. My new songs still celebrate life and our global family, but now my appearances are before older audiences that include college students,[1] parents, educators, economists, policy makers, and professionals from many walks of life. My work is now part of a bigger quest that seeks to answer the question: *How can we turn our troubled world around, and work toward creating a nurturing world fit for all children?* It has moved me to "sing" a new paradigm into being: a compassionate revolution I call Child Honoring.

Since the 1970s, we have witnessed a rapid shift in societal mores and in planetary health, with serious consequences for children and families. In Canada and the United States, an increasingly violent and sexualized media culture reaches younger and younger kids. Alcohol and drug use, casual sex, and bullying have become prevalent among preteens and teens, and pandemic numbers of child sexual abuse cases are a grave concern. The gap between rich and poor has widened and more families live in poverty. Alongside these worrisome trends, by the mid 1990s, books such as *Our Stolen Future*[2] and *Raising Children Toxic Free*[3] detailed the pervasive chemical contamination in the biosphere and in our bodies, as well as young children's unique vulnerability to toxic chemicals. They revealed something profound: Chemical pollution is so prevalent worldwide that every baby is now born at risk.

The unique susceptibility of infants to even the minutest doses of toxicants[4] led me to wonder in what other ways they were most vulnerable. I explored the *interrelated* factors that impact early childhood, connecting the dots between economic and environmental conditions and their effect on child health and learning: for example, between a living wage and family nutrition, between accessible child care and employment prospects for single parents, and between the way paper is bleached and the state of breast milk. Over the past decade, in consultation with a broad range of experts in diverse fields, I developed an integrated philosophy that addresses the personal, cultural, and planetary conditions that affect formative human development.

Child Honoring is a vision of hope and renewal in response to a time of unprecedented social and ecological breakdown worldwide. It is a *metaframework* for addressing the major issues of our time, and for redesigning society towards the greatest good by meeting the priority needs of the very young.

A THEFT OF FUTURES

> Losing my future is not like losing an election or a few points on the stock exchange.
> Severn Cullis-Suzuki, age 12, Earth Summit, Rio De Janeiro, 1992

For a civilization and planet in systems failure, metaphors abound: the end of empire, a new *Titanic* headed for disaster, downed canaries in a coal mine. To me, our current unsustainable state on a globe with failing life support adds up to a colossal theft, a theft of futures—the futures of our children. How have we let this happen?

"We the undersigned, senior members of the world's scientific community, hereby warn all humanity of what lies ahead. A great change in our stewardship of the earth and the life on it is required, if vast human misery is to be avoided and our global home on this planet is not to be irretrievably mutilated." That stark warning in 1992 by the Union of Concerned Scientists was formally endorsed by 1,670 distinguished senior scientists (among them 104 Nobel laureates of many disciplines) from 71 countries from China to Chile, India to Ireland, the United States to the United Kingdom. But governments and the mass media ignored it.[5]

Despite the technological gains in the 50-plus years since I was a boy (space missions, instant communication, nanotechnology), our lives are still haunted by the demon of nuclear weapons and a hideous global arms trade. True, we've made tremendous advances in medicine, engineering, and science, and in life expectancy. Car engines start reliably. We have all sorts of material comforts. We're finally generating solar, wind, and hydrogen power. We can see sharp close-up images of the landscape on Mars. And yet, in the human mission to make peace on Earth, to care for the less fortunate, and in our stewardship of the planet, we're losing ground.[6]

Rachel Carson's *Silent Spring*, published in 1962, was hailed as a brilliant wake-up call. But by 1990, mass demonstrations that put Earth on the cover of *Time Magazine* (Planet of the Year) failed to produce substantive change in business, the engine that drives society. Sustainable development, a key phrase at the 1992 Earth Summit, has not lived up to its promise. In *Earth in the Balance*, Senator Al Gore (before he became Vice-President), urged a green "Marshall Plan" for Earth's revival; but *ecology-as-central-organizing-principle* wasn't heard of again.

The birth of a responsible commerce movement and the growth of ethical investment funds has not yet shaken business-as-usual. With corporate globalization we have witnessed the accumulation of money and markets at all cost. The 1990s, a period of record corporate profits, saw massive job losses coupled with a greater-than-ever income gap between rich and poor. With communism's demise, capitalism's triumph turned global commerce into a 24/7 gold rush. For all the admirable work of so-called civil society (tens of thousands of nongovernmental organizations [NGOs] worldwide), no countervailing idea has emerged to slow the worldwide shopping frenzy.

Since the grassroots uprising during the World Trade Organization's 1999 meeting in Seattle, millions have marched worldwide to protest the global money cartel and the financial organizations (such as the International Monetary Fund and World Bank) whose loans and programs often hurt the countries they're supposed to help. This response to globalization's excesses is one sign that a tipping point may be near.[7] E.O. Wilson, one of the world's most respected and influential scientists, likened the antiglobalization outcry to the Earth's immune system rising up to expel a disease. "The protest groups are the world's early warning system for the natural economy. They are the living world's immunological response."[8]

Among progressives, some anticipate a global economic collapse; they doubt that anything less will precipitate systemic change. Many, however, are forming "local living economies" to proactively grow networks of local entrepreneurs whose goods and services both build community and offer a safety net in case of international supply and distribution shortages.[9]

The onset of global warming brings the end of the fossil fuel era, and with it the need for a quick turn to clean energies to avert unimaginable hardships. Fortunately, there is an infinitely renewable energy within each one of us: In the pulse of the human heart, in the boundless love we feel for our children and grandchildren, there is a tremendous power that, when tapped, can turn this world around.

THE CHILD HONORING LENS

> We are conducting a vast toxicological experiment in which the research animals are our children.
> —Dr. Philip Landrigan, professor of pediatrics, Mount Sinai School of
> Medicine, New York

> The feeling appropriate to an infant in arms is his feeling of rightness, or essential goodness . . . that he is right, good and welcome in the world.
> —Jean Liedloff, *The Continuum Concept*

Across all cultures, we find an essential humanity that is most visible in early childhood—a playful, intelligent, and creative way of being. Early experience lasts a lifetime. It shapes our sense of self and how we see others; it also shapes our sense of what's possible, our emerging view of the world. The impressionable early years are the most vulnerable to family dynamics, cultural values, and planetary conditions. At this critical point in the history of humankind, *the irreducible needs of all children can offer a unifying ethic by which the cultures of our interdependent world might reorder their priorities.*

Child Honoring is a vision, an organizing principle, and a way of life— a revolution in values that calls for a profound redesign of every sphere of society. It starts with three givens: first, the primacy of the early years—early childhood is the gateway to humane being. Second, we face planetary degradation unprecedented in scope and scale, a state of emergency that requires a remedy of equal scale, and that most endangers the very young. And third, the crisis calls for a *systemic* response in detoxifying the environments that make up the ecology of the child. This is a "children first" approach to healing communities and restoring ecosystems; it views how we regard and treat our young as the key to building a humane and sustainable world. (It's not about a child-centered society where children rule, nor a facile notion of children being all things nice, and it has nothing to do with permissive parenting; none of these is desirable.) Child Honoring is a global credo for maximizing joy and reducing suffering by respecting the goodness of every human being at the beginning of life, with benefits rippling in all directions.

It's a novel idea—organizing society around the needs of its youngest members. Just as startling is the finding of neuroscience that a lifetime of behaviors is significantly shaped by the age of four, and that, developmentally speaking, the preschool years are more important than the school years. (Although people can and do change throughout their lives, it's much harder to alter the core emotional patterns of one's earliest years. What's more, a strong positive foundation at the start of life can help mitigate the wounding of later trauma.) In the words of Stanley Greenspan and Stuart Shanker, founders of the Council of Human Development,[10] "Early childhood is the most important time in a human being's development."

What does it mean to honor children? It means seeing them for the creatively intelligent people they are, respecting their personhood as their own, recognizing them as essential members of the community, and providing the fundamental nurturance they need in order to flourish. As formative growth is simultaneously affected by the personal, cultural, and planetary domains, sustainability strategies must take all three into account.

Children are not a partisan concern, and Child Honoring is not pitted against person or ideology. Its allegiance is to the children and their families. It speaks emphatically for the birthright of the young of every culture to love, dignity, and security. At the same time, it encompasses the whole of life; first years' benefits trickle upward and enrich later years. It takes people of all ages to cocreate humane societies. The focus on early life simply underscores a key developmental tenet. In fully honoring children, we would honor the lifelong web of relations that brings them forth and sustains them.

Child Honoring involves honoring all life, and ultimately means living in reverence with the mystery of creation. In our quantum universe where everything is interrelated, the child is a "holon," something that is both "whole," and a part of something bigger. Just as in quantum physics *observation affects outcome,* so too in human relations, with respect to the very young, *regard shapes development.* How we regard a child is the vital mirror with which that child's innate potential comes alive.

Children who feel seen, loved, and honored are far more able to become loving parents and productive citizens. Children who do not feel valued are disproportionately represented on welfare rolls and police records. Much of the criminal justice system deals with the results of childhood wounding (the vast majority of sexual offenders, for example, were themselves violated as children), and much of the social service sector represents an attempt to rectify or moderate this damage, which comes at an enormous cost to society. Most of the correctional work is too little, too late.

Child Honoring is a corrective lens that, once we look through it, allows us to question everything from the way we measure economic progress to our stewardship of the planet; from our physical treatment of children to the corporate impact on their minds and bodies; from rampant consumerism to factory schooling. It offers a proactive *developmental* approach to creating sustainable societies. As a creed that crosses all faiths and cultures, Child Honoring can become a potent remedy for the most challenging issues of our time.

At stake for our species is nothing less than the right to be human, the right to *remain* human in the magical world that gives us life—before it's too late.

Babies today carry toxic chemicals barely known 50 years ago, born into a degraded biosphere. That's the extent to which business-as-usual has failed children, both worldwide and here at home. It has endangered their well-being and undermined family life, as Sharna Olfman's book *Childhood Lost* dramatically reveals. The moral imperative is to undo the damage wherever possible, to take action to restore children's diminished futures.

Urgently we need to create a culture of deep compassion, one in which the primacy of the early years guides public policy, the admired life blends material sufficiency with more noble aims, and our children learn to become responsible global citizens. A culture in which corporate ingenuity is redirected to profit all shareholders of the planet, and in which our economy (as a subset of nature) becomes a means to this end, not an end in itself. A culture in which "the good life" speaks not to purchasing power but to the quality of our existence—our relationships with one another, between cultures, and with Nature. A culture that puts self-confidence ahead of consumer confidence, and affirms developmental health as the true wealth of nations.

But how do we get there? Eminent thinkers such as Lester Brown, Maurice Strong, Hazel Henderson, Vandana Shiva, Amory Lovins, and others (including many contributors to this volume) have written important books on a range of economic, cultural, and environmental breakthroughs that, in my view, are practical and much needed. But I want to stress that effective strategic planning must embrace—as a priority—the universal needs of the very young. Their well-being will comprise the true test of all our efforts.

COVENANT AND PRINCIPLES

One morning in late 1996, the phrase "Child Honoring" woke me up from a sound sleep. In that pivotal moment, I realized that all my years of singing and talking with young children, learning all I could about child development—and then of watching, with growing alarm, the disintegration of communities and the deterioration of our planet—had been a preparation of sorts, a way of showing me the link between the state of the world and the health of its children. I knew I had to speak out in a new way on behalf of the world's young. This sparked a dialogue with people in a wide range of disciplines.

On New Year's Eve, 1998, on the University of Virginia campus, an important part of the Child Honoring vision emerged. I'd been visiting with Bill McDonough, then dean of architecture, who began his sustainable-design course each year with the question, "How do we love all the children?" Bill spoke of the importance of not imposing "remote tyranny" on children to come, of society's current activities not compromising their future lives. (This was the same message I'd heard 12-year-old Severn Cullis-Suzuki deliver in 1992 at the Earth Summit in Rio de Janeiro.) Later that night, I pulled a copy of the Declaration of Independence from a bookcase and began reading. In those pages, there was no mention of children. I wondered what a similar emancipatory proclamation about them might say, and began writing what became "A Covenant for Honoring Children"—a declaration of duty to this and future generations.

An early supporter of the covenant was Dr. Philip Landrigan, a pediatrician and director of the Center for Children's Health and the Environment, who invited me to speak at the New York Academy of Medicine. After a day of scientific and medical presentations, my talk "Child Honoring: The Loving Challenge" was greeted with a rousing ovation. Encouraged, I accepted invitations to speak at Parliament Hill in Ottawa and at a number of conferences, including the World Bank's "Investing in Our Children's Future." At Harvard, I spoke of Child Honoring as the next *ecological* paradigm, stressing its integrated nature as expressed in the following piece I began writing in Virginia:

A COVENANT FOR HONORING CHILDREN

We find these joys to be self-evident:
That all children are created whole, endowed with innate
intelligence, with dignity and wonder, worthy of respect.

The embodiment of life, liberty and happiness,
children are original blessings, here to learn their own song.
Every girl and boy is entitled to love, to dream, and to
belong to a loving "village." And to pursue a life of purpose.

We affirm our duty to nourish and nurture the young,
to honor their caring ideals as the heart of being human.
To recognize the early years as the foundation of life, and to
cherish the contribution of young children to human evolution.

We commit ourselves to peaceful ways and vow to keep
from harm or neglect these, our most vulnerable citizens.
As guardians of their prosperity we honor
the bountiful Earth whose diversity sustains us.
Thus we pledge our love for generations to come.

The following Child Honoring principles elaborate the essential themes
of the covenant, and suggest a way to embrace the young of every culture as
treasure and inspiration. Taken together, they offer a holistic way of reversing
the deterioration of natural and human communities, and thus brightening
the outlook for our children and the world we share. They also form a basis
for a multifaith consensus for societal renewal based on the universal and
irreducible needs of the very young.

Respectful Love is key. It speaks to the need to respect children as whole
people and to encourage them to know their own voices. Children need the
kind of love that sees them as legitimate beings, persons in their own right.
Respectful love fosters self-worth—it's the prime nutrient in human development. Children need this not only from parents and caregivers, but also from
the whole community.

Diversity is about abundance: of human dreams, intelligences, cultures,
and cosmologies; of earthly splendors and ecosystems. Introducing children
to biodiversity and human diversity at an early age builds on their innate
curiosity. Not only is there a world of natural wonders to discover, but also a
wealth of cultures, of ways to be human. Comforted by how much we share,
we're able to delight in our differences.

Caring Community refers to the "village" it takes to raise a child. The community can positively affect the lives of its children. Child-friendly shopkeepers, family resource centers, green schoolyards, bicycle lanes, and pesticide-free
parks are some of the ways a community can support its young.

Conscious Parenting can be taught from an early age; it begins with empathy for newborns. Elementary and secondary school curricula could teach
nurturant parenting (neither permissive nor oppressive) and provide students
with insight into the child-rearing process. Such knowledge helps to deter
teen pregnancies and unwanted children. Emotionally aware parents are
much less likely to perpetuate abuse or neglect.

Emotional Intelligence sums up what early life is about: a time for exploring emotions in a safe setting, learning about feelings and how to express them. Those who feel loved are most able to learn and most likely to show compassion for others. Emotional intelligence builds character and is more important to later success than IQ. Cooperation, play, and creativity all foster the "EQ" needed for a joyful life.

Nonviolence is central to emotional maturity, to family relations, to community values, and to the character of societies that aspire to live in peace. It means more than the absence of aggression; it means living with compassion. Regarding children, it means no corporal punishment, no humiliation, no coercion. "First do no harm," the physicians' oath, can apply to all our relations—it can become a mantra for our times. A culture of peace begins in a nonviolent heart and a loving home.

Safe Environments foster a child's feeling of security and belonging. The very young need protection from the toxic influences that permeate modern life—from domestic neglect and maltreatment to the corporate manipulations of their minds and the poisonous chemicals gaining access to their bodies. The first years are when children are most impressionable and vulnerable; they need safeguarding.

Sustainability means living in a way that does not compromise the lives of future generations. It refers not merely to conservation of resources, renewable energy development, and antipollution laws. To be sustainable, societies need to build social capacity by tapping the productive power of a contented heart. The loving potential of every young child is a potent source for good.

Ethical Commerce is fundamental to a humane world. It requires a revolution in the design, manufacture and sale of goods, supported by corporate reforms, "triple bottom line" business, full-cost accounting, tax and subsidy shifts, and political and economic cycles that reward long-term thinking. A child-honoring protocol for commerce would enable a restorative economy devoted to the well-being of the very young.

The contributors to *Child Honoring: How to Turn This World Around* include leading thinkers in the fields of psychology, education, economics, business, governance, and religion. Together, they show how the universal human symbol and reality—the child—can inspire a peacemaking culture for our world.

Part I

Universal Needs:
Keys to the Garden

Section I A

Personal Child:
Primacy of
the Early Years

Chapter 1

The Emotional Architecture of the Mind[1]

STANLEY I. GREENSPAN AND
STUART G. SHANKER
WITH BERYL I. BENDERLY

In recent years, through our research and that of others, we have found unexpected common origins for the mind's highest capacities: intelligence, morality, and sense of self. We have charted critical stages in the mind's early growth, most of which occur even before our first thoughts are registered. At each stage certain critical experiences are necessary. Contrary to traditional notions, however, these experiences are not intellectual, but rather, subtle emotional exchanges. In fact *emotional rather than intellectual interaction serves as the mind's primary architect.*

While charting these earliest stages in the growth of the mind, we have been confronted with mounting evidence that such growth is becoming seriously endangered by modern institutions and social patterns. There exists a growing disregard for the importance of mind-building emotional experiences in almost every aspect of daily life including child care, education, and family life, and extending to how we communicate, govern, and build international cooperation. Ironically, the very mind that created a complex society is now that same society's potential victim.

The elevation of the intellectual over the emotional aspect of our minds has deep-seated origins. Ever since the ancient Greeks, philosophers have elevated the rational side of the mind above the emotional and seen the two as separate. Intelligence, in this view, is necessary to govern and restrain the base passions. This concept has been profoundly influential in Western thought; indeed, it has shaped some of our most basic institutions and beliefs. Because of this dichotomy, our culture has an immense, long-standing intellectual and institutional investment in the notion that reason and emotion are separate and irreconcilable and that, in a civilized society, rationality must prevail. But are these long-held assumptions correct? Striking new results from a variety of disciplines—from research into infant development, neuroscience, and clinical work with infants, children, and adults—are revealing the limitations of these traditional beliefs.

Unfortunately though, the perennial dichotomy between emotions and intelligence persists because, until recently, there has been little inquiry into the way emotions and intelligence actually interact during early development. Historically, emotions have been viewed in a number of ways: as outlets for extreme passion, as physiological reactions, as subjective states of feeling, as interpersonal social cues.[2] Our developmental observations suggest, however, that perhaps the most critical role for emotions is to create, organize, and orchestrate many of the mind's most important functions.[3] In fact, intellect, academic abilities, sense of self, consciousness, and morality have common origins in our earliest and ongoing emotional experiences. The emotions are, in fact, the architects of a vast array of intellectual operations throughout the life span. Indeed, *emotions make possible all creative thought.*

Support for the link between emotions and intellect comes from a number of sources including neurological research, which has found that early experiences influence the very structure of the brain itself.[4] The importance of emotional experience for high-level intellectual and social capacities is supported by studies showing that areas of the brain having to do with emotional regulation, interaction, and sequencing (the prefrontal cortex) show increased metabolic activity during the second half of the first year of life—at a peak time in the formation of attachments with their caregivers and in their demonstration of increased intellectual ability as evidenced by their ability to solve simple problems and to search for hidden objects.[5] In general, during the formative years, there is a sensitive interaction between genetic proclivities and environmental experience. Experience appears to adapt the infant's biology to his or her environment.[6] In this process, however, not all experiences are the same. Children seem to require certain types of emotional interactions geared to their particular developmental needs.

Such research leads to the question of what types of early experience are most helpful to the child's growing intellect. Should a toddler's growing memory, for example, be met with flash cards showing pictures and words, or natural interactions that include words and imaginative play? Should young children be taught geometry as soon as they can appreciate spatial relationships, before they have the capacity for complex causal thinking?[7] As we will see, such precocious activities are not the foundations of true learning. Our research points towards a new understanding of how the mind develops in the earliest stages of life, one that integrates the child's experience of emotional interactions with the growth of intellectual capacities and, indeed, the very sense of self. The following pages explore this developmental perspective and its implications for how we bring up our children, function as adults, and participate in our society.

THE DUAL CODING OF EMOTIONS AND PERCEPTIONS

A baby begins the lifelong task of learning about the world through the materials at hand, which at this stage of life are the simplest of sensations, such as touch and sound. How babies learn to attend to, discriminate among, and comprehend these sensations has been well known for many years. Infants' increasingly complex emotions are also well described in other studies. Relatively ignored in these investigations of initial perceptions and cognition, on the one hand, and emotional development on the other is a seemingly obvious observation whose importance cannot be underestimated. In the normal course of events, each sensation, as it is registered by the child, also gives rise to an emotion.[8] That is to say, the infant responds to it in terms of its emotional as well as physical effect on him. Thus a blanket might feel smooth *and* pleasant or itchy *and* irritating; a toy might be brilliantly red *and* intriguing or boring, a voice loud *and* inviting or jarring. Mom's cheek might feel soft and wonderful or rough and uncomfortable. The child might feel secure when Mom gives a hug, or frightened if she jerks away. As a baby's experience grows, sensory impressions become increasingly tied to feelings. It is this *dual coding* of experience that is the key to understanding how emotions organize intellectual capacities and indeed create the sense of self.

Human beings start to couple sensations and feelings at the very beginning of life. Even infants only days old react to experiences emotionally, preferring the sound or smell of Mother, for example, to all other voices or scents. They suck more vigorously when offered sweet liquids that taste good. Somewhat older babies will joyfully pursue certain favorite people and avoid others. By four months of age children can react to the sight or voice of a particular person with fear.

The first sensory experiences an infant has occurs within the context of relationships that give them additional emotional meaning. Whether positive or negative, nearly all of children's early emotions involve the persons on whom they depend so completely for their very survival, and who discharge their responsibilities in a manner that can range from all-encompassing nurturing to near-total neglect. Having a bottle might mean the bliss of love and satiation with a warm, generous mother or hunger, frustration, and fear with a peremptory attendant who snatches the nipple away on schedule. Playing with Mother's hair may occasion giggles or an angry scolding.

As infants grow and further explore their world, emotions help them comprehend even what appear to be physical and mathematical relationships. Simple notions like *hot* or *cold,* for example, may appear to represent purely physical sensations, but a child learns "too hot," "too cold" and "just right" through pleasant or painful baths, chilly or comforting bottles, too much or too little clothing—in other words, through sensations coded with the child's emotional responses. Rather more complex perceptions like *big* or *little, more* or *less, here* or *there* have a similar foundation. "A lot" is a bit more than makes a child happy. "Too little" is less than expected. "More" is another dose of pleasure or, sometimes, of discomfort. "Near" is being snuggled next to Mother in bed. "Later" means a frustrating stretch of waiting.

Abstract, apparently self-contained concepts, even those forming the basis of the most theoretical scientific speculations, also reflect at bottom a child's felt experience. Mathematicians and physicists may manipulate abstruse symbols representing space, time, and quantity, but they first understood these entities as tiny children toddling toward a toy in the far corner of the playroom, or waiting for Mother to fill the juice cup, or figuring how many cookies they could eat before their tummies hurt. Einstein and other thinkers such as Schrodinger came by their most penetrating insights through "thought experiments." The grown-up genius, like the adventurous child, continues to take imaginary rides on intergalactic elevators or beams of light or capsules hurtling through space. Ideas are formed through playful explorations in the imagination, and only later translated into the rigor of mathematics.

Although time and space eventually take on objective parameters, the emotional component persists. For a physicist used to measuring nanoseconds with precision, half a minute on hold on the telephone might feel like half an hour. A topology professor late for a plane and lugging a heavy suitcase might see a flight of stairs as a slope steeper than a mountain. For these sophisticated thinkers, as for an infant wriggling toward a toy far out of reach or a toddler enduring the minutes until Mother gets home, a few yards or a few minutes can reflect felt emotional experience.

Indeed, before a child can count, she must possess this kind of emotional grasp of extension and duration. She must be able to express, perhaps with gestures before she can do so with words, whether an object is far away or a snack is coming soon. Numbers eventually objectify the "feel" of quantity, giving it logical parameters. For a child without an intuitive sense of *few* (somewhat less than she wants) or of *many* (lots more than she can hold), no matter how precisely she might be able to recite their names, numbers can have no real meaning, and operations like addition and subtraction cannot describe realities in her world. Working with children facing a variety of challenges who could nonetheless count and even calculate, we found that numbers and computations lacked significance for them unless we created an emotional experience of quantity by, for example, arguing with them about how many pennies or candies or raisins they should receive—in other words, by engaging their interest.

Each sensory perception therefore forms part of a dual code. We label it both by its physical properties (bright, big, loud, smooth, and the like) and by the emotional qualities we connect with it (we might experience it as soothing or jarring, or it might make us feel happy or tense). This double coding allows the child to "cross-reference" each memory or experience in a mental catalogue of phenomena and feelings and to reconstruct it when needed. Filed under both "eating" and "feeling close with Mother," for instance, each feeding eventually joins with other experiences to build up a rich and detailed but inherently subjective description of a child's emotional and sensory worlds. Emotional organization of experience, as we will see, by helping to establish meaning and relevance, supports the development of logic.

But how can a handful of emotions organize so vast a store of information as is housed in the human brain? To fine-tune our selections, we modulate our emotions to register an almost infinite range of subtle variations and combinations of sadness, joy, curiosity, anger, fear, jealousy, anticipation, and regret. We possess an extraordinarily sensitive "meter" on which to gauge our reactions, and in a certain sense it almost possesses us. Anyone who pays attention to the subjective state of his body will almost always perceive within it an emotional tone, thought it may be elusive or hard to describe. One might feel tense or relaxed, hopeful or fatigued, serene or demoralized. This inner emotional tone constantly reconstitutes itself in the innumerable variations that we use to label and organize and store and retrieve and, most important of all, make sense of our experience.

Our entire bodies are involved. Our emotions are created and brought to life through the expressions and gestures we make with the voluntary muscle systems of our faces, arms, and legs—smiles, frowns, slumps, waves, and so forth. The involuntary muscles of our guts and internal organs also play a role; our hearts might thump or our stomachs register the "butterfly" sensation of anxiety. Emotions like excitement, delight, and anger are primarily controlled by the voluntary system. Others, including fear, sexual pleasure, longing, and grief, are mostly involuntary. Some responses, like the intense fight-or-flight alertness stimulated by adrenaline, affect us more globally and belong to portions of the nervous system formed early in evolution. Those involved in social reciprocity, the ones that signal reactions and that negotiate acceptance, rejection, approval, annoyance, and the like, belong to more recently evolved parts of the nervous system and rely on the highest capacities of the cortex.

Emotions and Judgment: Learning to Discriminate and Generalize

This explanation of how emotions organize experience and ultimately thinking solves one of the enigmas that has mystified modern psychology: How does a child know when to take a behavior or skill or fact or idea learned in one situation and apply it in another? How, in other words, does she figure out how and when to generalize? How does she discriminate among situations—at home, church, school, Grandma's house—and select particular behavior—laughing loudly, sitting quietly—for the appropriate situation? How, in short, does she learn to perceive relevance and context?

The key to the puzzle lies in the fact that emotion organizes experience and behavior. Consider, for example, how a child learns when to say hello. This seemingly trivial skill is based on the mastery of subtle, complex cues. A youngster must learn to use the greeting only with those for whom it is appropriate. Teaching him some general principle, such as "Greet everyone who lives within three blocks of our house," won't work; he can't stop to ask people their addresses. Nor will "Greet everyone you see" suffice; he might give a warm smile to a would-be thief or kidnapper. Nor can we count on "Greet only our friends and members of our family"; there are many old chums and distant relatives he hasn't met. Even if he could learn a set of rote rules, by the time he decided whether to say hello, the person would be gone.

Instead, through countless encounters in his early years, the child works out the problem for himself. As he goes about his daily life, he eventually comes to associate saying hello with a particular emotion—the warmth of seeing someone he or his family knows. That friendly feeling, he learns, calls for the most basic unit of social discourse, a smile and greeting. Having learned through experience what is actually a very abstract principle, "Say hello when you feel friendly toward someone," he can apply it appropriately wherever he goes. Strangers don't rate a hello because he doesn't feel friendly toward them; they don't fit the emotional context. Neither do people—even kith and kin—who make him worried, cautious, or uncomfortable. Such folk instead get downcast eyes, a quizzical face, or scrutiny from behind Mommy's or Daddy's legs. But for the rest of his life, whenever the child feels friendly in an unfamiliar situation, he will recognize the familiar emotional context and say or communicate something like "hello."

A child discriminates not by learning conscious or unconscious rules or examples but by carrying his own set of emotional cues from situation to situation. Whenever this "discrimination meter" composed of past emotional cues confronts new circumstances that reproduce a familiar feeling, the child will tend to produce the relevant behavior. Without this highly accurate meter, however, reacting appropriately becomes difficult.

Thus our ability to discriminate and generalize stems from the fact that we carry inside us as we go from one situation to another the emotions that automatically tell us what to say, do, and even think. Long before a baby can speak much, even before she reaches 18 months of age, she has already developed this capacity to size up a new acquaintance as friendly or threatening, respectful or humiliating, supportive or undermining, so that she can behave accordingly. Before she has words to describe her reaction or can even think consciously, for that matter, this ability to discriminate emotionally begins to operate a "sixth sense," allowing her to negotiate social situations.

At any level higher than the most concrete, thinking involves the ability to form abstract concepts. The question of how this ability arises has long challenged educators, psychologists, and child development specialists. We know how to promote memory and how to teach counting. But how do you teach someone to be more abstract, to progress beyond concrete ways of thinking? Must we depend on the child's learning abstract thinking on her own? If she can't, must we assume that it is a fixed limitation? Viewing intellect as based on emotion gives a new perspective on the process of learning to abstract. From this novel vantage point, we have the ability to fuse various emotional experiences into a single, integrated concept.

The abstract concept represented by a word like *love,* for example, begins to be formed not from any dictionary definition but, literally, in the heart.

A baby may well first know it as hugs and kisses and a readily accessible nipple. Over the next few years, she learns that it also has to do with admiration, security, pride, forgiveness, and the ability to recover from anger and retain a sense of security. The concept soon widens to include aspects of companionship, a variety of pleasures, and the demands of loyalty. The child learns that disappointment and dissension don't seem to destroy it. In adolescence, sexual longing is added to the mix, along with jealousy, perhaps, and pride. In adulthood the concept broadens further to encompass a sense of commitment and the willingness to work hard to sustain family life. As our emotional experience and the richness and reach of the loves we can feel continue to grow, so does our understanding of love. Where once it was an undifferentiated sense of well-being, it can unfold into a wide spectrum of loves—brotherly, erotic, filial, maternal, altruistic. It encompasses the devotion of a long-married couple, the inseparability of army buddies, the intimacy of best friends, the ecstasy of romance, the poignancy of posthumous memory, the awe and reverence a believer feels toward God. The concept of love can thus become very complex and abstract as we incorporate into it many challenges in many contexts: fulfilling our responsibilities, seeking our happiness, coping with loss and disappointment, coming to terms with other people's vulnerability and fallibility. To the concrete thinker, love is hugs and kisses and happiness. To the abstract thinker, it is far less simple, a many-layered formulation acquired gradually from life's experiences.

Concepts like *justice* and *mercy,* though seemingly more abstract still, also prove to have similarly emotional foundations. How do we come to an understanding of what is fair, what is just, what constitutes suitable retribution and atonement? How do we measure a person's guilt or decide what sort of punishment he merits? Once again, we refer to notions that we have formed through specific emotional experiences.

A child may think justice is hitting back the child who hit him or taking away the toy he grabbed. Through years of fights in the schoolyard, struggles on the playing field, temptations to cheat on tests, promises to shield a friend who has shoplifted or to exact vengeance for a slight, he eventually develops a far more complex picture of what it means to be fair. But always, no matter how long he lives, no matter how learned a philosopher or legal scholar he may become, that sense remains grounded in felt, lived experience of justice and injustice. Only the abstraction of lived experience provides the basis for reasoning at this level. As we saw with the concept of love, an abstract notion of justice differs from a concrete one in that it integrates the essence of disparate and even competing experiences of just behavior into a body of principles that will stand up to logical analysis. The ability to scrutinize emotionally created ideas and organize them logically is related to the maturation of the brain and central nervous system but also to the accumulation of experiences that challenge and give form to this biological potential.

Many of the experiences that help shape logical capacities are at least in part emotional in nature. It begins with a child's first insight that "My smile leads to Mommy's smile" and continues with the recognition that reaching up results in getting picked up, or saying "I'm mad" makes Mom look sad. Before the child can understand the difference between fantasy and reality, she must experience her own intentions or wishes having an effect on others. It is the emotional bridge between her wish, intent, or emotion and another's response that establishes the foundation for logic and reasoning. Thus both the creative, generative aspects of thinking and the logical, analytical aspects derive in part from emotional experience. The most highly intellectual endeavors combine generative and analytical thinking. They are the product of our accumulated wisdom, our level of understanding based on our ability to abstract from lived emotional experience.

A FULLY HUMAN MIND

The concept of emotional experience as the foundation of intelligence offers a better understanding of human nature and relationships. Though this runs counter to the prevailing view of the human being as a conglomeration of rationally based skill and capacities on the one hand and emotions on the other—a view that pervades our culture and social institutions—it also suggests new avenues for dealing with such issues as child care, education, conflict resolution, family disintegration, and violence.

The work of computer scientists to synthesize intelligence illustrates especially pointedly the limitations of a view that separates cognition and emotion. To be sure, researchers trying to replicate human thought have had many successes and raised challenging questions. They have postulated different types of perceptions and different kinds of consciousness. They have constructed neural loops equipped with feedback circuits in imitation of those in the brain. But though they have programmed computers to exceed humans by far in rote calculations and other tasks, they have not succeeded in making computers that can arrive at the complex perceptions and thoughtful judgments that human beings, even small children, do with apparent effortlessness.

Proponents of the computer's ultimate ability to rival the human mind claim that inadequate capacity alone explains the failing of technology to replicate human consciousness to date. But they do not generally consider the most fundamental limitation of artificial intelligence: the computer's inability to experience emotion, and thus to use it to organize and give meaning to sensation, which remains simply inputs of data. No matter how sophisticated the technology may become, it is unlikely that a machine will ever acquire the "emotional software" possessed by a small child. Even a pet dog, despite the fact that its nervous system is in some respects quite different from our own, can respond in a more "human" manner than the most brilliantly designed computer because it does experience emotions and, to the limits of its ability, can learn from what it feels. No computer is likely ever to have anything like the uniquely human "operating system" composed of feelings and reactions that would enable it to "think" like a person. The basic element of thinking—the true heart of the creativity central to human life—requires lived experience, which is sensation filtered by an emotional structure that allows us to understand both what comes through the senses and what we feel and think about it as well as what we might do about it.

This realization compels us to reconsider our social priorities. *If our society were truly to appreciate the significance of children's emotional ties throughout the first years of life, it would no longer tolerate children growing up, or parents having to struggle, in situations that cannot possibly nourish healthy growth.* Mastering our current social challenges requires that we discard older views that divide the mind into distinct segments, that see intellect and emotion as separate, even contradictory, elements. These out-dated distinctions have too long permitted us to ignore every child's need for a stable, loving setting in the early years, the very environment that well-functioning nuclear and extended families seem tailor-made to provide. The fundamental capacities of mind that develop in the enveloping intimacy of the child's first home are maintained, reinforced, and brought to full fruition through similarly compelling emotional exchanges that are, ideally, repeated in other places and with other persons throughout the developmental stages. Emotion shapes not only human intelligence but also an individual's psychological defenses and coping strategies—indeed, the entire structure of personality.

We can no longer afford to ignore the emotional origins of intelligence. The common origins of emotions and intellect demand a concept of intelligence that integrates those mental processes that have been traditionally described as cognitive and those qualities that have been described as emotional, including the sense of self or the ego, the awareness of reality, conscience, the capacity for reflection, and the like. The mind's most important faculties are rooted in emotional experiences from very early in life—before even the earliest awareness of symbols, conscious or unconscious.

If early emotional experience is the basis of our intellectual capacities as well as of our moral sense and creativity, we must give it higher priority in our personal, community, and national planning. The challenges that face us—ecological, economic, and military—require collective action. Such challenges require the development of our individual minds and the opportunity for each and all of us to attain full humanity.

Attention to emotional experience is then not purely a humanitarian or aesthetic activity, but one that is crucial to human survival. Putting the care of children, relationships, and the quality of emotional experience first in families, education, and the institutions of social welfare is, I believe, our human imperative. Cultures that regard parenthood not as a private concern and a distraction from work but as the most challenging, rewarding, and most socially useful task any adult could undertake would encourage and support far greater parental involvement than many of today's children now experience. For the long-term good of each child, and of society as a whole, the demanding project of raising a member of the next generation of adults needs recognition not merely as a family's privately chosen responsibility but as work done for our common benefit. Creative, contributing, compassionate citizens have always been our nation's most vital resource. Those who labor to produce them need recognition and support.

If the split between, on the one hand, subjective, spiritual, and emotional, and on the other, objective, rational, and materialistic conceptions of human nature continues to divide us as it has long done in Western thought, we may continue on our present course. We may look to mechanistic and materialistic solutions, such as tougher social policies and more prisons, instead of attempting to meet emotional needs in a framework of appropriate structures and discipline. From the view that emotional experience constitutes the foundation of the human mind and that providing it positively is the essence of the demanding but infinitely valuable task of raising children, it follows that child rearing and family life deserve the highest priority among the many conflicting demands made on individuals, and in society.

Chapter 2

Starting off Right

PENELOPE LEACH

Different parents in different families, in different communities in different cultures, rear children in different ways and children can flourish or fail to do so within any of them. The human genome provides initial flexibility because evolutionary success depends on our ability to adapt to unforeseeable diversity. And yet, in spite of our species' extraordinary capacity to adapt to a wide range of physical and cultural conditions, human children share universal needs that must be met to ensure their survival and optimal development. And the most important of these is a relationship with at least one loving and consistently available parent (or caregiver). But if parents are to have the physical and emotional resources to foster secure and responsive bonds with their young, they in turn need ongoing support from their extended families and communities. The pages that follow highlight the power and importance of our very first relationships, and parents' equally compelling need for both practical and emotional support.

THE UNIVERSAL NEED FOR ATTACHMENT

Every baby needs at least one special person to attach himself to. It is through this first love relationship that he will learn about himself, other people, and the world. It is through it that he will experience emotions and learn to recognize and cope with them. And it is through this baby-love that he will become capable of more grown-up kinds of love; capable, one far-distant day, of giving children of his own the kind of devotion he now needs for himself.

The idea that early relationship experiences have both immediate and long-term effects on developing children is not new. Attachment theory, developed by the British psychiatrist and psychoanalyst John Bowlby[1] in the decade after the Second World War, has provided a framework for studies, led by psychologist Mary Ainsworth,[2] which have demonstrated that certain patterns of attachment relationships during babyhood are associated with characteristic processes of emotional regulation and social relatedness throughout life.

Because attachments between caregivers and infants are critical for survival and have an enduring impact on psychological well-being, nature has not left their formation entirely to chance. Babies are born predisposed to seek out engagement with other humans, and in turn to be engaging to them. It is not by chance but by design that babies are born with soft skin, round faces, a natural desire to seek out contact comfort, and cries that tug at our heartstrings.

From birth, a baby is naturally drawn first and foremost to other humans. As the first few weeks pass, he begins to find faces fascinating. Every time his mother's face comes within his short focusing range he studies it intently from hairline to mouth, finishing by gazing into her eyes. He listens intently to her voice, kicking a little when he hears it, or becoming still as he tries to locate its source. Soon he will turn his eyes and his head to see the person who is talking. If his mother picks him up, he stops crying. If she cuddles and walks him, he usually remains content. He clearly likes and needs his parents, and this can be a source of comfort and encouragement to the parents of this new human being.

But in case these responses to parents' care are not enough to keep them caring, the baby has a trump card still to play: smiling. One day, as he is studying mother's face in his intent and serious way, his face slowly begins to flower into the small miracle of a wide toothless grin. For most parents, grandparents, and caregivers, that's it—he is the most beautiful baby in the world and the most lovable baby in the world (no matter how often he wakes in the night). While the baby smiles it looks like love, but he cannot truly love anyone yet because he does not know one person from another. His early smiles are an insurance policy against neglect, and for pleasant social attention. The more he smiles and gurgles and waves at people, the more they will smile and talk to him. The more attention people pay him, the more he will respond, drawing them ever closer with his throat-catching grins and his heart-rendingly quivery lower lip. His responses create a self-sustaining circle: his smiles leading to caregivers' smiles, and their smiles to more from him.

By the time he is around three months old it becomes clear that the baby knows his mother and other adults who are special to him. It is not that he smiles at them and whimpers at strangers—he still smiles at everyone—but that he saves his best signs of favor, the smiliest smiles, for the people he knows best. Week by week he becomes increasingly sociable and increasingly fussy about whom he will socialize with. He is ready to form a passionate and personal emotional tie with somebody and if his mother is available at all, she will probably be his choice. But the blood-tie is not an automatic qualification. The privilege has to be earned not just by birthing him, but by mothering him. And mothering does not just mean taking physical care of the baby. His first love is not "cupboard-love," rooted in the pleasures of feeding. Babies make their primary attachments to people who mother them emotionally, talking to them, cuddling them, smiling and playing with them. Of course babies need good physical care too; feeding is their greatest pleasure in life and therefore, the act of feeding a baby links physical with emotional care. But babies don't only need to feed when they're hungry, they also need someone to be available when they need company—one who notices when they smile and smiles back, who listens and responds when they "talk," who plays with them and brings little bits of the world for them to see.

Building on Parent-Child Bonds

Every baby needs a mother or mothering person who identifies with him so strongly that she feels the baby's needs as if they were her own. A newborn is still physiologically and psychologically an extension of his mother. If a mother feels upset when her baby feels upset, she will immediately want to comfort and reassure him; to "regulate" his emotions so that he feels comfortable again. This early emotional regulation involves sensing the baby's feelings and responding to them physically. The caregiver does this with facial expressions, with tone of voice, with touch and holding. Sometimes she will soothe a crying baby by first joining him in verbal expressions of distress ("Oh, dear . . . ") and then leading him gradually, with a quieter and gentler tone, towards calm. When her baby is tense, she may soothe him by rocking or wrapping him when he is frightened, she may hold and cuddle him; and if he is sad or bored, she might engage and distract him by smiling, while bobbing her face to and fro. By all these, and many other means, she moves her baby out of an uncomfortable state back to feeling comfortable again.

In order to respond empathically to their children, parents need to be comfortable managing their own feelings at the same time as they track their child's. If parents are acutely uncomfortable managing their own anger and hostility, for example, they will find it difficult to tolerate and regulate those states in their children. The caregiver who cannot bear anger in herself is likely to feel very distressed and uncomfortable when her one-year-old screams with rage. Urgently wanting to push such feelings away, she may bring herself down to baby-level and yell at the child, "Shut up!"

Monitoring and regulating an infant's states provides the child with much more than momentary comfort. In interaction with parents, basic states like "feeling happy" or "feeling unhappy" get differentiated into a range of feelings like feeling amused, affectionate, interested; or annoyed, angry, or disappointed. As well as being quick to notice and respond to those feelings in the baby, parents also have to help the baby to become aware of her own feelings; telling and showing her what kind of "unhappy" she is feeling; identifying feelings and labeling them clearly so the baby will recognize them next time. These early lessons enable the infant to grow into a child and an adult who has learned how to monitor and recognize her own states and manage them effectively. If the mother has such difficulties with recognizing and regulating her own feelings that she can't feel with her baby, he may be left without any clear sense of how to keep himself on an even keel. The more consistently, and therefore predictably, parents and other caregivers respond to the baby, the sooner clear patterns of action and reaction will start to emerge: "I cry and she comes." "I do this and that happens."

Different theorists refer to these unconsciously acquired expectations using a number of different terms. John Bowlby called them "internal working models."[3] Daniel Stern[4] calls them "representations of interactions that have been generalised" (RIGS). Robert Clyman calls them *procedural memory*.[5] Wilma Bucci calls them *emotion schemas*.[6] Regardless of the particular terminology that is used, all agree that *these unconscious assumptions exist in everyone, that they are based on these earliest experiences and that they are of fundamental importance.* The most crucial assumption of all is that people will be emotionally available to help notice, process, and regulate feelings and thus help the child learn to retain or restore emotional balance.

Patterns of Attachment

Newborn babies have a built-in drive to develop and practice every aspect of being human, yet each aspect of their growing up depends on partnership with adults. Premature attempts to bring organized routine to new babies, intended to diminish the acute stresses of early parenthood, will actually increase them. The erratic and inconsistent neonatal behaviors that drive some parents crazy will change, and can only be changed, when the infant's physiology has matured and steadied so that compared to a newborn he has become a relatively settled baby. The more generously his earlier needs are met, the sooner that will be, and this parental generosity also pays a long-term dividend. Newborn babies want nothing that they do not need and therefore do not know how to demand anything more. Having their real needs met, readily and lovingly, throughout the first weeks and months teaches them that this new world and its adults are benevolent and can be trusted, and these early lessons form the basis of their confidence in others and in themselves, from infancy to old age. An attitude towards the world of basic trust facilitates the development of self-esteem, as well as the capacity to cooperate with others and to cope with occasional frustrations or disappointments. Even six weeks' total indulgence of a baby's needs will still be paying off when she is 6 months, 6 years, or even 16 years old. Secure attachment to a caregiver is the emotional foundation that enables children to enter adulthood with the confidence and adaptability to make the most of whatever possibilities life offers them.

Secure Attachment. By the end of the first year there are clearly visible differences in the behavior of babies who have secure as opposed to insecure relationships with their parents. Observed with their mothers in the playground or the supermarket, securely attached children show a greater joy for life as it is in the moment, and are more willing to do as they are asked even if it is not fun. Any young toddler can throw a tantrum when the checkout line is too long or the favorite swing is occupied, but the securely attached child displays less frustration and aggression and gets over it faster. And he is very much easier to bring back to cooperation with a joke or a hug. Secure attachment provides a child's launch-pad to exploration and adventure, as well as to love. The firmer and more trustworthy that pad, the better the take-off and the more successful the flight!

Insecure Attachment. If secure attachment is a protective factor, insecure, or anxious, attachment makes children increasingly vulnerable to life's events. There are three recognized categories of which the third is so serious as to count as a disorder in its own right.

Avoidant attachment is the name given to a strategy that is often developed by babies whose parents have discouraged emotional displays, are slow to offer sympathy or comfort, and discourage overt signs of either affection or distress. Convinced that other people do not see them as worth loving (or even responding to), such babies tend to develop low self-esteem and eventually high levels of aggression. As the child gets older, close relationships are avoided; he may have few friends at school and no "best friends." As an adult, he may mask his emotional insecurity and friendlessness by burying himself in work and material acquisitions. Alternatively, he may retreat behind obsessional and ritualistic behaviors.

Ambivalent (or *resistant*) *attachment* stems not from parenting that is cold and repressive but from the baby's experience of inconsistent parenting. Such a child can never be sure if his distress or anxiety will be noticed and suitably responded to. Although his parents are sometimes nurturing and protective they are sometimes the opposite and the inconsistency makes it very difficult for the baby to feel that it is safe to explore the world. The child may be easily upset but have no confidence that comfort will be forthcoming. When he is upset he tries to get close to the parent or caregiver, but because he cannot count on a helpful response he often becomes angry and resists contact—helpful or not. As adults, such children have serious problems with relationships. They may withdraw and become loners or become clingy and dependent; either way they are easily overwhelmed by their own emotions.

Avoidant and ambivalent attachments are far from ideal. However, they are at least coherent, providing the child with a set of unconscious strategies for relating to others which he will carry with him into adulthood. These are internal working models of what once did, and are now expected to, occur in interpersonal exchanges.

Disorganized (controlling) attachments occur when children get nothing, or worse than nothing, from parents who may have so many unresolved emotional issues or hardships from their own past, and/or in their present lives, that they either have no mental space for their baby or actually pose a threat through neglect or abuse. It is difficult to imagine a more terrible conflict. The baby is biologically programmed to seek safety through closeness to the parents, yet the parents themselves are the source of fear. This prevents the child from developing any faith in the world of relationships, leaving him with no coherent means of relating to other people. As eloquently summarized by Karr-Morse, a family therapist and former consultant to Brazelton's "Touchpoints" program, and Wiley, a lawyer charged with restructuring Oregon's child care:

> Abuse and neglect in the first years of life have a particularly pervasive impact. Pre-natal development and the first two years of life are the time when the genetic, organic, and neurochemical foundations for impulse control are being created. It is also the time when the capacity for rational thinking and sensitivity to other people are being rooted—or not—in the child's personality.[7]

Disorganized attachment poses a major risk factor for future psychological disturbances in childhood. It has been found to be associated with "failure to thrive"—a syndrome in which the infant's physical and psychological development begins to stall or regress, sometimes ending in death. According to Alan Schore,[8] who has integrated attachment and neuropsychological research, severely disturbed attachment relationships derail brain development in ways that compromise the child's ability to regulate emotions and cope with stress.

Attachment Theory Meets Neurological Research

New techniques for imaging living, working brains have transformed research on brain development. Although we have known for several decades that attachment relationships are of the utmost importance for infants' physical and psychological well-being, recent neurological research has demonstrated that the quality of the caregiver-infant bond directly influences the development of brain structures that are responsible for social and emotional functioning throughout our lives.

At birth, the human brain is very immature. To reach the level of development that most mammals achieve *inside* the womb takes most of the first year of life for the human infant. In the early weeks and months of life, the hippocampus, temporal cortex, prefrontal cortex, and anterior cingulate grow so rapidly that the brain more than doubles its weight by the end of the first year. Because so much more human brain development occurs *outside* of the womb (compared to all other species), human children undergo an unusually long period of complete dependency, necessitating intense and long-lived social bonds between caregivers and offspring. And the quality of brain development in the early months and years of life is shaped to a significant degree by the nature of these intense social bonds. Although at birth the baby's brain has all of the neurons (brain cells) that she will ever need, she now needs the loving human attention that will stimulate her brain cells to make rich and "intelligent" connections within and between different regions of the brain. It is no coincidence that there is a dramatic burst of new synaptic connections in the prefrontal cortex during the second half of the first year, corresponding exactly with the period when the attachment relationship between baby and her parents is reaching peak intensity.

For optimal growth and development, the human brain requires a balance between different biochemicals. Positive, enjoyable interactions with parents— especially with mother—encourage that balance. Early positive experiences produce increased glucose metabolism, which in turn stimulates the development of neuronal connections. A chemical called norepinephrine plays an important role in our ability to concentrate and maintain sustained effort. Infants who have experienced neglect or separation from their mothers tend to have low levels of norepinephrine.

The capacity for pleasure and optimism depends on the number of dopamine and opiate receptors that develop in the baby's brain, especially in the prefrontal cortex. A baby who has lots of warm, rewarding contact with mother will form more dopamine synapses. Dopamine is a neurotransmitter which is released from the brainstem, and makes its way to the prefrontal cortex where it enhances the uptake of glucose, helping new tissue to grow in the prefrontal brain. It also produces an energizing and stimulating effect that makes the individual feel good. Dopamine flowing through the orbitofrontal cortex helps it to do its job of evaluating events and adapting to them quickly. It also helps the child become a person who can stop and think about choices and their positive rewards. A baby who is deprived of affectionate early contact with his mother, and therefore lives with high levels of stress, will have a permanent scarcity of dopaminergic neurons because stress hormones, such as cortisol, effectively "turn them off."

GOOD PARENTING TAKES MORE THAN GOOD INTENTIONS

After 30-odd years in child development research and a good many passing on the findings to parents and using them myself in bringing up my own children, I believe that most parents do everything they can to facilitate the health and happiness, growth and development of their babies; and to support them throughout their childhood years. "Good parenting"—the kind that fosters secure attachment—cannot be formally taught; it has to evolve out of the unique interaction between individual children and their parents or special adults. However, if parenting cannot be taught, it can and must be supported both practically and emotionally if parents are to have the security and self-confidence to tune in and respond to their children.[9] Across the globve, though, it seems as if parents are increasingly under siege. The forces restricting good parenting are as varied as the circumstances in which children are being brought up, but one way or another they all reduce parents' ability to be fully physically and emotionally present for their babies as they grow into children who are loved, loving, and lovable.

If a mother or mothering-person who is there for a baby, tuned in to her moods and feelings and sensitively responsive to her, is the crucial factor in every child's optimum development, then parents must be—and must feel themselves to be—supported from outside in whatever ways enable them to give of themselves to their babies. A mother who dies of AIDs is not in any sense there for her baby. Caught in war or famine, her baby starving, she has no space to respond to anything but his hunger and her fight to keep him alive.

Today, the very survival of more than half the world's children—numbering more than a billion—is under threat from the AIDs epidemic, war, terrorism, disease, and famine. Under such circumstances, parents' time and energy is taken up with the constant battle for survival. And parents' bonds with even the most cherished and doted-upon infant may be ruptured because when prospects for survival are precarious, and parents lack the means to intervene effectively, it may become painful to invest themselves fully in their babies.

When we think about the kinds of support parents need, we have to start from the basics—such as secure supplies of adequate food, clean water, sanitation, and high-quality, accessible health care—and be aware of the millions of parents who have none of those. Against staggering odds, many nonetheless forge secure bonds with their children. Some benefit from traditions of social support for mothers and children which the postindustrial West has largely lost. But some seek a better future for their children by leaving them to be cared for by grandparents while they travel to the West to care for ours. The money we pay them for housecleaning or child care may go to purchasing grade school education or medicine for children whose circumstances are unfathomable to us and who remain conveniently invisible in countries that we might have difficulty locating on a map. And yet, even when parents do manage to raise their children successfully under conditions of extreme deprivation, it is tragic that they are must work so hard against such odds. Other children are even less fortunate. Twenty-nine thousand children are dying every day—mostly of preventable causes. More than three million are enmeshed in the sex trade, and still countless others become child soldiers.

While secure attachment is not uniquely a requirement of the West, neither is it guaranteed by privilege. While some Western countries such as Sweden and Germany have prioritized support to families in the form of generous parental and child sick leave, subsidized high-quality child care, socialized medicine, flexible work arrangements, and affordable housing, other countries such as the United States have not done so. In the current global economy, the chasm between rich and poor in the United States continues to widen, and as many as 20 percent of American children are growing up in poverty without reliable access to health care. But even for families in the West who do have access to material comforts, and can purchase the best child care and education, many lack the social and emotional support that would enable them to revel emotionally in their children. Western culture with its emphasis on individual rights and privileges and rampant consumerism is antithetical to attachment parenting that requires caregivers to interrupt activities that generate individual success and money. In response, an entire industry of parenting advice books has been created which teaches parents how to "manage" their children and their time efficiently.

Mothers as Managers

Mothers "managing" and "disciplining" their infants from the time they are newborns has become an increasingly visible phenomenon in the West. The phrase "controlled crying" epitomizes the approach that owes much to the concept of "sleep training" formulated by Ferber a generation ago. The delayed-response (to crying) method, which is often referred to among parents as "Ferberizing," originally aimed to train babies from four to six months of age to go to sleep without adult soothing and to go through the night without attention. Now though, Ferberesque arguments and techniques—the diametric opposite to sensitive responsiveness—are being generalized from sleep-problem solving to ordinary practice and from the middle of an infant's first year to the whole of it. Generalized from sleeping patterns to all behaviors, and recommended as an overall strategy through which mothers can avoid and/or manage all the difficulties and conflicts that may arise in caring for babies, the phrase "controlled crying" has slipped out of the problem-solving literature and into popular advice on child care, both in print and on the Internet, and with it the notion that mothers can and should control every aspect of their babies' lives. Detailed and prescriptive plans for the exercise of such maternal control, manipulation, and management, covering every minute of the 24 hours with exact times at which the baby must eat, sleep, and exercise, are reaching a wide public. It seems surprising that in the midst of physical plenty and in the face of all that is known and published about the importance of parental sensitivity and responsivity, so many mothers, including older and better-educated women, welcome this World War Two–era, Truby King–like advice. No similarly authoritarian approach to babies is seen anywhere in the developing world. The truth is that in the present social context of, say, North America, any set of strategies that empowers women to control infants' behavior and limit their demands is attractive to many and may be especially appealing to those who are least able to allow themselves to be guided by what they feel.

Once a woman has decided to adopt such a scheme, no further judgments or decisions are required. Following each day's routine is mindless (though far from effortless) and assures her of the rightness of doing things she might otherwise have been uncertain about and had to work out for herself. The idea of closing the door on a baby and leaving him to cry, for example, can be simultaneously tempting and shameful. Good-enough mothers can be tempted and may or may not find themselves ashamed. But if leaving the baby is part of "settling him" in a prescribed way at a scheduled time in a day whose every moment is programmed to do what is right for him, a woman can feel like a good mother even whilst he cries, ignoring rather than hearing him.

The Western trend towards adopting external-control methods with children is not designed to deal with real problems in the here-and-now but with projected problems in a fraught future. Societal pressures to minimize the effect a child has on their lifestyle make parents so anxious (lest babies take over their lives and control *them*) that they gladly adopt programs for managing and controlling their babies' lives instead. Sadly, parents may thereby delay, even perhaps distort, the relationship of mutual regard that is at the heart of enjoyable and effective parenting. The more responsive, loving experience a baby gets, the more she will flourish today and the more resources she will have to cope with difficulties tomorrow.

Here is the sad irony. In many Third World nations, traditional social structures are conducive to the formation of secure attachments between mothers and infants who are traditionally embedded in close extended family and community networks. However, these are often unable to provide parents with the physical conditions they need for adequate parenting in the form of food, safety, health care, and clean water. In contrast, Western parents by and large have far better physical conditions within which to rear children, but are struggling to do so in a *cultural* climate that undermines attachment parenting.

CONCLUSION

In order for children to grow up fulfilling every aspect of their genetic potential, intensive personalized and long-lasting care is not a theoretical ideal or a Western conceit but a human basic. Babies have to be fed, warmed, and protected, and we are good at that in the developed world and could do it worldwide on little more than beer money if we really cared. But essential though it is, physical care is not enough. If that is all babies are given, many fail to realize their full potential, some fail to thrive, and some die. The end of infancy alters the necessary commitment of parents or their surrogates but does not end it. Human brains are most sensitive when growing most rapidly. But while this means that the first two years of life—and especially the very first—are the most important to a lifetime, neural connections continue to be made throughout childhood, mediated by empathic responses, emotional education, and unconditional love. All children under seven need constant adult protection. In middle childhood, survival and life-skills, along with morals and manners, go on being learned over at least five more years of close emotional apprenticeship to adults. Even then, on the edge of puberty, it takes people at least five further years of physical growth and intellectual and social maturation to refine those skills so that the adolescent can begin to function as an adult within the value system of his or her particular culture.

So even if we truly gave emotional and practical support to new mothers, encouraging them to explore and embrace the new world of parenthood, it would not be enough. The parents of a baby are parents forever and this needs to be acknowledged and celebrated. Parents and parent-figures are crucial to every phase of this long human childhood, not least because it is individual parents who most passionately want to meet the needs of their own children, and passion is part of what is needed. The support societies give to parents and caregivers in this vital role is a telling criterion of their priorities and, ultimately, of their humanity.

Chapter 3

Self, Identity, and Generativity

Sharna Olfman

How do newborns who are barely aware of their own existence, and have no language or mobility, develop into children with a healthy sense of self, and adults who possess the desire and ability to care for the next generation? The quality and course of children's developmental journey is powerfully influenced by the ways in which parents respond to their biological and existential needs. But parents do not live in a vacuum; the experiences and environments that they (consciously or unwittingly) provide for their children, and protect them from, reflect values and beliefs that have been shaped by their culture. During the first years of life, parents are the conduits of their culture, which is mirrored in the identities their children acquire, and ultimately, in the ways in which they will parent their own children. But cultures also entail systems of governance, education, economy, and religion that may support or undermine parents' efforts to nurture their children's development.

CULTURAL RELATIVISM AND UNIVERSAL HUMANISM

In the wake of World War II, when racism led to the systematic slaughter of millions of Jews across Europe, many progressive thinkers embraced and promoted a worldview called "cultural relativism" in which all human cultures were deemed to be of equal value. At that time, cultural relativism was widely perceived as an antidote to racism. It encouraged a deeper appreciation of the wisdom, spirituality, and artistry of diverse cultures, many of which had been dismissed or disparaged by Western intellectuals as "primitive" and inferior because of their lack of technological sophistication or economic prowess. Individual and cultural diversity *is* a defining feature of our humanity. Nonetheless, when we reflect upon the fact that:

- Half of the world's children are starving, or dying from diseases that we know how to prevent, or being exploited as soldiers and sex workers;
- Millions of children from wealthy nations are routinely subdued by psychiatric drugs so that they can "fit in" to deadening systems of education while struggling with obesity-related illnesses and consuming hours of violent media each day;
- Our planet is being destroyed by a toxic brew of synthetic chemical compounds;

we are driven to question whether in fact, all cultures *are* equally humane.

At this critical juncture, it is imperative that we rediscover and renew the worldview of "universal humanism," which emphasizes our *shared* humanity. In so doing, we address children's *essential needs* that *all cultures* must meet to ensure that they reach their full human potential with the will, competence, and resources to care for the next generation.

Globalization makes the project of understanding what it means to be human all the more urgent. As technologies enable ever more rapid international communication and travel, the Earth is being rapidly transformed into a global village with an increasingly homogenous culture. At the present time, however, global culture is created and defined by corporations whose values and goals are promoted efficiently and relentlessly around the world by powerful media conglomerates. But corporate culture is indifferent at best, and hostile at its worst, to the world's children, and it is killing our planet. And so, while preserving the richness of local cultures, we must strive to create an overarching, *child honoring* global culture, codified in international laws and practices—that is, defined *not* by elite corporate interests that serve the few, but by *humane consideration of children's intrinsic human needs.*

In the pages that follow, I discuss the nature of children's essential needs. Next, I consider how these needs express themselves at different stages of development, and how caregivers and society at large must meet them, to ensure that children develop to the fullness of their human potential. My reflections owe much to the work of psychoanalysts Erich Fromm and Erik Erikson.

BIOLOGICAL NEEDS

While children have a multitude of biological needs that must be met to ensure their physical survival—for food, water, warmth, and so forth—I will focus on two innate needs that, when neglected, threaten children's *psychological* rather than their *physical* integrity. These are the need for a loving, reliable, and sustained relationship with a caregiver—which psychologists call attachment—and the need for play.

Attachment

In the words of Robert Karen, author of *Becoming Attached*: The concept of attachment

> encompasses both the quality and strength of the parent-child bond, the ways in which it forms and develops, how it can be damaged and repaired, and the long-term impact of separations, losses, wounds, and deprivations. Beyond that, *it is a theory of love and its central place in human life.*[1]

Penelope Leach has already described the critical role of attachment for children's development, in chapter 2. Here I will address its evolutionary origins. In my anthology *Childhood Lost,*[2] anthropologist Meredith Small explains that humans, like all primates, are designed to care for their young for many years, but that evolutionary pressures have rendered the human caregiver-child relationship especially intense and long-lasting. About four million years ago, our hominid ancestors began to walk on two legs instead of four, and this necessitated changes in our musculature and pelvic architecture that resulted in a much smaller pelvic opening. And then, one and half million years ago, there was an evolutionary push for larger brains. In consequence— if human babies and mothers are to survive childbirth—babies must be born "too soon," neurologically unfinished compared to other primates, and in a physically and emotionally very dependent state. But prolonged dependence could not have occurred if there hadn't been a gradual evolutionary shift in parental behavior that deepened our capacity to respond to infant needs. Human infants, therefore, are designed by evolution to be "attached" both emotionally and physically to their caregivers.

Studying modern hunter-gatherer and horticultural groups reveals the rich diversity of beliefs, values, and lifestyles that is typical of our species. But despite these variations, a common pattern emerges: in the preindustrial milieu, infants are in almost constant skin contact with their caregivers, who respond immediately to their needs and never leave them to cry. *And this style of care is precisely what a half century of "attachment" research tells us infants need for optimal psychological and neurological development.*

But beyond the early months and years of life when attachment relationships protect and support us, the human brain takes *two decades* to develop—far longer than any other species. This is because our brains are designed to grow in response to the environments in which we are raised and—as we begin to establish our sense of identity—to the experiences and conditions that we select for ourselves. Indeed, it is the very immaturity of our brains throughout childhood, adolescence, and young adulthood that permits our unique capacity to adapt to and to create a seemingly endless variety of physical and cultural environments. And so, relationships with our loved ones continue to play a powerful and formative influence on our development, long after the first years of childhood.

Play

Play is an integral part of childhood, and an invariant feature of human development across cultural and socioeconomic boundaries.[3] It has a central role in the lives of all young primates and most young mammals, underscoring its lengthy evolutionary history and adaptive value.[4] Research has established a strong correlation between the period of greatest playfulness and the time when brain connections are most actively made.[5] Children "grow" their brains through the act of play. Thousands of studies spanning four decades have established incontrovertibly that creative play is a catalyst for social, emotional, moral, motoric, perceptual, intellectual, linguistic, and neurological development.[6] Recollections of child holocaust survivors reveal that even in the degraded and desperate circumstances of the concentration camps, play sustained them.[7] Many of our greatest thinkers locate their capacity for original and profound thought in their imaginative abilities, first developed through creative play in early childhood.[8]

EXISTENTIAL NEEDS

In addition to attachment and play, which are so deeply inscribed in our primate ancestry, humans share *existential* needs that are born of our specifically human capacity for self-consciousness which makes us aware of our mortality, our vulnerability, and our singularity—to an extent unparalleled in the animal world. Psychoanalyst Erich Fromm identified six uniquely human needs that arise from the conditions of our existence, which I summarize below:

- *The need for relatedness and unity.* Awareness of our separateness creates a need to love and care for others, to feel at one with humanity and with nature. Here we see that loving relationships have both biological and existential origins.
- *The need for transcendence and a sense of effectiveness.* Humans alone are aware that they can create life. In the act of creation, we transcend ourselves as creatures. To create presupposes love for that which one creates. When incapable of creativity, we seek transcendence through destructive acts.
- *The need for rootedness.* Separated from our mothers at birth, and from the safety of their care in late childhood, we need to establish a sense of rootedness, stability, permanency, and security.
- *The need for a sense of identity.* Self-awareness imbues us with a desire to establish a sense of identity, to be able to say "I am I."
- *The need for a frame of orientation and an object of devotion.* Enveloped in a vast and mysterious universe, we need a set of beliefs about the meaning of life and the course of our destiny.
- *The need for active engagement.* We need to be actively engaged in making meaning and in living.[9]

Cultural and familial conditions that support our existential needs for relatedness, transcendence, rootedness, identity, meaning, and engagement, promote a life-loving or *biophilious* orientation.[10] In Fromm's words, when our existential needs are fully met, we are "fully human," and we

> live in harmony with ourselves, with our fellow human beings, and with nature. . . . We carry within ourselves all of humanity; in spite of the fact that no two individuals are the same, the paradox exists that we all share in the same substance, in the same quality; that nothing which exists in any human being does not exist in myself. I am the criminal and I am the saint. I am the child and I am the adult. I am the man who lived a hundred thousand years ago and I am the man who, provided we don't destroy the human race, will live a hundred thousand years from now.[11]

By contrast, when the expression of our existential needs is blocked, we acquire a destructive, or *necrophilous* orientation to life. In 1973, Fromm wrote:

> [The necrophile] turns his interest away from life, persons, nature, ideas—in short from everything that is alive; he transforms all life into things, including himself and the manifestations of his human faculties of reason, seeing, hear-

ing, tasting, loving. . . . The world becomes a sum, of lifeless artifacts; from synthetic food to synthetic organs, the whole man becomes part of the total machinery that he controls and is simultaneously controlled by. . . . He aspires to make robots as one of the greatest achievements of his technical mind and some specialists assure us that the robot will hardly be distinguished from living men. This achievement will not seem so astonishing when man himself is hardly distinguishable from a robot.[12]

STAGES OF PSYCHOSOCIAL DEVELOPMENT

Having identified our core biological and existential needs, I will now consider how these needs are given expression at different stages of development, and how they must be met by caregivers—who in turn must be supported by the wider culture—in order for us to acquire a "fully human" sense of self, identity, and generativity. I will use Erik Erikson's "Psychosocial Stages" as a framework.[13] Erikson believed that each stage of the life cycle carries with it a central psychological challenge that is catalyzed by our unfolding biological needs. However, whereas Erikson (who was a pupil of Anna Freud's) emphasized the sexual drives as the engine of early development, I place greater emphasis on the role of attachment, play, and existential needs.

Infancy: Trust versus Mistrust

According to Erikson, the central psychological challenge for the infant is to establish a basic sense of trust. When an infant's needs for nourishment, warmth, and comfort are addressed in a timely, purposeful, and loving fashion by her primary caregivers, then she is likely to develop an attitude of trust in others, in the world, and in herself, and she will carry within her an attitude of hopefulness.

The conditions that foster trust and hopefulness in infancy are one and the same as those which lay down the foundation for secure and loving attachments. But the capacity to love requires awareness that you are a *separate* human being, who loves another. During the first year of life, there is a dawning awareness of selfhood, which is facilitated by and reflected in the infant's burgeoning capacity to "hold the world in her head" through the act of symbolization. Now the infant can recognize and express the words for *mama* and *baby*. In so doing, she demonstrates that she knows that her mother continues to exist, even when she cannot be touched or seen. The universally loved game of peek-a-boo enables the baby to affirm again and again that the people and things that populate her world, herself included, continue to exist, even when they are temporarily out sight.

As we begin to acquire a sense of self, and therefore an awareness of our separateness, some of our existential needs are activated, in particular the need for relatedness, which we initially express through our attachment relationships. And so we see that the need for loving relationships, beginning in infancy, is primed by our biological heritage, as well as a condition of being human.

Establishing a trusting and hopeful orientation towards life can be threatened in myriad ways. Many regions of the world today are ravaged by war, famine, disease, and environmental decay, and even the most loving mother cannot instill trust when she herself is enveloped in or overwhelmed by violence, malnourishment, or illness. By the same token, even the most beloved infant cannot be made to feel secure if illness, fear, or hunger make her inconsolable. In less extreme circumstances, when parents must work away from home, but lack adequate social supports such as flexible working hours, living wages, maternity leave, health insurance, affordable and regulated child care, and child sick leave, then despite the best of intentions, they may fail to foster a sense of security and trust in their child.

Even when our physical needs are met, and we are economically secure, cultural values and practices that are prevalent in many wealthy countries can undermine loving relations between mothers and infants. In the West, the premium placed on independence and privacy, when taken to extremes, can undermine healthy development in the early months and years. We are so keen to foster independence in our children, that from the time they are born, we physically separate them from ourselves, and place them on feeding and sleep schedules. However, *healthy* independence can only emerge after infants have known a deep sense of security and trust. Because child care and health are deemed to be private and personal matters, there is a widespread conviction—particularly in the United States—that government should not intervene, thus undermining efforts to create humane public policies to protect and support children and families.

The technologies of infant care—bottles, cribs, playpens, mechanical swings, electronic gadgets that simulate the sound of the heartbeat and "sing" to the infant, "laptops" that the baby can "interact" with while strapped to car seats or high chairs, and video series that allegedly build better brains—undermine responsive human interaction, and healthy development, at every turn. And many of these gadgets are made of synthetic materials that are toxic to the infant's growing brain and body (over and above the toxins that they are exposed to in our air, soil, and water). In our consumer culture, parenting has become just another marketable commodity. There is no money to be made in informing parents that breastfeeding, holding, and singing to their infants are optimal for their development.

Toddlerhood: Autonomy versus Shame and Doubt

Between the ages of 18 months and 3 years, several developmental milestones are achieved that encourage the child's capacity for autonomy and the desire to exercise her will. Compared to the infant, the toddler has far greater mobility, neuromuscular control, language, and a more vivid awareness that she is her own person endowed with agency and desire. And yet, just as she acquires more skill and independence, her growing self-awareness puts her in touch with her ongoing *de*pendence on others and her vulnerability to the elements at large. As a result, during toddlerhood, the child experiences an intensification of her existential needs for active engagement with the world and human connection, which motivate her to be more physically competent, while at the same time ensuring the ongoing presence of her loved ones, who she is more consciously aware of relying upon. And so, towards the end of toddlerhood, the child is at turns, more active and willful, and more vulnerable and anxious to please her caregivers.

In order to support children's growing autonomy, caregivers must allow them to experience and express their own agency, whether it be initiating and negotiating a climb up a hill, feeding themselves, or choosing what toy to play with. At the same time, they must limit their children's will in ways that ensure their safety (and that of others). They must be clear that certain actions, such as hitting another child or throwing their food on the ground, are not acceptable. In Erikson's words, the child who successfully negotiates this stage evidences "a capacity for 'free will,' for 'good will,' and for 'willful self-control.'"[14] By contrast, children whose parents are overly protective, overly punitive, or who provide no protection or prohibitions, will be overwhelmed by feelings of self-doubt and shame.

In the late 1940s, Erikson interviewed female elders from the Oglala subtribe of the Sioux from South Dakota, and the Yurok, who lived on the Pacific coast along the Klamath River, in order to learn about their traditional infant and child care practices. He noted that while we think of these (and other indigenous cultures) as "collectivist," and of our own Western culture as "individualist," that in fact, their early child care practices are *more* conducive to the acquisition of a secure and intact sense of self, and the capacity for free will, than are modern Western childrearing practices. Erikson learned that during infancy and toddlerhood, circa the late nineteenth and early twentieth centuries, the Oglala Sioux and the Yurok met their children's physical needs for food, warmth, and contact comfort as they arose; scheduled times for feeding and sleeping were unheard of. And during toddlerhood, harsh toilet training and shaming remarks about the body were virtually nonexistent.[15]

By contrast, wrote Erikson in *Childhood and Society*, Western parents "implant the never silent metronome of routine into the impressionable baby and young child to regulate his first experiences with his body and with his immediate physical surroundings. Only *after* such mechanical socialization is he encouraged to proceed to develop into a rugged individualist. He pursues ambitious strivings, but compulsively remains within standardized careers."[16] Erikson went on to say that increasingly, children are being raised as "efficient machines" in order to fit into the machine world. These sentiments are resonant with Fromm's description of the "necrophilous" individual described earlier, who, denied the opportunity to express his needs for relatedness and efficacy in the early years, turns away from life and takes more pleasure in relating to his "machines." These prescient ideas, which Erikson and Fromm expressed in the mid-twentieth century, are doubly relevant today, when we consider the number of hours each day so many of us spend "wired"—to computers, television screens, game systems and ipods, and out of "touch" with human communities and the world of nature.

Early Childhood: Initiative versus Guilt

Early childhood is distinguished by the child's capacity for imaginative play. In my anthology *All Work and No Play*, Jeffrey Kane explains that when children "make-believe," they do not merely mimic their role models— whether they be a loved one, an animal, or a mythical character—but they *become* them in their play. He also emphasizes the critical importance of playing in natural settings. When a young child has the gift of time to gaze with wonder and then *embody* a butterfly in her play—as opposed to studying a fact sheet on butterflies at school—she trusts the discoveries of her senses and her bodily experiences. She begins to understand what it means to be a butterfly in relationship to other natural delights in her environment, and in the process, she acquires a deep empathy with her subject. She is also acquiring the potential to *initiate* new scientific or artistic discoveries by developing her imaginative capacities as opposed to memorizing other people's decontextualized discoveries whose meaning and relevance may elude her. At this stage of development, the existential need for transcendence through the act of creativity gains expression. Also, while "playing her way into" the various humans and creatures of nature who are a part of her life, whether they be bakers, fire fighters, kittens, or flowers, her empathy for and sense of unity with her world is further awakened.

The child who is not constrained in her role playing when, for example, it crosses gender or ethnic lines, who is given age-appropriate permission to be curious about her body and how it is different from other bodies, whose artistic productions are not ridiculed, is opening herself up to a wealth of possible futures and to a faith in her ability not merely to follow, but to participate in creatively shaping her world. At the same time, parents must restrict play that is destructive. So, for example, play that is ceaselessly violent, or in which another child is habitually victimized, should of course be prohibited.

In view of the central role of creative play in natural environments for healthy development, it is of the utmost concern that so much of children's playtime today is lost to "screentime," early academics, and structured activities. When we have never played in natural settings, when we have never imaginatively lived as a tiger or a rabbit, but have only been taught atomistic facts about mammals in school, or when Disney versions of these creatures override our own imaginings, then like Plato's cave dwellers, our knowledge of the world will be a shadow knowledge handed to us by others, as opposed to knowledge gained firsthand that is deeply experienced and trusted. In the absence of empathy for and understanding of our place in nature, we may grow up to feel no qualms about using science and technological discoveries to dominate and mine the world for resources, imperiling ecosystems and human health in the process.

Middle Childhood: Industry versus Inferiority

Middle childhood begins at six or seven years, an age when children all around the world typically begin formal schooling or apprenticeships. This timing is not mere coincidence, but reflects (as was the case in the stage of autonomy) the maturation of a number of lines of development in concert with each other, including the intellect, neuromuscular coordination, and dexterity. At this stage, "children learn by virtue of their trust, autonomy, initiative, and industry that confident, independent, and active productivity is satisfying because it allows them to join and to effect changes in the adult human community."[17] During middle childhood, our existential needs for relatedness, effectiveness, and active engagement are increasingly expressed through the mastery of valuable skills, and played out among a widening circle of friends and communities, including classmates, teammates, and schools.

While historically, and to this day, there are many parts of the world in which children's labor enslaves them and robs them of their health and dignity, children are *also* disadvantaged when they have *no* meaningful contribution to make to the productive work of their families or the wider community. So often today, in industrialized nations, children are kept "out of sight" through screens that silence them, or they are kept busy through structured activities that build skill sets that benefit the child but no one else. Also, far too many students graduate from high school without a single well-cultivated practical skill. A sense of industry is incumbent upon age-appropriate opportunities to make *real* contributions that foster a sense of competence and membership in community.

Adolescence: Identity versus Role Confusion

The central challenge of adolescence is to establish a sense of identity—a commitment to a set of roles, beliefs, values, communities, and future goals. All of the psychological milestones that have been reached up to now are reworked, and consolidated over the course of the adolescent period. *Trust* must blossom into an enduring faith in the beliefs that the adolescent has embraced, and this may include a faith in God; *autonomy* becomes the freedom to find her own path in life; *initiative,* whose foundation was laid in the make-believe play of early childhood, must evolve into experimentation with (and then commitment to) the roles that define her; and *industry* must be applied with rigor and discipline to her chosen goals. All of her existential needs for relatedness, effectiveness, rootedness, identity, active engagement, and a frame of orientation are "in play" during the work of identity formation.

While parents, teachers, and the wider community must remain available as sources of love, wisdom, and support, their caregiving during her childhood has already laid down the foundation she needs to search for her identity. If she was raised within a *stable* family and culture, she is more likely to have the psychological tools necessary to experiment with *new beliefs and values.* In addition, her search for identity will be much less conflicted if the *values* of her culture are humane and support her strivings for self-actualization.

In view of this, we can see why technologically advanced, consumer culture may not be conducive to healthy identity formation. As screen technologies continue to mushroom and transform children's lives, their parents may not feel that they have the wisdom to compete with the information superhighway. They may feel at a loss to understand let alone guide their children's lives, which may be radically different from their own childhoods. Furthermore, in so many respects, consumerism has distorted our values, beliefs, and goals, creating a vacuous context for self-actualization.

Young Adulthood: Intimacy versus Isolation

The young adult who has achieved a strong and healthy sense of identity is more capable of experiencing mature intimacy that is based upon respectful partnership rather than on dependency, submission, or domination. Intimacy based on principles of equality and reciprocity, as well as erotic passion, sets the stage for the challenge of generativity.

Adulthood: Generativity versus Self-Absorption

Erikson coined the word *generativity* to refer to the desire and the ability to care for the next generation, which he recognized as the central psychological challenge for mature adults. While having and raising children is the most direct way of expressing generativity, all of the choices that we make and the activities that we engage in have the potential to be generative, whether it be mentoring younger colleagues, taking care of the earth, making works of art that inspire others, or participating in the political process. As I discussed earlier, human infants and adults are biologically primed to form attachments with each other. But our desire to ensure the well-being of the next generation is also a reflection of our existential needs for relatedness and transcendence.

GENERATIVITY IN CRISIS

Every day, as I ride the bus, take my children to the library, or stroll in my neighborhood, I witness acts of patient, loving kindness on the part of caregivers towards their young charges that restore my faith in human nature. But when I step back and consider the dire conditions under which so many children in the world today are being raised, I cannot escape the feeling that we are in the midst of an unprecedented failure of generativity on a global scale. Historically, such failures were limited to particular cultures in particular places. But corporate culture in its current incantation, which has imposed itself worldwide, is undermining the ecological integrity of our planet, the

viability of local economies, the means to ensure essential services to communities and families, and the values that undergird and invigorate our feelings
of responsibility towards the next generation. When a culture is grounded in
a humane worldview, then parenting is guided by coherent and meaningful
intentions. But when our core cultural values keep us mired in poverty, or
encourage us to locate our worth in our earning power and our own immediate pleasures, then the will and the means with which to raise our children is
undermined, and our children will not acquire the qualities they will need to
raise *their* children to a wholesome maturity. By the same token, we must not
forget that we *are* the culture, and in the pages that follow we will see how,
together, we can restore our voices, reclaim our values, and "*turn this world
around, for the children.*"

Section I B

Cultural Child: Compassionate Village

Chapter 4

The Benefits of Partnership: When Children Are Honored There Is Peace and Prosperity [1]

Riane Eisler

Millions of us are working for a more equitable, caring, peaceful, and sustainable society—a society where children are truly honored. Today, these goals are seriously threatened, both in the United States and worldwide. We are at a historic juncture that challenges us to go deeper, to reexamine the very foundations on which human society rests.

Family relations are microcosms of broader social relations. A central lesson from history is that regressive leaders promote authoritarian and violently punitive family relations to perpetuate oppressive political and economic structures. The reason for this is that how these primary relations are organized directly influences what people consider normal and moral in *all* relations—public as well as private. Family relations affect how people think and act. They also affect how people vote and govern, and whether the policies they support are just and democratic, or violent and oppressive.

To ensure that our children thrive, and even survive, in this age of nuclear and biological weapons, we must build foundations for a world where peace isn't just an interval between wars. This means starting with our foundational relations—the relations between women and men and between parents and children, without which none of us would be here. *We must ensure that all children worldwide grow up free from domestic and other forms of intimate violence.*

Family relations based on domination and submission transmit lasting lessons about violence. When children experience violence, or observe violence against their mothers, they learn it's acceptable to use force to impose one's will on others. Indeed, the only way they can make sense of violence coming from those who are supposed to love them is that using violence to control others must be natural, even moral.

We're sometimes told violence is human nature. But this ignores what we know from sociology, psychology, and, most recently, neuroscience: that violence is learned. We know that what happens during a child's early formative years is a major factor in whether people commit violence, be it in their families or within the family of nations. As findings from Harvard University, Maclean Hospital, and other research institutions show, the brain neurochemistry of abused children tends to become programmed for fight-or-flight, and thus for violence.[2]

Not everyone from families based on domination and submission fits these patterns—but many people do if they don't gain access to more egalitarian relationship models. Studies show, for example, that men from authoritarian, abusive families tend to vote for so-called strong-man leaders. Also, they tend to support punitive rather than caring social policies.[3]

To build cultures of justice, safety, and genuine democracy, we need families where women and men are equal partners, where children learn to act responsibly because adverse consequences follow from irresponsible behavior, where they learn to help and persuade rather than hurt and coerce, where they're encouraged to think for themselves.[4]

It's not coincidental that throughout history the most violently despotic and warlike societies have been those in which violence, or the threat of violence, is used to maintain domination of parent over child and man over woman. It's not coincidental that the 9/11 perpetrators came from cultures where women and children are terrorized into submission. Nor is it coincidental that Afghanistan under the Taliban in many ways resembled the European Middle Ages—when witch burnings, public drawings and quarterings, despotic rulers, brutal violence against children, and male violence against women were considered moral and normal. It should also not surprise us that those in the United States pushing crusades against "evil enemies" oppose equal rights for women and advocate punitive childrearing.

If we're serious about moving to cultures of equity and peace, we must take into account the link between intimate violence and international violence. If we don't, we won't have the foundations on which to build a more peaceful, equitable, and sustainable future.

CULTURES OF WAR/OPPRESSION AND PEACE/EQUALITY

Terrorism and chronic warfare are responses to life in societies in which the only perceived choices are dominating or being dominated. These violent responses are characteristic of cultures where this view of relations is learned early on through traditions of coercion, abuse, and violence in parent-child and gender relations.

Yet none of the conventional social categories takes the relationship of intimate violence and international violence into account. Indeed, classifications such as religious versus secular, right versus left, East versus West, and developed versus developing do not tell us whether a culture's beliefs and institutions— from the family, education, and religion to politics and economics—support relations based on nonviolence and mutual respect, or rigid rankings backed up by fear and force. Each of these categories looks only at a particular aspect of society, rather than its total configuration.

Based on three decades of research studying societies across cultures and epochs, looking at both the public and personal spheres, I discovered cultural configurations that transcend conventional categories. Since there were no names for these configurations, I coined the terms *partnership model* and *dominator or domination model.*[5]

Hitler's Germany (a technologically advanced, Western, rightist society), Stalin's USSR (a secular leftist society), Khomeini's fundamentalist Iran (an Eastern religious society), and Idi Amin's Uganda (a tribalist society) were all violent and repressive. There are obvious differences among them. But they all share the core configuration of the domination model. They are characterized by top-down rankings in *both* the family and state (or tribe) maintained through physical, psychological, and economic control; the rigid ranking of the male half of humanity over the female half; and a high degree of culturally accepted abuse and violence—from child- and wife-beating to chronic warfare.

The partnership model, on the other hand, is based on a democratic and egalitarian structure in *both* family and state (or tribe) and on equal partnership between women and men. There is little violence, because rigid rankings of domination, which can be maintained only through violence, are not part of the culture. Since women have higher status, stereotypically feminine values have social priority.

When I say stereotypically, I mean traits classified by gender to fit the domination model. In this model, so-called masculine traits and activities, such as toughness and "heroic" violence, are more valued than nonviolence

and caregiving, which are associated with the half of humanity in dominator tradition barred from power. I am not speaking of anything inherent
in women or men. Men can be caring and conciliative, and women can be
cruel and controlling. As we see all around us, what is considered normal for
women and men can change.

What I am talking about is simply this: that how a society structures the
primary human relations—between the female and male halves of humanity,
and between them and their children—is central to whether it is violent and
inequitable or peaceful and equitable. And although this too is not noted in
conventional analyses, it is also central to whether people have a higher or
lower general quality of life.

PROSPERITY AND THE PRIMARY HUMAN RELATIONS

Where the rights of women and children are protected, nations thrive. In
fact, a study of 89 nations by the organization I direct, the Center for Partnership Studies, shows that the status of women can be a better predictor of the
general quality of life than a nation's financial wealth. Kuwait and France, for
example, had identical GDPs (Gross Domestic Product). But quality of life
indicators are much higher in France, where the status of women is higher,
while infant mortality was twice as high in Kuwait.[6]

The social investment in caring for children characteristic of the partnership model actually contributes to prosperity. We can end poverty and solve
other seemingly intractable global problems once we have policies that invest
more of our resources in caring for children. This is particularly urgent as we
move to a postindustrial economy where the most important capital is what
economists call "human capital."

Finland is a good example. Like other Nordic nations, Finland's economy
is a mix of central planning and free enterprise. In the early twentieth century,
Finland was very poor. That changed as the country invested in its human
capital through child care (both day care and allowances for families), health
care, family planning, and paid parental leave.

Like other Nordic nations that have what economist Hilkka Pietila calls
a caring state,[7] Finland now regularly ranks near the top in United Nations
Human Development Reports—far ahead of the United States, Saudi Arabia,
and other wealthier nations.[8] It even ranked ahead of the much wealthier and
more powerful United States in both 2003 and 2004 in the World Economic
Forum's World Competitiveness Rankings.[9] The reason is that Nordic nations
have the characteristic partnership configuration.

First, Nordic nations have both political and economic democracy. While there are differences in status and wealth, these are not extreme, as there is not the huge gap between haves and have-nots characteristic of the domination model. These nations conducted the first experiments on teamwork and other aspects of industrial democracy, and also created environmentally responsible industrial practices such as Sweden's Natural Step.[10]

Second, in Nordic nations a much higher percentage of legislative seats are filled by women than anywhere else in the world: approximately 40 percent. As is the case when the status of women rises, the status of traits and activities such as nonviolence and caregiving stereotypically considered feminine are socially supported, and this has been a major factor behind the more caring Nordic policies. Another, and related factor, is a prominent men's movement working to disentangle masculinity from domination and violence.

These nations also have policies that promote nonviolent relations—the third part of the core partnership configuration. They pioneered education for peace, have low crime rates, often mediate international disputes, and invest heavily in aid to developing nations. Not only that, their government policies either discourage or legally prohibit physical discipline of children in families.

We see the same configuration of nonviolence coupled with respect for women and children among the Minangkabau, an agrarian culture of 2.5 million people in Sumatra.[11] Here, anthropologist Peggy Sanday reports, violence isn't part of childrearing, women aren't subordinate to men, and nurturance is part of both the female and male roles. The Teduray, the people of a tribal culture in the Philippines, also don't discipline children through violence, nor is violence integral to their male socialization. As anthropologist Stuart Schlegel writes in *Wisdom from a Rain Forest,* the Teduray value women and men equally, and elders—both female and male—mediate disputes.[12] Similarly, there is compelling evidence of prehistoric societies in most early centers of civilization that oriented to the partnership model—more equitable and peaceful societies where women were not excluded from power and violence was not idealized.[13]

RELIGION AND VIOLENCE

At the core of most religious traditions are teachings of caring and nonviolence. Unfortunately, for much of recorded history, religion has been used to justify, even command, violence against women and children. Indeed, the subjugation of women and children is still the central message of some fundamentalist religious leaders today—leaders who, not coincidentally, also advocate "holy wars."

Fortunately, today many religious and secular leaders are speaking out against international terrorism and wars of aggression. But we urgently need to hear their voices raised also against the intimate violence that sparks, fuels, and refuels international violence. Far too many customs and public policies still accept, condone, and even promote violence against women and children.

Consider these statistics: The United Nations reports that each year 40 million children under the age of 15 are victims of family abuse or neglect serious enough to require medical attention.[14] The UN also reports that a woman is battered, usually by her intimate partner, every 15 seconds in the United States, that in Africa, Latin America, and Asia up to 58 percent of women report having been abused by an intimate partner, and that each year an estimated 2 million girls undergo some form of female genital mutilation,[15] In China and India, millions of baby girls are killed or abandoned by their parents; and "honor" killings by other family members result in the death of thousands of women in Middle Eastern and South Asian countries.[16] The World Health Organization (WHO) reports that 20 percent of women and 5 to 10 percent of men have suffered sexual abuse as children.[17] Another WHO report found that child abuse alone costs the United States economy $94 billion a year.[18]

I am passionately involved in an initiative to change this intolerable situation. The Spiritual Alliance to Stop Intimate Violence (SAIV) aims to end violence against women and children by engaging the moral authority of spiritual and religious leaders. More than 80 percent of the world's people identify with a religious faith and look to religious leaders for guidance. SAIV was formed to encourage enlightened spiritual and religious leaders to speak out against intimate violence as strongly as they do against terrorism and war. This is essential, not only for the many millions whose lives are taken or blighted by terror in the home, but for us all, because intimate violence teaches that it is acceptable to use force to impose one's will on others.

SAIV has gathered a council of leaders who are prepared to break the silence on this pivotal issue. Among them are Queen Noor and Prince El Hassan bin Talal of Jordan; Archbishop Desmond Tutu of South Africa; A.T. Ariyatne, leader of the Sarvodaya peace movement of Sri Lanka; Ela Gandhi, granddaughter of Mohandas Gandhi; Irish Nobel Peace Laureate Betty Williams; Bill Schulz, director of Amnesty International; Kalon Rinchen Khando, Tibetan Minister of Education for the Dalai Lama; Harvey Cox, professor at the Harvard Divinity School; Jane Goodall; Deepak Chopra; and Raffi. The SAIV website (*www.saiv.net*) offers materials for violence prevention as well as articles showing the link between intimate and international violence for religious and spiritual leaders, health professionals, policy makers, teachers, parents, and social activists.

SAIV is part of a global movement to change traditions of violence in family and other intimate relations. It reflects a growing consciousness that we can't leave family values to those trying to turn back the clock—that we must shift matters affecting women and children to the front of the progressive agenda.

A REVITALIZED PROGRESSIVE CULTURE

Progressives worldwide urgently need a social and political agenda that takes into account both the public sphere of politics and economics, and the personal sphere of human relations. Only in this way can we build foundations for cultures of equity and peace rather than war and intolerance.

The "culture wars" launched in the United States by the so-called Christian fundamentalists pay close attention to relations between women and men, and parents and children. The rightist-fundamentalist political agenda centers on reimposing male-headed family where women render unpaid services (with no independent access to income) and children learn that orders must be obeyed on pain of punishment.

The progressive family agenda I propose is informed by the principles at the core of *both* religion and humanism: principles that support caring and equity. It is *not* about discarding religion. It's about building on the partnership elements of religion that support compassion, justice, and nonviolence, while rejecting those that justify domination, violence, and injustice—*starting with our primary relations.*

It is critically important to redefine the meaning of family values. Rather than focusing on current notions of what *form* constitutes a moral family, progressives should focus on what kinds of family *behaviors* are respectful and just, and on changing those traditions and policies that are violent and unjust.

A progressive platform on family relations is based on a fundamental principle: transforming the model for personal, social, economic, and political relations from domination to partnership. It has three goals:

- To help develop and disseminate progressive values that promote intimate relations based on *partnership*—mutual respect, accountability, and caring.

- To show how the current definition of traditional family values is based on a selective reading of scriptures that supports a system of top-down rankings of *domination* backed by fear and force.
- To show why a more just, democratic, and peaceful world requires a reframing of ethics for family relations.

WHAT WE CAN DO

We can all work for a pro-family, pro-child, pro-democracy political culture that:

1. Focuses on the rights of children to have a chance to grow up healthy and to thrive, including the right to shelter, nutrition and health care, a clean environment, and freedom from violence.
2. Promotes equality between women and men.
3. Supports all families, whether children are parented by a man and woman, a single parent, or two parents of the same gender.
4. Promotes an economic system where the drive for productivity does not overshadow the value of having parents spend time with their children.
5. Supports parents with policies such as a living wage, paid parental leave, high-quality child care, and preschool education for all children.
6. Protects reproductive freedom and promotes family planning and sex education as the best way to prevent abortions (as do nations with far lower abortion rates).
7. Provides education for nonviolent family relations and parenting courses for both boys and girls (as offered by Nordic nations, which have longer life spans and rate at the top of the U.N. Human Development Reports).
8. Promotes real educational reform through small classrooms and small schools where every child can have individual support and attention.
9. Confronts corporate practices that harm children—from marketing unhealthy food and drinks to toxic dumps and pollution—and addresses global warming and other ecocrises that threaten our children's future.
10. Ratifies United Nations conventions to protect women and children.[19]
11. Takes a strong stand against intimate violence—the violence against women and children that is a mainspring for learning to use violence to impose one's will.

CONCLUSION

In his *Covenant for Honoring Children*, Raffi writes: "We commit ourselves to peaceful ways and vow to keep from harm or neglect these, our most vulnerable citizens."

This is the vow we must all keep. We can do so by joining the movement to stop intimate violence and by inviting responsible policy makers, leaders, the media, and the general public to look with fresh eyes at the meaning of the terms *family, values,* and *morality.* We must redefine these terms to evoke partnership, mutual respect, and caring—not domination, top-down control, and coercion.

Our world urgently needs a progressive family culture that truly honors children as the very basis for partnership societies.

We stand at a crossroads. The mix of high technology and the dominator model may take us to an evolutionary dead end. There is movement toward partnership, but traditions of domination and violence persist. We need the spiritual courage to stand up to these coercive traditions. Working together, we will succeed in laying the child-honoring foundations from which a secure, prosperous, and sustainable future can be built—for ourselves, our children, and generations still to come.

Chapter 5

Educating the Whole Child

EDUCATING YOUNG CHILDREN FOR A HEALTHY LIFE BY JOAN ALMON

EDUCATING A CULTURE OF PEACE BY RON MILLER

ECOLITERACY BY FRITJOF CAPRA

EDUCATING YOUNG CHILDREN FOR A HEALTHY LIFE BY JOAN ALMON

When I began teaching young children in Baltimore in 1971, I had one clear ideal: I was convinced that there was a spark of spirit and creativity in every human being, and I was sure there was a way to educate children that would honor that spark and keep it alive. Early in my career as a kindergarten teacher, I was introduced to Waldorf education, with its emphasis on nurturing the physical, soul, and spiritual nature of the child. As I began to incorporate elements of this approach, daily I witnessed how children can flourish and grow when provided with a healthy education that resonates with their natural developmental needs.

Over the years, as I learned more about wider trends in early childhood education, I met and observed many outstanding teachers who were struggling to honor children in systems that placed everything else first before children's well-being: test scores, politics, and preparing children as foot soldiers in the global economy. I began to witness firsthand the negative impact on young children of educational approaches with little understanding or regard for their needs.

Out of concern for the increasingly unhealthy trends in education and in other arenas of children's lives both here and in Europe, I joined together with an international coalition of childhood experts in 1999 to form the Alliance for Childhood. Our primary task is to educate the public about the decline in children's health and well-being, while working for social change. In the pages that follow, I will outline the healthy essentials of early childhood education, which first appeared in an Alliance publication called *Fool's Gold.*

HEALTHY ESSENTIALS OF EARLY CHILDHOOD EDUCATION

Loving Relations with Caring Adults

It is widely recognized that of all the things children need for healthy development, loving relations with caring adults is of prime importance. When pediatrician T. Berry Brazelton and child psychiatrist Stanley Greenspan wrote their book, *The Irreducible Needs of Children: What Every Child Must Have to Grow,* "ongoing nurturing relationships" topped their list of essential needs and was deemed by them the most important of all.

As a teacher I certainly found that my relationship with each child was the most central and critical factor in their school experience. In the few instances where I had difficulties in developing a warm relationship, I could see that the child was suffering and could not fully participate in the kindergarten. I was grateful that almost always, I could resolve these difficulties, sometimes through the help of a parent or a colleague. I was then astonished at how quickly the child's relationship to me and the classroom changed.

The current practice of changing teachers every year makes it much more difficult for a teacher and child to form a deep bond. This is especially important in child care where children spend long hours with caregivers. Yet many child care centers are age stratified and some even change caregivers every six months. I find it much better to integrate young children across age lines and have been in some excellent child care centers where the age range in a group goes from infants to six-year-olds. It is very family-like and very warm.

If teachers are going to succeed in forming consistent, caring relationships with children, they must be allowed to educate young children in such a way that the child feels unhurried. I recall one teacher saying she wanted to put a sign over her door announcing that no one should enter her kindergarten who was in a hurry. Indeed, in her kindergarten it always seemed there was lots of time for everything, including relating to one another.

Creative, Social Play

Creative, social play is a key element in early childhood education. I am referring to play that children initiate themselves, by telling their own stories and playing them out with others or alone. Creative play is the time-proven way that young children absorb life and make it their own, developing social and emotional skills, as well as physical and intellectual ones, along the way.

Although creative play costs nothing and is highly effective, it has become a seriously endangered activity, pushed aside by the demands for early academic achievement, long hours spent in front of screens where children absorb other people's imaginative stories but do little to create their own, and a heavy reliance by parents on organized activities rather than giving children a chance to explore and learn on their own.

In its effort to better understand the loss of play, the Alliance for Childhood has been gathering reports from kindergarten teachers. In a small pilot study in Atlanta, experienced kindergarten teachers spoke of the disappearance of play from their classrooms because of mandated curriculums. They described how they were required to abandon creative play in favor of learning centers, which at first allowed open-ended exploration on the part of children that remained quite playful. Now, however, the learning centers have "defined outcomes," so the children have to be guided through learning experiences. While one private school teacher spoke of how her school still honored creative play, the public school teachers said that there was no room left in their curriculum for play.

What was most disturbing was the statement repeated by the teachers that when they did give their children time to play, the children did not know what to do with it. "They have no ideas of their own" is a remark we frequently hear.[1] Looking ahead, there is cause for serious concern about the barrenness of life when we can no longer think for ourselves or sustain democracies, which rely on the free thinking of their citizenry.

It is therefore essential that we create preschool and kindergarten curriculums that feature open-ended, creative play. To succeed, we will need to intervene and bring many children back into the world of play in their daily lives both in and outside of the classroom, and we will need to educate early childhood teachers, child care providers and others who work with children in the ways of bringing play alive again. Two key elements in bringing children back to play include the following:

- Young children have a deeply felt desire to participate with the adults around them through imitation. If we cook or do other real work that is comprehensible and meaningful (as opposed to sitting at a keyboard, and staring at squiggles on a screen), they are often at our feet, wanting to participate at least for a short time, *and then they are inspired to play.* But even if they do not imitate us directly they are taking in our inner mood and outer gesture, and this inspires their play. Observing adults engaged in purposeful physical work is children's primary mechanism for learning about their world. And then they make these lessons their own through play, during which time they give meaning to the gestures, attitudes, feelings, and actions that they have observed in us.

• The second key element for promoting play is to provide *simple* materials that are very open-ended such as logs and branches for building, stones, cloths, ropes, and other basic play materials. Giving children defined toys narrows their play options, whereas open-ended materials allow them to try on every aspect of life. Such materials also cost little and hold up for years. Over the years my classroom grew simpler and simpler, while the play grew more robust.

Arts and Hands-on Activities

Children are highly creative by nature and love to express themselves with any material at hand. It is widely recognized that artistic activity enhances a child's abilities in many areas. The National Association for the Education of Young Children (NAEYC), the world's largest early childhood organization, describes early artistic activity in this way:

> It is now agreed by many in the field that exploring and creating with art materials helps children become more sensitive to the physical environment (for instance, shape, size, and color); promotes cognitive development (decision-making, nonverbal communication, and problem solving); and increases their social and emotional development (a sense of individuality, appreciation of others' work, and sharing). Young children who are encouraged to engage in expressive art activities also gain a sense of accomplishment and grow toward achieving independence and autonomy.[2]

Another aspect of artistic activity is that it requires a hands-on relationship with the materials of life. Hands-on activity is another dying element of childhood, replaced by hours of passive screen viewing or interaction via keyboards and other computer devices. Not many children grow up knowing how to sew, cook, garden, do woodwork, knit, or crochet. Yet all of these contribute greatly to children's creativity and their ability to think and express themselves. As Frank Wilson, neurologist and well-known author of *The Hand,* explains, an unusually large part of the brain is linked to the hand. When children learn about the world or express themselves using their hands, there is much brain stimulation. He, too, is concerned that children have less and less opportunity to use their hands creatively and that this will have a negative effect on brain development.

Nurturing a Love of Nature

Young children have an inborn love of nature. Take a fussy infant outdoors and he nearly always calms down. The trees and sky, the air and wind, all seem to speak their own language and the young child is open to that language and is at home with it. Yet increasingly, children are growing up indoors or in cars with little free access to the outdoors. As Richard Louv points out in his book, *Last Child in the Woods,* today's children know far more about environmental risks than did his generation, but they have far less chance to relate directly with it. Too often they are not developing the personal love for nature that is so beneficial to them as an individual and so vital for their care of the Earth.

Expressed differently, young children have a natural relationship with the world of nature that can be developed into a lifelong bio-philia, a love of nature, or it can be diminished and subverted into bio-phobia, a fear of nature. If we are to preserve our endangered environment, a love of nature will be needed. However, it is important not to burden young children with an intellectual view of nature and its current degradation. Rather, one wants to work with children's own openness to nature to help them feel at home in it. Gradually they can learn the art of protecting nature or of cultivating it in ways that sustain it.

Some kindergartens here and abroad are developing outdoor programs that may include long, daily walks and play in natural settings. The forest kindergartens of Denmark and Germany have the children out in the woods all morning. This may seem a bit extreme, but so is the opposite tendency in this country to keep young children indoors all day. There are now many elementary schools that have completely eliminated recess time and schools are actually being built with no playgrounds at all.

As much as young children need time in nature, they also delight in small hands-on experiences of nature in the classroom such as planting grass or moss gardens in plates and tending them. Children's joy in watching their grass grow is palpable and learning to water the garden each day is a power-ful lesson in caring for the earth. Going for daily walks, even if it is only to a nearby tree if one is in an urban setting with no parks nearby, helps attune children to nature through all the seasons and all forms of weather. Whether we can offer young children a little or a lot of nature, what is important is that their encounters with nature consist of direct, hands-on, open-hearted experiences. Videos simply cannot provide that.

A Sense of the Sacred

Woven through all of these healthy essentials is a child's deep-rooted sense that there is a sacred element to life. Sometimes he or she will speak of it in terms of angels or God, and sometimes it is not named but is felt deeply, nonetheless. The realization that there is a spiritual dimension to life colors and fills young children's whole sense of being, and their sense of the world.

Children have an innate sense of the sacred but it can be easily forgotten through the deluge of modern, commercial life. Yet children long to find their connection to the sacred again. One example was a young four-year-old who begged her parents to leave her alone with her newborn sister. The parents were reluctant at first, but as the child was so insistent, they positioned themselves in an adjoining room and listened in via a baby monitor. They heard their child walk over to the cradle and whisper, "Tell me about God; I am forgetting."

This sense of the divine or the sacred can be kept alive in early childhood education through a deep respect for the creation of the world and all its manifestations, for the life of festival celebrations, for the sacredness of birth—and also of death when that enters the kindergarten through the death of a pet or a beloved relative. All of life offers moments of affirming the sacred, if we ourselves recognize it and honor it.

Educating Children for Peace

In a time when children are bombarded with messages about war and terrorism, it is especially important to also educate them in the ways of peace. Of course at a young age we do not want to make it an intellectual education about the difficulties of the world, but rather offer young children experiences that lay a foundation for a lifelong dedication to peace.

The Alliance for Childhood has prepared 10 steps for educating children for peace.[3] Some relate strongly to childhood essentials that we have discussed here, such as finding peace in nature and making time for creative play, which is such a good release for anger and upset. Another is to create a peaceful space at home or school where children can seek solace and inner centeredness.

It can be a small space, but there can be lovely colors, flowers or plants, and artwork. This is quite a contrast to the time-out chair, a punishment tool used widely for discipline. We could call this a "tune-in" chair, for it helps the child center and tune into themselves again. In my experience, even a very disturbed child is likely to get centered within a few minutes in such a setting. I discovered the power of such a chair as a new teacher when I worked with a very disturbed child from a difficult home. I soon learned that to punish her with time-out did more harm than good, yet her behavior was often out of control, and something was needed. I took a lumpy old armchair, put a beautiful blue cloth on it and called it our resting chair. When she was in need of calm and peace she would go to the chair and curl up. After a few minutes she was centered again and able to participate with us all. In later years I used a rocking chair or at times even a large basket lined with sheep's skins. The idea was always the same: here is a place of peace. The children loved it and took to it very well.

Finally, there are ways to gently introduce children to real-life problems by letting them help through hands-on activities. Perhaps they will bake bread or cookies for a family in the class where there is illness or a newborn baby. Most children love to draw cards or make simple gifts to help in times of trouble. Children have a natural altruism, and cultivating it through simple deeds that meet real needs is a way to prepare them for a life of giving and helping on the earth. However, we do need to be careful not to fill them with problems larger than they can carry. Emphasize the active ways they can help, rather than the enormity of the problem.

CONCLUSION

Worldwide, educators, policy makers, and parents are wrestling with the best ways to educate children. Too often, however, "best" is measured according to abstract goals for preparing children for the global market-place. In the process we are placing dangerously high levels of stress on the children, and they are suffering needlessly. We know so much about healthy child development, and if we could overcome fear and resist the need to hurry children, we could actually raise and educate children in wonderful ways. A recent book, *In Praise of Slowness* by Carl Honoré, is filled with positive examples of individuals and groups who have stepped out of the fast lane and opted for a slower and richer path of life.[4] He urges similar approaches in the raising of children and gives several examples of schools, including Waldorf schools, where the natural pace of child development sets the tone for the education, rather than the education accelerating the development of the children.

It is certainly not too late to slow down and put children at the center of education. There is always the fear that they will not learn enough. I don't know where that fear comes from, for my experience is that children enjoy working hard—not because we have created a test or set a bar that is impossibly high, but because they want to learn and are willing to go to great lengths when they are encouraged to be active in their own learning.

Among the greatest gifts we can offer children is a willingness to admit that we have made a mistake in the way we have shaped their education and then strive to do it right. It is time to be honest, own up to our failures, and work together to create healthy schools, families, and communities for the sake of the children and for us all.

Educating a Culture of Peace [5] by Ron Miller

The institutions and cultural values associated with the rise of modernity have had momentous effects, both positive and negative, on traditional social organization. Individualism, democracy, and material prosperity have opened up new vistas of equality and opportunity for many millions of people. Yet they have also shattered communal relationships and sense of responsibility toward local environments, exacerbating social inequality and ecological degradation. The modern, technologized world has uprooted the stability of traditional cultures, whose people now face wrenching choices and radical dislocations, not only from generation to generation, but often from one month to the next. Every aspect of our culturally mediated identity—from our economic activities and religious understandings to our food preferences and courtship rituals—is challenged or altered by the hypnotic power of mass media, the dizzying speed of technological innovation, and outbursts of mass violence, both sudden (for example, September 11) and endemic (in many parts of the world), all of which have pervasive global influence.

Consequently, the way *education* has been understood for many centuries, as the transmission of a shared social reality, is obsolete and inadequate for addressing the severe challenges of our time. As John Dewey observed more than a century ago, the challenges of modernity ought to cause us to radically rethink the purpose and process of education. To sustain a democratic culture in the face of rapid change and extreme conflict, he argued, requires the cultivation of *critical,* not merely technical, intelligence. Rather than instilling obedience and conformity, education for modern times must enable individuals to think deeply and creatively, and to work collaboratively as students and citizens to alter social practices that hinder their freedom or welfare. Education, he asserted, cannot simply look to the past but must be responsive to the pressing issues and dilemmas of a changing world. An education that is relevant to our time cannot simply aim for *transmission,* but must support cultural *reconstruction* or *transformation.*

Unfortunately, in these troubling times many societies are choosing reactionary responses to the unsettling consequences of modernity. This is most evident in the various forms of religious and cultural fundamentalism that have arisen from the Middle East to the American heartland, and in attempts by ruling elites, religious hierarchies, and male-dominated institutions to maintain their control in the face of the moral confusion and psychological disorientation that modernity has brought in its wake. Yet even the most advanced forces of modernization, otherwise so disdainful of traditional restraints, have adopted the educational mode of *transmission* to instill and reinforce a semblance of cultural stability. Ignoring the need for critical intelligence in sustaining a democratic culture, the leaders of government, business, and other powerful social institutions have forged authoritarian educational systems intended to mold a national—and indeed, global—consensus in support of their own economic and political fundamentalism.

By defining learning reductionistically as quantifiable performance on academic tests, these "standardistos" (as teacher-author Susan Ohanian aptly calls them) have isolated education from any meaningful engagement with the disturbing moral, political, and economic realities of our age and made schools the training grounds for mindless conformity and quiescent citizenship. By repeatedly threatening that young people, local communities, and even national economies will fail—that is, become outcasts—if their standards are not worshiped, the elites have persuaded whole populations to maintain, indeed to rigidify, the familiar, old-fashioned ways of teaching that rely on the forcible transmission of approved facts, beliefs, and attitudes.

The construction of this educational empire (which is, in fact an education *for* empire) is wrong for many reasons, according to those of us who envision a more caring and democratic culture than the one now unfolding. When education-as-transmission is transplanted from its heritage within the archaic, local, tradition-bound community to the modern nation-state and multinational corporation, powerful elites obtain compelling influence over the ideas and attitudes of huge masses of people. A pervasive academic monoculture seriously restricts opportunities for creative exchange of diverging intellectual, or ethical perspectives. Teachers become technicians rather than mentors; students become workers (or customers) adhering to prescribed tasks (or consuming an endorsed product) rather than curious, critical thinkers in search of wisdom and meaningful identity.

There is another major reason why present educational regimes are dangerously inadequate: The world is in crisis, suffering from insane violence, degradation of nature, rampant greed and commercialization, and loss of meaning and community, but the consuming goal of our schools is to train young people to compete in the job market, reinforcing the domination of the global corporate economy, which fuels many of these problems. Moreover, modern schooling, like any transmission-oriented model, prevents young people from recognizing or addressing critical problems in the world around them. So long as they are made to merely memorize the so-called facts presented in authorized textbooks, students are isolated from the difficult choices they will need to make, and the complex issues they will need to understand, if they are ever to respond effectively to this suffering world. If we don't involve young people in reconstructing our societies, in building a culture of peace, justice, and compassion, their future looks bleak indeed, no matter what marketable skill their school provides them. If education embodies a people's vision of the future, what future do we wish for our own children?

I stand with other visionary educators who, for the past 40 years at least, have passionately decried the failure of modern schooling to address the crisis of our age. During the period of intense cultural critique in the 1960s, opponents of the expanding technocracy such as Paul Goodman, John Holt, George Dennison, Ivan Illich, and A.S. Neill clearly saw the need to free education from the grip of corporate interests and standardized, bureaucratic management.[6]

More recently, writers such as Douglas Sloan, David Purpel, Nel Noddings, James Moffett, Deborah Meier, and various others have rejected the dominant emphasis of the professional education literature on standards and testing to argue that educating for a democratic and humane society requires qualities such as freedom, creativity, social responsibility, and commitment to moral and ethical ideals that transcend self-interest and corporate profits. The increasingly rigid and constricted scope of present-day public schooling is a key component of the destructive global technocratic monoculture now emerging, and it needs to be addressed just as urgently as the economic and environmental challenges that concern so many of us.

Riane Eisler, author of the international bestseller *The Chalice and the Blade* (1987), is perhaps the best known of the *cultural creative* writers to focus on the importance of education in reversing the destructive tendencies of both authoritarian traditions and modern technocracy. After exploring the broad sweep of cultural history and identifying the ruinous effects of a dominator cultural orientation on modern social institutions, Eisler concluded that her vision of a partnership-oriented culture could be achieved, in large part, through a deliberate change in educational practices. *Partnership education* is a coherent cluster of attitudes, goals, teaching approaches, design elements, and curriculum decisions meant to awaken young people's compassionate awareness of the huge oral and cultural choices that lie before them. In her book *Tomorrow's Children,* which spelled out the approach of partnership education, Eisler used the phrase "caring for life" to describe its essential underlying moral orientation: Where a dominator culture gives priority to top-down control, power, and authority, whether in intimate or international relations, a partnership culture seeks to protect the delicate variety, interdependence, and integrity of living beings, human and nonhuman. An attitude of reverence for life is the fundamental basis for a partnership culture, a caring and humane culture, a culture where peace rather than violence prevails. And this attitude can be cultivated, and must be cultivated, in the adult society's interactions with its children—that is, through education.

Partnership education, as I understand it, is not a method to be slavishly practiced. Rather it is a philosophical attitude, a specific expression of an educational orientation that has been called "progressive" and "holistic" at various times over the last century. The theme, if not the exact phrase, of *caring for life* appears commonly in the work of educators within this philosophical tradition, for they understand that to *educate* (literally to call forth) a human being is to nourish the mysterious life forces that give birth to our existence—exactly the opposite intention of drumming in obedience to stale cultural programming.

In a world suffering from obscene violence and wanton desecration, it is time for us to let go of the dominator cultural programming that was inflicted upon us, long enough to give our children a glimpse and a hope of a more peaceful, joyful, and caring world. A culture of peace honors the essential needs and aspirations of all human beings and recognizes, also, that our needs must be seen in the context of the fragile and interconnected web of life. A culture of peace nurtures strivings for mutual understanding, tolerance, and cooperation, rooted in empathy and compassion. Surely this must become the primary goal of education in our time.

ECOLITERACY[7] BY FRITJOF CAPRA

Over the past 10 years, my colleagues and I at the Center for Ecoliteracy have developed a special pedagogy, called Education for Sustainable Patterns of Living, which offers an experiential, participatory, and multidisciplinary approach to teaching ecological literacy. We are sometimes asked: "Why all these complexities? Why don't you just teach ecology?" In the following passages, I show that the complexities and subtleties of our approach are inherent in any true understanding of ecology and sustainability.

The concept of ecological sustainability was introduced more than 20 years ago by Lester Brown, who defined a sustainable society as one that is able to satisfy its needs without diminishing the chances of future generations.[8] This classical definition of sustainability is an important moral exhortation, but it does not tell us anything about how to actually build a sustainable society. This is why the whole concept of sustainability is still confusing to many.

What we need is an operational definition of ecological sustainability. The key to such a definition is the realization that we do not need to invent sustainable human communities from zero but can model them after nature's ecosystems, which *are* sustainable communities of plants, animals, and microorganisms. Since the outstanding characteristic of the biosphere is its inherent ability to sustain life, a sustainable human community must be designed in such a manner that its ways of life, businesses, economy, physical structures, and technologies *do not interfere with nature's inherent ability to sustain life.*

This definition of sustainability implies that in our endeavor to build sustainable communities, we must understand the principles of organization that ecosystems have developed to sustain the web of life. This understanding is what we call *ecological literacy.* In the coming decades the survival of humanity will depend on our ability to understand the basic principles of ecology and to live accordingly.

We need to teach our children—and our political and corporate leaders!—the fundamental facts of life: for example, that matter cycles continually through the web of life; that the energy driving the ecological cycles flows from the sun; that diversity assures resilience; that one species' waste is another species' food; that life, from its beginning more than three billion years ago, did not take over the planet by combat but by networking. Teaching this ecological knowledge, which is also ancient wisdom, will be the most important role of education in the twenty-first century.

The complete understanding of the principles of ecology requires a new way of seeing the world and a new way of thinking in terms of relationships, connectedness, and context. Ecology is first and foremost a science of relationships among the members of ecosystem communities. To fully understand the principles of ecology, therefore, we need to think in terms of relationships and context. Such contextual or systemic thinking involves several shifts of perception that go against the grain of traditional Western science and education. They are shifts from the parts to the whole, from objects to relationships, from contents to patterns, from quantity to quality, from structures to processes, from absolute knowledge to contextual knowledge.

This new way of thinking is also emerging at the forefront of science, where a new systemic conception of life is being developed. Instead of seeing the universe as a machine composed of elementary building blocks, scientists have discovered that the material world, ultimately, is a network of inseparable patterns of relationships; that the planet as a whole is a living, self-regulating system. The view of the human body as a machine and of the mind as a separate entity is being replaced by one that sees not only the brain, but also the immune system, the bodily tissues, and even each cell, as living, cognitive systems. This view no longer sees evolution as a competitive struggle for existence, but rather as a cooperative dance in which creativity and the constant emergence of novelty are the driving forces.

Consequently, teaching ecology requires a conceptual framework that is quite different from that of conventional academic disciplines. Teachers notice this at all levels of teaching, from very small children to university students. Moreover, ecology is inherently multidisciplinary, because ecosystems connect the living and nonliving worlds. Ecology, therefore, is grounded not only in biology, but also in geology, atmospheric chemistry, thermodynamics, and other branches of science. And when it comes to human ecology we have to add a whole range of other fields, including agriculture, economics, industrial design, and politics. Education for sustainability means teaching ecology in this systemic and multidisciplinary way.

When we study the basic principles of ecology in depth, we find that they are all closely interrelated. They are just different aspects of a single fundamental pattern of organization that has enabled nature to sustain life for billions of years. In a nutshell: nature sustains life by creating and nurturing communities. No individual organism can exist in isolation. Animals depend on the photosynthesis of plants for their energy needs; plants depend on the carbon dioxide produced by animals, as well as on the nitrogen-fixed by bacteria at their roots; and together plants, animals, and microorganisms regulate the entire biosphere and maintain the conditions conducive to life. Sustainability, therefore, is not an individual property but a property of an entire web of relationships. It always involves a whole community. This is the profound lesson we need to learn from nature. The way to sustain life is to build and nurture community.

When we teach this in our schools, it is important to us that the children not only *understand* ecology, but also *experience* it in nature—in a school garden, on a beach, or in a riverbed—and that they also experience community while they become ecologically literate. Otherwise, they could leave school and be first-rate theoretical ecologists but care very little about nature, about the Earth. In our ecoliteracy schools, we want to create experiences that lead to an emotional relationship with the natural world.

Experiencing and understanding the principles of ecology in a school garden, or a creek restoration project, are examples of what educators nowadays call *project-based learning*. It consists in facilitating learning experiences that engage students in complex real-world projects, reminiscent of the age-old tradition of apprenticeship. Project-based learning not only provides students with important experiences—cooperation, mentorship, integration of various intelligences—but also makes for better learning. There have been some very interesting studies on how much we retain when we are taught something. Researchers have found that after two weeks we remember only 10 percent of what we read, but 20 percent of what we hear, 50 percent of what we discuss, and 90 percent of what we experience. To us, this is one of the most persuasive arguments for experiential, project-based learning.

Community is essential for understanding sustainability, and it is also essential for teaching ecology in the multidisciplinary way it requires. In schools, various disciplines need to be integrated to create an ecologically oriented curriculum. Obviously, this is only possible if teachers from the different disciplines collaborate, and if the school administration makes such collaboration possible. In other words, the conceptual relationships among the various disciplines can be made explicit only if there are corresponding human relationships among the teachers and administrators.

Ten years of work have convinced us that education for sustainable living can be practiced best if the whole school is transformed into a learning community. In such a learning community, teachers, students, administrators, and parents are all interlinked in a network of relationships, working together to facilitate learning. The teaching does not flow from the top down, but there is a cyclical exchange of knowledge. The focus is on learning and everyone in the system is both a teacher and a learner.

In the conventional view of education, students are seen as passive learners, and the curriculum is a set of predetermined, decontextualized information. Our pedagogy of education for sustainable living breaks completely with this convention. We engage students in the learning process with the help of real-life projects. This generates a strong motivation and engages the students emotionally. Instead of presenting predetermined, decontextualized information, we encourage critical thinking, questioning, and experimentation, recognizing that learning involves the construction of meaning according to the student's personal history and cultural background.

Education for sustainable living is an enterprise that transcends all our differences of race, culture, or class. The Earth is our common home, and creating a sustainable world for our children and for future generations is our common task.

Chapter 6

Transcendent Spirit

CHILD HONORING AND RELIGION: ISSUES AND INSIGHTS BY HEATHER EATON
SPIRITUALITY AND THE CHILD BY MATTHEW FOX

CHILD HONORING AND RELIGION: ISSUES AND INSIGHTS BY HEATHER EATON

Your children are not your children. They are the sons and daughters of Life's longing for itself. They come through you but not from you, and though they are with you, yet they belong not to you.

—Kahlil Gibran

Child Honoring is a revolutionary project. It is a vision of immense importance, and is a bold and challenging response to the myriad troubles within human societies and the Earth community. Its principles require a radical change of consciousness, and a fundamental reorientation of social values and structures. First impressions of the Child Honoring paradigm do not reveal the profundity and depth of what the world would be like if children were honored and their welfare put at the heart of societies. As a mother, an ecofeminist, and as someone who considers herself to be socially aware, until recently, I assumed that the world of children was on my radar screen. After conversations with Raffi, and on considerable reflection, I have come to realize that children are *not* on the social, political, ecological, or feminist radar screens: not in an effective way. We live in an adult-oriented world. Child honoring requires a genuine awakening to the realities of children, and a rethinking of social, political, ecological, and religious priorities.

CHILD HONORING AND RELIGION

The intersection of religion and children is interesting, surprising, disappointing, and one of great potential. At the initial stages of my investigation, and as a professional theologian, I assumed there would be abundant materials on religion and children. This is not the case. In fact, I was shocked at how little is available, with its narrow focus on how to transmit religious teachings *to* children. I found almost nothing from the viewpoint and realities of children themselves. And yet, religions, at times, have viewed the infant and young child as an essential manifestation of the Sacred.[1] I would like to offer an overview of the contributions, ambiguities, and potential that religions can offer to a child-honoring revolution. I will explore the following five aspects of the intersection of religion and children:

1. Religious teachings and traditions
2. Religion, culture, and children
3. Religion, beliefs, and the transmission of faith
4. Children as spiritually aware
5. A new religious moment

RELIGIOUS TEACHINGS AND TRADITIONS

Religions, as symbolic and social worldviews, have been present from the earliest times of human culture, and in innumerable forms.[2] They influence virtually all aspects of human life: from the cosmological horizon to social norms, and from cooking details to the most intimate moments of life. Religions offer elaborate stories, rituals, symbol systems, and social codes that orient and guide human communities. Overall, they relate to ultimate values that motivate and activate a deep energy within us.

Religions are broad and deep. Each has a point of origin, teachings and texts, dogmas, beliefs and rituals, ethics, and universal truth claims. At a deeper level, religions begin and end in mystery. They are about experiences of an ineffable dimension of life: the mysterious, living, overwhelming yet affirming sense of the wonder of life. Religious sensitivities urge us to identify with something larger than ourselves: they stir the lure of the beyond and an attraction to a transcendent dimension of life. Religious experiences tend to affirm that life is utterly precious, priceless and of infinite value, even in the face of despair, meaningless, and death. Religions discern the patterns, coherence, and archetypes hidden within the mysteries of life, and name these as Sacred. For Hinduism and Buddhism it is the Dharma or law; for Confucianism, the Li; for Daoism, the Dao or the Way; for Judaism, the Torah; in some Indigenous traditions it is the Great Spirit; and for Christianity, the Logos.

Religions often contain tenets that are opposed to what is revealed through other forms of knowledge, such as science. They are fraught with bias, irrationality, and at times unintelligible beliefs. Most espouse beliefs aimed at social control; they can abuse their power and oppress undesirables, and often constrain women. Recent attention has been given to the ambivalent role of religions in both oppression and liberation, in creating conflict, and in its resolution and reconciliation.[3]

Contemporary religions have faced many issues, such as women's autonomy, human sexualities, massive poverty, global inequities, and ecological ruin. When the multireligious and radical plurality of the world confronts religious truth claims, religions generally respond in one of two ways. They retrench into rigid and distilled beliefs and moral judgments, or they renegotiate their understandings within the altered social parameters. Whatever one's religious stance, at the very least, religions are complex phenomena, and their impact on social realities cannot be underestimated.

Religious texts contain only sporadic passages about children. In some passages children are described as particularly blessed and to be cherished. They are said to reveal the Sacred, and in the monotheistic traditions (Judaism, Christianity, Islam) have a more direct relationship with God. There are also troublesome stories of children being sacrificed, raped, eaten, sold, and left to die. Still other stories talk of children only in terms of their value to adults. They are often seen as possessions. When children are referred to as blessings or heirs, it is usually only the sons; the daughters by contrast, are often regarded as a curse. These varied descriptions of children in texts remind us that there is no "pure religion" to which to appeal, and no historical manifestation of religion that was not deeply flawed and biased. In every era, religions are renegotiated and reinterpreted.

Nonetheless all religions have core traditions and teachings on personal and social ethics, nonviolence, the common good, equitable sharing, and care for the vulnerable. They teach the value of human life, and a sense of the Sacred. Can these now be reinterpreted and oriented towards honoring children?

RELIGION, CULTURE, AND CHILDREN

When examining the relationship between religion and children, it is necessary to be context-specific: Buddhism in Vietnam is not the same as in North America or Tibet. Christianity is lived differently in Sweden or Indonesia, in Latin America or China. Cultural context plays an enormous role in how religions are lived and how children fare. Furthermore, in strongly religious patriarchal cultures, children must show obedience to their father and to religious leaders. In such societies as these, there are distinct constraints on both girls and boys. Often, girls are given less to eat, and receive little or no formal education. They will enter adulthood with few rights, and with minimal sexual and reproductive freedom. And boys are educated with patriarchal biases. This does not mean that the creative, inquisitive, and wonder-filled world of all young children is stifled. Rather, it is that the cultural and religious contexts place restraints on respecting and honoring children. Upon close examination, however, it is unclear where religious edicts end and cultural bias begins.

In North America, with its diverse cultural influences, there is an overarching, albeit weak, tradition of respect for children. This is further weakened by a rabid consumer ideology that is force-fed to the young. Religions add to this potpourri. While some blend with the dominant culture of secular consumerism, others desire to limit certain cultural norms in ways that can be either progressive or regressive. Some religions come into conflict with prevailing cultural values with regard to gender roles, dress codes, scientific beliefs, and sexuality. They can even motivate racism, misogyny, homophobia, and other problems. Sometimes children are placed at risk when a remedy of healing prayers rather than medical care is used to treat illness. Religions can and do encourage followers to reject overly consumer-oriented and competitive values, and to participate more fully in the life of the community. At one extreme, religious practices can threaten human rights, and at the other, it is the wisdom from within a given religious tradition that challenges social oppression. It is a mixed bag!

RELIGION, BELIEFS, AND THE TRANSMISSION OF FAITH

As we have seen throughout the millennia, each successive generation passes on its cultural and religious traditions. Many groups fear that their faith will be lost unless the next generation receives, accepts, and lives it similarly to their parents.

Many religions believe that they contain ultimate and absolute truths, which often include their patriarchal biases. Practitioners of these religions believe that children must be taught the truth. Dogma and beliefs are stressed over religious experiences; this approach tends to treat other religions as inferior or simply wrong. Some religions are more flexible and view the different religions as valid alternative paths to a point of unity. They teach tolerance and an appreciation for diverse religious experiences. In reality, however, each tradition has degrees of fundamentalist, conservative, liberal, radical, and inclusive approaches. The transmission of the faith to children differs in each case.

Despite these differences, however, religions are virtually always *taught* to the young. This means that children are expected to passively receive the foundational claims. Obedience is subtly or blatantly the norm. In Christian contexts, for example, children are taught that Jesus saves. From what, one might ask, and kids do. From your sins. What sins . . . Not sure . . . You just have to believe. The problem is that usually children are initiated into religion via the beliefs, dogmas, and rituals; not via the road of religious experiences.

But when religious beliefs or dogmas are separated from religious experiences—wonder, awe, reverence, amazement, and a sense of the Sacred—then they are like bones without flesh, or lungs without air. Without the grounding religious experiences, dogmas, beliefs, and symbolic language sound like a foreign language. They are unintelligible, and erode quickly into fundamentalism. It is essential to realize that religious experiences must take precedence over the beliefs that nurture and sustain them. For religions are about the art of living.

There is little value in the transmission of faith by the passive learning of beliefs that barely make sense to a child. This is especially true in a climate where the freedom and integrity of creative and discerning children is already diminished. Children usually have an innate sense of truth-telling; they are not attracted to what does not make sense, and are deeply hurt when they are deceived. They possess dignity, integrity, and emotional intelligence. Religious transmission of truncated, disconnected beliefs is unhelpful, even harmful. I agree with Alice Miller's conclusion that such practices amount to society's betrayal of children.[4]

Yet, revising beliefs and truth claims is difficult, because religions are complex. They are woven into both personal identity and into our social worldview. They are not simply customs and practices, or places of comfort in challenging times. Peoples' religious beliefs and commitments are interconnected and integral to their self-understanding. To unravel someone's closely held religious beliefs is to unravel their sense of self. As a religion professor, I have seen people cling to obviously erroneous beliefs rather than reexamine them; reexamination is simply too threatening. It is understandable (yet not acceptable) that the Catholic Church condemned Galileo. He discovered that it was the Earth that revolved around the sun, not the other way around. But the official Christian dogma held firmly that the Earth was the center of the universe, and many other Christian beliefs and dogmas hinged on this. The church could not tolerate the potential domino effect of changes in belief. Instead, it suppressed a factual truth. Religions become unintelligible when they divorce themselves from the ever-changing world as it is.

Young people have an inquisitive and daring spirit, and they are keenly interested in the world. Religions need to be cognizant of the contemporary world of children and bring into dialogue what they are learning from many sources. Religions need to support, not compete with, their life-affirming experiences. As says Buddhist Thich Nhat Hanh:

> People usually consider walking on water or in thin air a miracle. But I think the real miracle is not to walk either on water or in thin air, but to walk on earth. Every day we are engaged in a miracle which we don't even recognize: a blue sky, white clouds, green leaves, the black, curious eyes of a child—our own two eyes. All is a miracle.[5]

CHILDREN AS SPIRITUALLY AWARE

Religions, like most of society, tend to be an adult-oriented phenomenon. The premise is that children need to be taught and initiated into the social customs and moral norms. This is of course true. But the emphasis on what needs to be taught often overrides what children themselves posses and can teach. Children need to be seen, not as future adults or as our future, but as people here and now who manifest attributes that are important for society as a whole.

Children who are nurtured and loved are curious, playful, receptive, relational, as well as uncertain. They live in a world of imagination. Imagination is not something opposed to reality, but rather the way we appreciate and give meaning to the depths hidden within reality. As Maria Montessori eloquently wrote:

> There is in the soul of a child an impenetrable secret that is gradually revealed as it develops. Human consciousness comes into the world as a flaming ball of imagination.[6]

Imagination is closely tied to creativity, ingenuity, and responsiveness to life's challenges. What we imagine is what we create. These days the world is overrun with conflict, violence, segregation, patriarchy, and ecological ruin. If we were to imagine that nonviolence and peace are possible, that diversity is beautiful, that equity is desirable, that we belong to the Earth, and that even our religious truth claims may not be the last word . . . then a different world may indeed be possible. But first it must be imagined!

Religious experiences can open us to a world of imagination and possibilities, of stunning elegance, of mysteries and adventure, of vistas beyond our knowing, and of a sacred dimension sustaining the whole. For children and mystics, "Even the tiniest caterpillar is a book about God," in the words of Meister Eckhart. Religions need to rediscover their roots in which awe and wonder are integral to religious experience. In this way, they can join with and celebrate the child. As Rabbi Abraham Joshua Heschel claims, "Wonder, not doubt, is the root of all knowledge."

It is my experience that children live in a world of wonder and awe, whose power is available to anyone who spends time in the natural world. Examples of such awareness are found in all religious traditions. The movement of the stars, the power of mountains, the invigorating quality of clean ocean air fills us with feelings of celebration and reverence.

Children can teach us about wonder, amazement, joy, dance, generosity, and unconditional love. They pour themselves into life, without reservation. They feel emotions fully—all of them! They are not moral angels or overly concerned with the common good. But they are fully alive and willing to engage with all senses and ways of knowing. It is the neglected or emotionally or physically hurt child who shows a fear of life.

The trouble is that many children are deeply hurt in their early years and carry on through life with fears, wounds, and constraints. They experience injustices, and feel despair about life, without protective boundaries. They live in an inner world of confusion and sadness. Dogmatic forms of religion can provide a compensation for these injuries, offering clear answers in an ambiguous world, and a desire for a better future, or heaven, sometime, somewhere else.

There is a fluid relationship between authentic religious experiences and the world of the young child. This needs to be nurtured in our time. As Rachel Carson commented,

> If I had influence with the good fairy who is supposed to preside over the christening of all children, I should ask that her gift to each child in the world be a sense of wonder so indestructible that it would last throughout life.[7]

A NEW RELIGIOUS MOMENT

There is no question that religions have resources that could support the Child Honoring initiative. The overall commitment to the common good, the conviction that all life has intrinsic value, and the intuition that there is something unique and special about the young child could all contribute to a new consciousness about children. Pragmatically, religions are highly influential social forces, and have access to more people than most other social organizations. Thus the potential for education is immense. If religious resources were actively oriented towards the principles of the *Covenant for Honoring Children,* we would see immediate changes in the lives of children, and in their communities. To heal children is to heal humanity. The time is ripe to make a new covenant with children.

I have described religious experiences through the classic lens of wonder and awe, for this is where religion and children readily meet. If religions were more focused on *experiences* rather than dogma and beliefs, they might be more oriented towards the world of children. If religious experiences were nurtured for everyone, then we would be moved to act from places deep in our being, beyond our dogmatic stances. We would find new images for describing a level of life only known as Sacred, Holy, Divine, Mystery, Great Self, Spirit, God/ess, Dao, and other innumerable names for the ineffable. When the Sacred is recognized, in whatever form and with whatever language, it is protected. If the Sacred was recognized in children, they would be cherished. If the Sacred was perceived in all religious traditions, then tolerance would give way to genuine appreciation for diverse traditions. If the Sacred was recognized within all life of the Earth community, then we would not be in an ecological crisis. People do not destroy what they experience as Sacred.

It is clear that religions are currently in transition. They did not emerge from civilizations that had to address the radical plurality and spiritual diversity that we face today. As mentioned, of the two responses to this challenge, one is to insist on absolute truth claims, which fosters fundamentalism. The other is to reevaluate the truth claims, the notions of revelation, and recover the basic religious insights. For those who take this road, there is no loss of faith, although perhaps a reexamination of some beliefs. Experiences of the Sacred expand and deepen. Life is enriched, more subtle, and opaque. This latter multifaith or interreligious approach, while more challenging, is the one I consider to be worthwhile in today's world.

While each religion has distinct contributions, common ground is necessary if we are to address the current global crises. It *is* possible to appreciate each religious tradition as offering specific insights and teachings within what Thomas Berry calls a tapestry of revelations.[8] It is interesting that young children have little difficulty in being in multireligious environments. They can navigate the beliefs and symbols, and attend diverse rituals without the religious borders adults find necessary.[9] Young adults (who are not archconservatives) are rarely attracted to religion these days because they *know* the world is multireligious and they *need* a religious response that takes this seriously. This is precisely the time for religions to unite, to reach consensus on the need to care for and honor children. It is time to encourage religions to make such a historic commitment.

Religions are in transition from another vantage point. Our generation is the first to have sufficient data to recognize the creative process, history, and evolution of the universe and of Earth. We belong to an emergent universe of some thirteen billion years, living on a fragile blue-green planet of four to five billion years. Humans are a very young species (two hundred thousand years or so) within a complex evolving community of life. We belong to the Earth, in every conceivable way! We cannot think of children's health without Earth health. Nor can we think of economics, psychology, sciences, and even religion without considering the centrality of the Earth. This is a new—and ancient—religious awakening!

If we could enter into this new religious moment, we would know of our belonging to Earth as a vital member of a community of life. We would not feel a desire to escape to an afterlife. We would perceive and respond with reverence to the Great Spirit hidden within every leaf and tree. Our role as adults would be to mentor this religious/spiritual awakening within children. We would agree with Thomas Berry, that it takes a universe to raise a child.[10]

Child Honoring is a profound part of this awakening. Not only are we realizing the breadth and depth of the cosmic and Earth reality in which we are embedded, but we see that the human child is a vital part of this consciousness. If we look we can discover the origins of humanity in the child; what is essential and most precious for a lifetime is present in children. Religions speak the language of awareness, awakening, wisdom, reverence, and responsibility—all are integral to understanding the unique place of humanity within the Earth community, most visible in the young child. Children *know* they are a part of something much bigger than themselves. The roles religion can and should play in Child Honoring are many, and necessary. The moment is now.

CONCLUSION

The crucial work of Child Honoring joins with other initiatives that see the need for genuine new insights if the future is to be viable. We are coming to realize that to nurture children is to nurture humanity, and to do so is to restore the Earth's biodiversity by a commitment to sustainable living. To care for the most vulnerable members of society—to put them at the heart of all decisions—is to care for the whole. This is a deep spiritual truth, a religious teaching of vital significance.

Child Honoring will require conscious choices and a reevaluation of the basic orientation of many, and perhaps most, societies. Yet within this divine, if troubled, milieu in which we live, there are hidden strengths, insights, wisdom, courage, justice, beauty, abundant joy, and a Sacred presence available to those who thirst. We can and need to thirst more for the well-being of the children. Perhaps we need to remember that they can teach as well as learn, lead as well as follow. In the wise words of Maria Montessori:

> Whoever touches the life of the child touches the most sensitive point of a whole which has roots in the most distant past and climbs toward the infinite future.[11]

SPIRITUALITY AND THE CHILD BY MATTHEW FOX

Psychologist Alice Miller made the compelling point that the West teaches the commandment to "Honor thy father and thy mother," but there is no commandment to "Honor thy children." There is a certain neglect of the child that religion often succumbs to. This is especially the case, I believe, in Western culture with its emphasis on competition and empirical science. In the West we are taught that we live in a mechanical universe and our bodies are machines and that no creatures other than humans have soul: animals, plants, rivers, mountains, lands do not have soul. Such a world is not just neglectful of children; it is expressly hostile towards them.

The child knows, quite instinctively, how full of awe and wonder nature is. How magical and full of soul life is. But if adults hold ideologies about the deadness and inertness of the world—orthodox science for several centuries—children's inner lives wither rather than blossom.

And adults, instead of honoring the child within, have grown up repressing, scolding, feeling shame or guilt about this child. It is a short journey from disparaging the inner child of the adult to disparaging the child who is not yet adult. We can call this adultism, and it is just as serious as racism, sexism, or any other ism. It is just less talked about, probably because adults do almost all the talking (and writing and publishing).

Adultism derives, as I argued in my book, *The Coming of the Cosmic Christ,* from adults repressing the inner child.[12] In an adultist society, the mystic gets aborted. In the modern era the mystic was neither honored nor understood. As Theodore Roszak observed, during the Enlightenment the mystic was held up for ridicule as the worst offense against science and reason. And so with the child. The child too was to listen and obey, to take orders, and stay out of the way. All too often, the child too is ridiculed for being an offense against the adult world of science and reason.

The great twentieth-century psychologist Otto Rank observed that: "Man has misinterpreted the child's inner life, which he can conceive of, it seems, only in terms of his own psychology. The child lives mentally and emotionally on an entirely different plane: his world is not a world of logic, causality, and rationalism. It is a world of magic, a world in which imagination and creativity will reign—internal forces that cannot be explained in terms of scientific psychology."[13]

Artist Suzi Gablik, author of *The Reenchantment of Art and Living the Magical Life,* describes her childlike way of experiencing the world: "to attune my mind to ways of seeing that have remained hidden or left out in our culture. . . . I personalize my belief that the universe is communicating with me in a conscious and intelligent way. In a world that mistrusts and rejects magic, I feel as if I am reclaiming an older, half-forgotten way of consciousness, deep down in the senses . . . heightening my mystical receptivity to experiences that don't fit into our rationalist view of the world." Recounting a mystical experience she underwent in the Southwest desert, Gablik writes: "after that experience, I never felt the same again about my past or the Western worldview—the rational, scientific conception of reality and the disenchanted philosophy which has shaped the twentieth century by breaking the back of alternative, more magical ways of thinking about life."[14] Such alternative, magical ways of thinking about life include the child's way of seeing life.

Consider what the French philosopher Gaston Bachelard teaches when he calls daydreaming "primordial contemplation." Children are experts at contemplation and daydreaming. But do we give them credit for their contribution? Or are we always trying to abort their daydreaming so that the rational will prevail? Some adults spend hours every day in contemplative exercises which often show little of the child's gift for contemplating and day dreaming.

Another issue in adultism is our images of Divinity. Many adults carry within them exclusive images of God as an Old Man, usually an old white man with a long white beard. Such stereotypes and projections carry on the work of adultism because, as Meister Eckhart observed, "all the names we give to God come from an understanding of ourselves." In 1987, Cardinal Ratzinger, in his role as Inquisitor General, was very upset by my calling God "child," even though many mystics of the West have done so, just as Eckhart did. If we do not see God as young, then we may have real difficulty in seeing the Divine in the child, and children as Divine—and as authentic images of God. Eckhart speaks against adultism when he says "God is novissimus—the newest thing there is." And God is "always new, always in the beginning," and when we feel renewed, we are ourselves young and in the beginning and with God.

Francis of Assisi, with his interpretation of the Christmas event, was especially keen on the memory of God as child. The manger and crèche rituals and traditions that he espoused ought not to be sentimentalized. They are not so much about a nostalgic return to Bethlehem and the "baby Jesus" as they are about the revelation that God comes to the lowly and as the lowly. God comes as a child, as the child in all of us, the smallest among us. God does not come so much to save the child as to announce to the world through the child that "good news" or breakthrough or change of heart is possible.

The wisdom tradition of Israel articulates the relationship between wisdom and children. "Out of the mouth of babes comes wisdom," we are instructed. Wisdom often plays like children. Indeed, the historical Jesus complained about his generation: "It is like children shouting to each other as they sit in the market place: 'We played the pipes for you, and you wouldn't dance; we sang dirges, and you wouldn't mourn.'. . . Yet wisdom has been proven right by her actions" (Mt. 11.16–19). And the Book of Proverbs, another book from Israel's wisdom tradition, has wisdom speaking: "I (Wisdom) was by God's side the master craftsperson playing with God day after day, ever at play in God's presence."

Play is a central feature of wisdom, central to the world of the child and the mystic alike. The thirteenth-century Beguine and mystic Mechtild of Magdeburg wrote: "I, God, am your playmate! I will lead the child in you in wonderful ways for I have chosen you. Beloved child, come swiftly to Me, for I am truly in you. Remember this: The smallest soul of all is still the daughter of the Creator, the sister of the Son, the friend of the Holy Spirit and the true bride of the Hoy Trinity."[15] Carl Jung agreed, saying that creativity comes only through play and fantasy.

In addition, the Christ who is slain on the cross in the person of Jesus was not named a "cosmic sheep" but a "cosmic lamb." The lamb archetype is significant for it is "the puer," "the puella," the child that gets slain by empires time and again. It is happening all over again in our day, in the American empire and beyond.

The truest victims of Empire are the children. They bear the brunt of all wars, including eco-wars or wars against the beautiful diversity of species. Their extreme vulnerability is most prone to assaults on psyche, soul, and body: by domestic coercion, cultural violence, and by the industrial pollution of air, water, and soils. They have the most years to live, and the most to lose.

Adults need to discover and rediscover the child within. This involves setting out on a kind of mystical journey. For to befriend one's inner child is to befriend the mystic in oneself. We can begin to see how radical the teachings of the historical Jesus were when he criticized adults telling them that it is they and not the children who have to change; and it is the children, not they, who are the teachers of what matters most. "Until you change and become like children you will never receive the kingdom and queendom of God." He challenges adults to welcome all that is alive and real of the child in them. Truly such a teaching honors the children and wisdom that comes through them. An alternative rendering of this saying of Jesus comes from Jesus scholar John Dominic Crossan.[16]

Crossan comments: "If we can leave aside our own dangerous and destructive romanticism of children, we should recall that in ancient patriarchal societies the newborn child could be easily abandoned (to slavery at best, death at worst) if the father did not lift it into his arms and declare it was to live as his child."[17] Jesus' teaching lifted up the self-image of children as it enlightened myopic adults.

As we have said, the child is not just outside us, but also inside. The child is us, not just the "other." And adults who do not heed this can easily fall into the trap of projecting ownership onto children, especially their own, *and thereby making children into our images instead of God's images.* Or as Otto Rank put it: "Parents and educators can learn from the child, indeed, must learn if the child is to be a living, valuable factor in their lives, and not merely an object for gratification of egoistic impulses."[18] Children are not here to be fodder for adult egos or their entertainment; they are not here to serve adults but to be served by adults, so they may grow into healthy adults who know about service.

One way that adults can learn to honor their inner child is through meditation, which is often described as a return to one's "original purity" (Buddhism) or "original blessing" (myself) or to "original wisdom" (Hildegard of Bingen). There is something about a return to one's origins that gets us going again, heals us, gives us energy, brings things together. There is a kind of holiness about beginnings, about origins. Rank called this a taste of the "unio mystica," the original mystical union that we all underwent in the womb but that was often disrupted when we were born. To return to our origin can be a refreshing thing, and that is what meditation helps us to do.

There are of course many kinds of meditation: from sitting to walking, from chanting to emptying oneself of all images and sounds, from singing to painting, from doing masks to doing clay, from drumming to dancing. Art as meditation is like child's play. It takes people back to their origins, to their childhood, when we sought out quite naturally a paintbrush, a piece of paper, scissors, a chant or a dance to express what was going on inside. Indeed, artists and children have a lot in common. Boudelaire declared that "an artist is one who can recover childhood at will." We might say that meditation and authentic prayer involve the art of recovering childhood at will, honoring the artist, the mystic, and the inner child inside each of us.

A common language of children and adults is art. And the art of arts is ritual. Community gatherings are where all ages and all stories are honored, aren't they? If you visit most houses of worship in our time, you will observe a great deal of reading, preaching, or being read to and preached at. You will also see a great deal of fidgeting by the children and you may also find rooms where fussing children can be kept out of sight and sound lest they disturb the adults. It appears that much modern worship—with its emphasis on text—excludes children.

These are some of the reasons that have led me to develop and participate in an alternative form of worship which I call "The Cosmic Mass." We do not sit and "read at each other" but rather we dance together amidst images from slides and videos while listening to music. No one has to invest in crying rooms for these services. Children of all ages participate and they are not bored. They love to dance with their parents and to observe adults dancing. Dancing is altogether natural for them.

A few years ago I was conducting a workshop in Florida and I invited the group to dance to music from a tape I brought with me that was representative of the music we employ at our Cosmic Mass. Afterwards a sophisticated woman in her 40s came up to me with tears on her cheeks and told me the following story. She was from Boston and was a practicing Episcopalian but she said her 11-year-old son for two years was unable to go to church with her. "He would shake if we even got close to church," she said. "I loved my faith and wanted to pass it on to him and was crushed by this problem. But in the middle of this dance I heard a voice that said: 'Here is a way you can pray with your son.' And these tears started and have not stopped." Yes, we need ways that adults and children can pray together as we move from modern to postmodern forms of worship.

By developing forms of worship that are *not* adultist and merely book-oriented and *do not* require reading skills to pray, we can include the child—both the child about us and the child within. And in the process, we can create true community, for community is by definition inclusive. It embraces all generations. It finds a common language by which varied generations can communicate, celebrate, and learn from each other. Ritual is one such language, a language essential to community.

Alice Miller wrote that suppressing the child "permeates so many areas of our life that we hardly notice it anymore. Almost everywhere we find the effort, marked by varying degrees of intensity and by the use of various coercive measures, to rid ourselves as quickly as possible of the child within us . . . in order to become an independent, competent adult deserving of respect."[19]

So essential is the celebration of the child to adult spirituality that I would propose this as a key litmus of spirituality and religion. Religion tends to offer itself only to the adult mind and agenda; while spirituality tends to include the child. By embracing the child with respect and love, both can speak not only to the corporal child, but to the child within—the mystic child, the magical child, the growing source of wisdom.

Chapter 7

Honoring All Life

LORNA B. WILLIAMS

Ten was a significant year. It was the year I came back to life and learned to speak again, a whole year after I returned home from "residential school" where my spirit was broken. I had lost the will to speak and lost the use of any language. Most importantly, I had lost the capacity to trust adults, those I loved and even myself. My parents, aunts and uncles, and the old people who surrounded me in my village, Mount Currie, British Colombia, Canada, helped me come back to life with their care and love. That same year, I witnessed my community disintegrate. It went from a healthy, caring, hard-working, orderly, community full of laughter to one of violence, uncertainty, anger, and irresponsibility. My life has been devoted to learning to understand the lessons from that year, when I was ten.

Residential schools were boarding schools operated by religious missionaries under the direction of the Canadian government. Indian Residential schools operated from 1763 to 1986. The purpose of the residential school was to remove Indigenous children from their families and communities, to wipe away the knowledge of their languages and to replace those languages with English; to erase their histories, stories, and songs; break their cultural traditions; and sever their relationships with the land and with their families in order to civilize, Christianize, and Canadianize them. For the children, the experience of forced removal was traumatic and destructive; it was equally destructive to the people left behind in the communities. With the children gone, the core of their world was detached. When the children returned they were strangers to their own families, to their community, and to the land.

I witnessed the effects of the residential schools in my community and in many other Indigenous communities. I saw children neglected, and living in poverty, without a single caring adult; I saw children caring for alcoholic and drug-addicted parents; I saw children parenting other children; I saw children exploited by adults and by older children; I witnessed children mistreated and disrespected by teachers, principals, physicians, health care workers, social workers, police, shopkeepers, and clergy. And yet, I also saw other children working alongside their families, their grandparents, fishing, gardening, hunting, berry picking, living happily on their land. I watched them playing in the forest, swimming, riding horses with nothing but a rope to guide the horse. I watched them sing and dance and learn their Indigenous languages while learning modern technologies. I saw that a child's spirit is both fragile and vulnerable and resilient and robust.

Healthy, caring communities produce healthy, caring, responsible children. And healthy, caring, responsible people create healthy, caring communities. First Nations worked at living life in a respectful, responsible, relational manner by practicing humility and acknowledging that we are only a small part of a greater whole. When each child in a community is honored and treated in an honorable way, all life is honored. While we cannot go back in time to relive the past, we can still learn from First Nations and other Indigenous people how they cared for and honored children to create healthy communities that cared for and honored all its members. In this chapter I will relate the child-honoring practices of my people—the Lil'wat—to demonstrate how societies can rebuild respectful caring societies after the world of children is torn by war, racism, and misguided government policies.

The Lil'wat believe that each child comes into the world with gifts to share. The responsibility of the family and community is to see these gifts and to nurture and support these gifts so they may emerge and flourish throughout the individual's life. The personal and unique qualities of each person are nurtured and recognized in every child as necessary for the well-being of the family, community, and nation. The process begins prior to birth.

Intentionality is built into the way the mother communicates with the unborn child during pregnancy. Mothers as well as other family members describe explicitly what they will do together once the child enters the world. They speak as though the child is already part of the family and community.

Young mothers and fathers-to-be are encouraged by the old people to live their lives in harmony and balance, not to overexert themselves in work or play. In order to help the unborn child maintain a state of balance, the family and community support the mother in keeping her balance, emotionally, mentally, physically, and spiritually. It is understood that how we feel affects the unborn child. Mothers are protected from becoming too distressed or upset—they are not to get too excited or frightened. Mothers are instructed not to eat food that is too hot or too cold, so as not to drastically change their body temperature. The entire family and community supports young mothers and fathers in maintaining balance and an even temperament.

Prior to hospitals and doctors, when a baby was born a midwife attended it, someone from the community, selected by the family. The newborn was considered to .have two mothers at the time of the birth, the birth mother and the midwife. The children the midwife helped bring into the world were considered to also be her children and she developed a special, lifelong relationship with them. At the time of birth, then, there was already a strong, positive, caring connection made with someone beyond the immediate family. The umbilical chord was placed in a tree in a quiet place so that the child would always maintain a connection with the land. Later, as children were born in hospitals, away from the community, they no longer had this connection with someone in the community or with the land and this further weakened the families and community.

Every child born in my family was brought to my uncle, who was the elder and leader in the family until he passed on. Whenever the child cried and could not be consoled we would bring him the child, and he would sing, and the baby would become calm and quiet. He was creating a connection for the child with the song and his voice. This is a good way of building trust. It is a powerful teaching to know we have a place in the life of our family, a place where we belong. The songs he sang all had an even tempo, a certain rhythm that created an environment of calmness and harmony, much like the quiet beat of the drum and the beat of the heart. From an early age the baby had strong relationships with significant people in the family and community. We learned from those who were significant in our lives.

Newborn babies and young children were given a name that would be associated with this early period of their lives; they would have this name until they received a formal name. The baby names were full of endearment, and demonstrated the love felt for the baby. The elders observed the qualities and characteristics of the child or the surrounding environment; if they recognized the qualities or characteristics of an ancestor the child would be given that ancestor's name.

The old people of the community would come and hold the baby and stroke the little nose, ears, forehead, cheek, arms, legs, and body. And they would say, "Oh baby, you've come to us and brought this good nose, mouth, strong legs, strong arms; you'll be able to help me with fishing, berry picking, root digging. You'll be able to run up the mountains to find the biggest berries for us. You'll be able to pack lots of fish. You'll run as fast as the deer." Their words to the baby were full of intention and reciprocity, transcendence and meaning. They expressed their intentions for future activities with the child and described what was important to the people, the land, their activities and values.

They were also very focused on the character of the child, commenting on the child's quickness to smile, curiosity, persistence, energy, calmness, attentiveness. They watched children who were quick to anger, those who were stubborn, willful, those who were quick to laugh; they noted those who tolerated teasing, those who didn't. They noted children who were playful, and those who cried easily; they noted the time of day when they fussed or liked to sleep, when they liked to be with people, and who made them laugh. They observed children at play; these observations gave them clues to determine the future role of the child in the community. These observations helped them make decisions about the names and mentors for the child. The names were chosen not only because the name suited the child but also as a challenge for the child to grow into. For example, if the child showed a fiery temperament, he or she would be given a name to balance that temperament to achieve harmony, not to eradicate the fire but to build its positive strength. The adults' responsibility would be to help the children channel his or her unique energies in positive ways.

From birth to around age six the children spent most of their time with the old people. Prior to age six, children, it was believed, were still connected to and remained close to the spirit world. During this period it was the family and community who learned from the child. They learned the child's natural tempo in life. Observing and knowing all the habits of a baby helped the adults to anticipate all its needs; babies were content, calm, and cried very little. Infants were never left alone and they were held as much as possible. To regulate and control one's own behavior was taught from a very early age in a preventative manner. Young moms were taught to prevent their children from doing something harmful, to anticipate what the children might do and not let them come to harm in the first place.

By age six children would spend less time with the old people and most of their time with their siblings and peers in the world outside, away from adults in the family. It was the time that children learned to be participants in the wider world, to learn to get along with others, establishing relationships with their peers and with the land.

The elders watched for the moment at around five or six years when children "awakened to the world." Children at this age learned to explore the limits of their bodies and their imaginations. Stories were an important part of mediating the world to children. Stories were told to young children about the dualities in human nature. The characteristics and qualities of being human are found in stories. For example, in the stories told even today, coyote, who has human qualities like greed, laziness, envy, and jealousy, is the central character. In many stories coyote becomes so overly focused on outsmarting someone, he forgets what is around him and always suffers the consequences. At bedtime, someone, most often the grandmother, would tell stories until every child was asleep.

Children learned how to be with the people in the community by participating in the life of the community. Older children assumed responsibility for the younger children, modeling what they learned from parents and others. Retelling what you knew by teaching others helped integrate new and old knowledge. By translating it into a form to be shared with others, one claimed ownership over what had been learned. Giving the older children the responsibility of caring for the younger children provided them with the opportunity to put into action what they had learned, and to develop their own creativity.

Another way that children learned at this stage was through play. Children constructed their own play, based on someone's experiences or ideas. They made the rules of play, designed the activities, chose the play environment, and made certain that everyone could take part. Some games lasted for days or several weeks. Children also learned how to include themselves in the play community. They played with very little interruption from adults during this period. The only time adults intervened was if children might seriously get hurt, and even then, the interruption was minimal. If adults noticed that a child was spending too much time alone, they would spend time with that child until they rejoined the group. Everyone in the community always knew where the children were playing and what they were doing. They kept each other informed about the activities of the young people. While the family and community worked, children worked alongside everyone, even the very young. Everyone had a role in contributing to the well-being of the family and community.

The child who showed that he or she could direct their own behavior signaled the next stage, around 9 or 10 years old. Demonstrating that they could concentrate on tasks until completion, working alongside other people without direction, and participating in the activities of the family and community showed they were ready for responsibilities. Often at this age young people were given tasks to do on their own without any detailed instructions. They had to figure out how to do the task on their own. In this way a young person developed a feeling of competence and independence. Gaining the feeling of competence requires that a significant person recognizes and acknowledges our growing competence.

During puberty it was the grandparents, aunts, and uncles who played a more important role in young people's lives than the birth parents. These relationships were nurtured from birth. A young adult needed guidance, which the aunts, uncles, and grandparents provided. Parents provided support and encouragement but other adults provided the intervention and teaching and in this way the young adult learned to have many and varied adult relationships.

In times past, a young woman would sit in seclusion during puberty training, away from the family and community. Her aunt, grandmother, and mother would help her to dig a small hole in the earth; they then built a tent from cedar boughs and animal hides. The hole inside the tent was lined with soft cedar and spruce branches. She replaced these every morning during her puberty training, which would last from four days to four months, or as long as four years. She and the elder women would determine the length of time depending on her overall health, spiritual, emotional, and learning needs. The training of a healer or spirit guide would take the longest period of time. As young women tend to become overly conscious of their physical bodies, during their puberty training they would sit secluded in mother earth; this encouraged them to go inward (to develop an inner relationship), and also to foster a relationship with the earth.

The young woman brought with her all her tools, and utensils for grooming, eating, and working. Members of her family made her the tools, such as awls, knives, and scrapers for basket making; patterns, needles, thread, and beads for buckskin work; and flatteners and threaders for bulrush mat making. Each day the young woman rose at dawn and prayed, before running about a mile or more to bathe in a stream. In winter, she first had to break the ice to get to flowing water. After a small breakfast she sat and made small berry-picking baskets out of cedar root. She would hang these on tree branches near trails. Anyone walking past them could take them; they would be given to small children to use when the family gathered to pick huckleberries each fall. This activity increased her skill and demonstrated to her that she could make things that were useful to others. It taught her how to share and she developed the habit of giving. Sharing is something that we learn first in our families and communities.

One common activity was to pick off the needles of an evergreen branch needle by needle. The needles on these branches could easily be removed by running your fingers along the branch in the opposite direction that the needles grow on the branch, a quick, efficient way to get the job done in a hurry. The young woman, however, had to pick each needle off one at a time. This exercise trained the young women's fingers, to make them more dexterous, accurate, and quick. Many of her tasks in life required these qualities. The exercise gave her an opportunity to feel the frustration that comes from doing a monotonous task; she experienced the frustration and learned to overcome it so she completed her task in a good, harmonious way. Much in life demands we know how to overcome frustration, monotony, and boredom. That's how we learn perseverance, persistence, and industriousness.

Young men spent time guided by their uncles, grandfathers, fathers, elder brothers, and other men in the community. Like the young women, their chosen profession in the family and community determined the type and duration of their training and who would be their guides and advisors. Young men tend to go inward so their training tended to bring them to wide, open spaces where they could establish a relationship with the universe. Their training was physically arduous. Even contemplative times were physically and mentally demanding. They were often given problems to think about; stories were told to them to make them think, or one of their guides would do something that was unexpected which caused them to ponder.

The puberty training of young men and women was intended to help them attain balance and harmony to overcome the egocentricity associated with adolescence. The experience helped them to realize that even when they spent time in solitude, they were never alone. During the puberty training, a vision, a song, and a dance emerged from each young person that was unique to him or her. These they shared with their guides, family, and community. Each winter the community sang each person's song while that person danced.

At this time each person also received a formal name, the name passed down through the generations; the name that came to the elders as they observed the qualities, characteristics, and traits of each person. The name connected the young person to his or her ancestors, because in that young person the elders saw qualities that previous nameholders had. The name served to connect the young people to their historical past and also served as a challenge to live up to. Each acquisition of a name was marked with a feast. When the name was announced in public, the new nameholder was introduced to each of the elders. They greeted the person, saying the new name many times; they described their own relationship to the previous nameholder (a relationship now transferred to the new nameholder), told stories about the person who last held the name, and told what they knew about the meaning of the name. Thus the young person's identity in the community was carefully fostered with a balance between unique individuality and connections to the community and ancestors. The new nameholder acknowledged the responsibility of holding the name for future generations.

Amongst the Lil'wat, as in many Indigenous communities, the belief is that when children come into the world they come with gifts that the community must nurture and support. The qualities of leadership are developed from birth, fostered, and recognized in every child. Every child is well prepared for adulthood. They are brought up to avoid conflict, so everyone can feel included and contribute to the family and community. Everyone both has a place and knows *how* to make a place for himself or herself in the community. They learn where they can put their strengths to make the community better and they learn their fundamental responsibility to the land and all that exists on the land.

Many people in Indigenous communities remember these ways, and they still are practiced in varying degrees. It is important for us to consider what kinds of things we can do today to help the children make a connection to community and family. To heal the pain of the Earth and to respect all our relations, we need to reconstitute the wisdom by which Indigenous people honor all life.

Chapter 8

The Great Turning [1]

DAVID C. KORTEN

Future generations, if there is a livable world for them, will look back at the epochal transition we are making to a life-sustaining society. And they may well call this the time of the Great Turning.

—Joanna Macy

We stand at a defining moment of choice unique in the human experience. It is the time of the Great Turning. The capacity to anticipate and choose our future is a defining quality of our species. Now the global spread of communications technologies combined with the crisis of planetary limits presents us with a unique imperative and opportunity to choose our common future with conscious collective intent.

CHOOSING OUR FUTURE

The defining choice is between two contrasting models for organizing human relationships that cultural historian Riane Eisler refers to as the dominator and partnership models. Empire is a metaphor for the dominator model, which has for some 5,000 years locked the dominant human societies into a relentless violent competition for dominator power—nation over nation, race over race, men over women, and rich over poor. Earth Community is a metaphor for the partnership model, which aligns with the four overarching organizing principles of the Earth Charter: (1) respect and care for the community of life; (2) ecological integrity; (3) social and economic justice; (4) democracy, nonviolence, and peace.[2] In the worldview of Earth Community the pursuit of dominator power is an immoral pathology contrary to the human and natural interest—a wasteful diversion of resources away from the important work of growing the generative potential of the whole of the community.

Empire assumes that we humans are by nature limited to a self-centered and ultimately self-destructive narcissism. Earth Community acknowledges and nurtures qualities for responsible service inherent in higher-order human capacities for love, compassion, and cooperation. A global awakening to the possibilities of the higher-order potentials of human consciousness sets the stage for an intentional collective choice to put the way of Empire behind us and bring forth the cultures and institutions of a new Era of Earth Community. Raffi's Child Honoring vision is perfectly aligned with this great turning.

The Era of Empire is in its death throes. Imperial economic and political systems organized to serve wealth and privilege without regard to social and environmental consequences are killing the Earth and destroying the fabric of civilization. At the same time, the revolution in technologies that has erased the geographical barriers to communication is enabling a grassroots cultural and spiritual awakening to the fact that we humans are one people who share one destiny on a small living planet. The choice is clear: either we join in common cause to birth the cultures and institutions of a new Era of Earth community based on the principles of the Earth Charter or we perish together.

To succeed in birthing the new era we must act with an uncommon clarity of mind and vision in this opportune moment to redirect our life energy from a habitual support of the old to a conscious building of the new. Each choice we make is a vote for the kind of future we bequeath to our children for generations to come.

FOR THE CHILDREN

The egregious consequences of Empire are nowhere more evident than in corporate globalization's war against the world's families and children. An economic system designed and managed to generate profits for corporate shareholders puts a crushing burden on the vast majority of parents struggling to do right by their children. It is nothing less than a crime against humanity. Although national conditions differ, parents around the world face a similar set of challenges to those in the United States as revealed by psychology professor Sharna Olfman in *Childhood Lost*:

- Inadequate parental leave and nonexistent child sick leave.
- A health care system that does not provide universal coverage for children.
- A minimum wage that is not a living wage.
- "Welfare to work" policies that require thousands of mothers to return to 40-hour workweeks, but fail to provide them with affordable, regulated, high-quality child care options.
- A two-tiered public education system that delivers inferior education to poor children and frequently ignores individual differences in learning styles.
- An entertainment and gaming industry that has been given the mandate to police itself, exposing children to graphic depictions of sex and violence, and undermining parental authority and values.
- An unregulated advertising industry that spends over $15 billion annually in direct marketing to children, shaping lifetime addictions to junk food, alcohol, and cigarettes, and contributing to a childhood obesity epidemic poised to become the leading cause of death in the United States.
- Weak environmental protection policies that have allowed thousands of toxic compounds to erode our air, soil, and water, many of which can undermine children's physical, neurological, and endocrine development.[3]

The list is a telling rejoinder to those who claim that there is no public interest beyond the aggregate of individual interests through the marketplace. These are burdens beyond the ability of even the wealthiest of individuals to resolve on their own and each is a direct consequence of the playing out of unregulated market forces. Markets alone cannot create suitable conditions for providing children and families with the support essential to navigate the path to healthy adult maturity. To raise healthy children we must have healthy, family-supportive economies, and that requires healthy, democratically accountable political systems responsive to peoples' real needs.

THE VALUES WE SHARE

Polling data affirm that the substantial majority of people share a desire for strong families and communities, a healthy environment, high-quality health care and education for all. They are likewise concerned about the unaccountable power of corporations and government and prefer to live in a world that puts people ahead of profits, spiritual values ahead of financial values, and international cooperation ahead of international domination. A stunning 83 percent of adults in the United States believe that as a society the United States currently focuses on the wrong priorities.[4]

The underlying values of this consensus cannot be categorized as either distinctively liberal or conservative. They are the values of the true political center, which is comprised of people who—irrespective of party affiliation—are committed to a politics based on principle, seek real solutions to real problems, and believe government should be accountable and serve the common good. So we might ask, if people are so united in their core values, why are they so divided in their politics?

The electoral systems that many mistakenly equate with democracy are designed to regularize electoral competition among factions of the ruling elite for control of the political system. This creates an inherent incentive for each faction to focus on portraying its opponents and their followers in the most unfavorable light while making promises to their own constituents that they have no intention of keeping. If the electoral process happens to produce some public benefit it is purely incidental to keeping the electorate divided into competing factions and thereby precludes a unified demand for systemic changes in the body politic.

Few nations appear to be more divided politically than the United States; yet Americans share an almost unanimous desire to strengthen the human connections of family and community and secure a positive future for their children. *Indeed, this may be the most politically potent issue of our time.*

More than four out of five Americans (83%) believe we need to rebuild our neighborhoods and small communities and are concerned that family life is declining.[5] Nearly all (93%) agree that we are too focused on working and making money and not enough on family and community. Ninety-four percent agree that we are too focused on getting what we want now and not enough on the needs of future generations.[6]

Our children agree. A poll of kids ages 9–14 commissioned by the Center for the New American Dream reports that 90 percent of respondents said friends and family are "way more important" than the things money can buy.[7] Fifty-seven percent would rather spend time doing something fun with mom or dad than go shopping at the mall.[8] Sixty-three percent would like their mom or dad to have a job that gave them more time to do fun things together. Only 13 percent wished their parents made more money.[9]

It is clear that if the institutions of governmental and corporate power were truly accountable to the public will, the United States would be pursuing very different policies both domestically and internationally. Captive to an imperial mindset, however, these institutions are defying and manipulating the public will to serve ends at odds with the national interest and most people feel powerless to do anything about it. But let us remember that human institutions are human creations. If they do not serve our interests we not only have the right to change them, we can in fact choose to do so.

My experience that a similar values consensus is emerging in almost every country in the world is confirmed by longitudinal data gathered from 43 countries by the World Values Survey from 1970 to 1994. These data reveal a growing acceptance of equal rights for women, a greater interest in the quality of life relative to pursuit of material gain, and an increasing sense of the importance of family life to individual and community well-being.[10]

We *can* create a world in which families and communities are strong, parents have the time to love and care for their children, high-quality health care and education are available to all, institutions are locally accountable, schools and homes are free of commercials, the natural environment is healthy and toxic-free, and nations cooperate for the global good. Wouldn't political coalitions devoted to creating such a world deserve to win sweeping majorities?

A CONSERVATIVE/LIBERAL ALLIANCE

The culture war in America is not between liberals and conservatives, who in fact share a great many core values, including a commitment to personal responsibility and democracy. It is between the Culture of Empire and the Culture of Earth Community. It is between those who deny the possibilities of our higher nature and those who seek to create a world in which they flourish. It is between a democratic politics based on principle and the common good, and an imperial politics of individual greed and power. It is between the realists of the true political mainstream who want to create a better world for all and a delusional minority of political extremists engaged in an economic war that hurts families and children, both here and abroad.

Call those of us on the side of Earth Community progressives—progressive conservatives and progressive liberals—for although we may have our differences, we share a commitment to creating a society governed by the people and dedicated to the ideals of liberty, justice, and opportunity for all. The politics of the progressive majority rejects both the extremist ideology of the far left that celebrates violent revolution and state control of every aspect of life, and the extremist ideology of the far right that celebrates imperial wars abroad, a theocratic state at home, and freedom for corporations to plunder planetary wealth to increase the fortunes of billionaires.

A politics of mature citizenship properly honors both the conservative values of individual freedom and responsibility and the liberal values of interdependence, equity, and justice for all. It brings together a conservative concern for community, spirit, and heritage with a liberal concern for inclusiveness and a world that works for the whole of life and for future generations. It recognizes the importance of local roots combined with a global consciousness. In the mature human mind these are complementary values that call us to a path of spiritual and mental health and maturity: to honor the children of every family, of every culture, of every continent.

Progressives of all stripes act from deeply shared values that resonate with the most basic of Christian values—do not kill, do not steal, love thy neighbor as thyself, and do unto others as you would have them do unto you. These are neither liberal nor conservative values; nor are they exclusively Christian values. They are universal human values shared by believers in Islam, Hinduism, Buddhism, and Native Spirituality, among others. From this foundation, we can find common ground even on those issues that presently divide us. For too long we have allowed extremists on both sides to define these debates in all-or-nothing terms that drive out the search for the common ground based on deeper spiritual principles.

IT'S ABOUT FAMILY AND COMMUNITY

We humans are born to learn and, through learning, to mature in our understanding of life and our relationship to one another. The foremost responsibility of a just society is to create a supportive context conducive to the formation of strong, loving, and stable families and communities. This principle is the foundation of a constructive dialogue on a range of potentially contentious questions.

What do children need from their parents and their community to advance toward their full emotional, moral, and intellectual potential? What diversity of forms might families take in fulfilling the developmental needs of both children and parents? What public policies best support and strengthen family units? What are the most crucial forms of support parents require from the larger society to fulfill their parenting role? What are the best ways to meet these needs?

These are questions equally important to liberals and conservatives, but their intelligent discussion has been precluded by the sound-bite politics of contending extremisms that have obscured even the most basic questions of what constitutes a loving family and good parenting. Consider the primary stages in the human life cycle: childhood, parenthood, and elderhood.

We learn in childhood to obey the word of our parents in return for the care that keeps us safe and healthy. Negotiating the passage from the dependence of childhood to the responsibilities of parenthood is one of the most difficult challenges of human life. It is all too easy to *become* a parent, but much more difficult to *be* a parent. The newborn child is wholly dependent on parents for both the physical and emotional care required for healthy development. Although there is no work more important to the society than parenting, the cultures and institutions of modern Empire provide virtually no support or preparation for the transition from childhood dependence to parental responsibility.

The final stage in the human life cycle, mature elderhood, is potentially the richest and most fulfilling. With a secure identity and no need to prove ourselves to the world, with a lifetime of experience on which to draw and our offspring in their own families and careers, we are thus free to explore, embrace, expand, and serve in previously inaccessible ways. Yet the cultures and institutions of Empire recognize elders mostly in their roles as retirees and consumers.

The contrast between how modern and traditional or tribal societies deal with the passage through these three basic stages of the life cycle is instructive. Modern societies characteristically segment the life cycle: a frenetic adulthood is fragmented between the enforced isolation and dependence of both childhood and elderhood.

While parents try to piece together a living income from multiple jobs, today's child is commonly parked in front of the television and prone to the power of corporate advertisers, warehoused in day care centers, or left to fend on the street without adult supervision. The child in such circumstances is expected mostly to keep out of the way of busy adults.

On reaching school age, the child is consigned to an educational facility in a state of enforced regimentation for a major portion of his or her waking hours. Although there are some wonderful schools that provide a rich learning environment, in the more typical school, the child's main activity is fighting off boredom while mastering the mechanics of reading, writing, and arithmetic, and memorizing large quantities of information unconnected with any other aspect of his or her life.

Typically, the experience of the child's parents is similarly fragmented and alienating. Struggling to support themselves and their families on multiple jobs offering less than a family wage and no benefits, they have little time for family or community, spiritual quest or leisure life. With few available options, most grit their teeth and tough it out. When and if retirement comes, it too often means enforced isolation and loneliness or confinement in facilities that offer only the company of other elders.

It is as if modern imperial societies are intentionally designed to keep our lives fragmented and disconnected in order to sell us the greatest number of things, while keeping us blind to the fact that caring relationships are the foundation of our very being.

The contrast to the traditional tribal community is stark indeed. In the traditional tribal village, the continuity and flow of life continuously underscores from the day of birth the individual's enduring connection to community, place, and generations past and future. Children grow up participating fully in the life of the community, which functions as a kind of extended family. Family, work, spiritual, community, and recreational life flow naturally one into the other. Children learn by doing under the watchful eye and coaching of parents and of elders revered for their wisdom and service. Older children learn parenting skills by participating in the care of younger children and in the life of hearth, field, and workshop.

At each stage in life's journey the individual members of the tribal society learn from the varied experiences of those who have lived a full life. Development of life skills relating to the tribe, to nature, and to the human spirit define the core of the curriculum. Public celebrations clearly mark graduation from the relationships appropriate to an earlier stage to those appropriate to the following stage.

When I turned 65, Timothy Iistowanohpataakiiwa, a Native American friend and elder, gave me one of the most important gifts of my life. In a simple native ceremony attended by a number of friends and colleagues, he initiated me as an elder in the human community and commemorated my graduation with the gift of an eagle feather from the headdress he had worn during his participation in the sacred Sundance festival. It totally changed my outlook on aging. Rather than feeling cast off to the isolation and irrelevance of retirement to await my final passage, I was initiated into elderhood as a mentor, teacher, and wisdom keeper.

VISIONING THE POSSIBLE

Traditional societies are structured around the needs of living. Contemporary societies are structured around the money-making interests of the corporate plutocracy. We have much to learn from the ways of more traditional societies that in many respects embodied an innate understanding of the developmental needs of children and of the human place within the larger web of life that modern societies have all but forgotten.

It is no great mystery. *If we were to redesign modern societies for living, we would place the needs of children, families, and communities front and center.* We would seek less money and more life. It seems to me quite a good bargain.

Systems of production and exchange would be localized to create a strong connection to place and community, thereby reducing the physical distance between home, employment, commerce, and entertainment. We would thus save time for family and community life and the energy otherwise expended in the needless movement of goods and people. Income and ownership would be equitably distributed and locally rooted to ground political democracy securely on a base of economic democracy and to achieve a more equitable, needs-oriented distribution of real wealth.

We would seek living-working arrangements that support sustained responsible engagement in family and community life by people of all ages. Older children would learn parenting skills by participating in the care and mentoring of younger children. Electronic media that use the public airwaves would inform, entertain, and facilitate learning and dialogue. Courses in developmental psychology and the skills of parenting and mentoring would hold a place in the formal educational curricula on a par with other subjects essential to responsible citizenship.

In the possible society of Earth Community, elders would remain active in community life in the full range of adult roles, particularly as educators and mentors. Those elders most revered for their mature wisdom would serve as advisors to those with the youth and energy to fill the more active leadership roles. Formal leadership roles would regularly rotate to enable sharing of the burdens and powers of office and access to the opportunities for learning that such positions afford. Formalized wisdom councils comprised of elders would serve as repositories of collective learning, provide needed continuity across administrations, and bring experienced talent to bear on addressing a wide variety of otherwise unmet health, education, or environmental needs.

All this and more is ours to choose. It is the time of the Great Turning, our time to "turn this world around," to take the step to species maturity and accept our adult responsibility to our children, one another, and the Earth. We are the ones we've been waiting for.

Section I C

Planetary Child: Earth Portrait

Chapter 9

The Environmental Life of Children

Sandra Steingraber

I live in a small village in upstate New York with my husband, two small children, and elderly dog. Our house is the little yellow Victorian just past the Baptist church on the north edge of town. It's the one with the tricycle and art easel on the front porch. A swing hangs from the walnut tree, and the lawn is littered with bamboo sticks of various sizes. (These serve as props for various *Peter Pan* reenactments.) A white picket fence lined with volunteer forget-me-nots runs out to a carriage house whose hayloft is home to an ill-tempered raccoon we'd like to evict. The sandbox under the spruce tree quarters a large and amiable toad whose specific whereabouts are investigated daily by children throughout the neighborhood. He can stay.

Yard work is not my forte. Raggedy stalks of pokeweed have taken over the south-facing slopes. I could mow them, but their berries feed migrating songbirds in the fall. A dying maple is home to a nesting pair of woodpeckers, so I have let it stand, as well. The ancient magnolia near the compost pile produced exactly three blossoms last spring, but because its gnarled branches are spaced just right for climbing, it too has been spared the saw. On the other hand, we really do need to do something about the geriatric gutters and downspouts that pour rain into the basement.

Jeff and I bought this house a year ago because we believed it would provide a good environment for our children. The local schools are highly rated. The public library is within walking distance. So is the farmers' market. The streets are quiet and flat—ideal for a kid ready to shed her training wheels. Around the corner and down the block is an art conservatory where my six-year-old takes piano lessons. She's already looking forward to the day she can ride her bike there and back all by herself.

Although some would find a 1,200-square-foot house (with no closets) too cramped for a family of four, my husband and I are mostly comforted by our home's modest size. It means we can run our household on a modest income, which, in turn, frees up time for toad investigations, walks to the library, and picnics at the nearby swimming beach. Jeff and I believe that, from the point of view of a child, the loving attention of one's parents—and a good climbing tree—count for more than closet space and cathedral ceilings. A toad in a sandbox and the sound of flickers drilling the trees bring more joy to a three-year-old, we suspect, than artful landscaping.

I am an ecologist as well as a mother. Therefore, I am concerned with more than just the quality of the environment within my children's yard and neighborhood. I attend conferences on global climate change, give lectures on the mercury contamination of fish, gather data on the link between air pollution and asthma, investigate industrial accidents, publish articles on the chemical contamination of breast milk. As such, I am deeply interested in the interplay between our personal environment (homes, lawns, marketplaces, schools) and the larger ecological world we all inhabit (including its systems of transportation, agriculture, energy, and toxics regulation). And I am particularly interested in the ways in which this interplay affects the development of children. After all, other than the 23 chromosomes that each of us parents contributes to our offspring during the moment of their conceptions, their growing bodies are entirely made up of rearranged molecules of air, food, and water. Our children are the jet stream, the global food web, and the water cycle. Their lungs absorb oxygen provided them by oceans of plankton and valleys of rainforests. Rainwater flows through their capillaries. Egg yolks, green beans, and peanut butter become their heart muscles, nerve fibers, and fingernails.

This truth was never more apparent to me than when I was pregnant. My breathing speeded up. My heart rate increased. I drank more water and ate more food. The whole ecological world seemed to be streaming through me. As I wrote in *Having Faith: An Ecologist's Journey to Motherhood,* "I myself was now a habitat. My womb was an inland ocean with a population of one."[1]

Whatever is in the environment is also in our children. We now know that this includes hundreds of industrial pollutants. A recent study of umbilical cord blood, collected by the Red Cross from 10 newborns and analyzed in two different laboratories, revealed the presence of pesticides, stain removers, wood preservatives, heavy metals, and industrial lubricants, as well as the wastes from burning coal, garbage, and gasoline. Of the 287 chemicals detected in the umbilical cord blood of these infants, 180 were suspected carcinogens, 217 were toxic to the brain and nervous system, and 208 have been linked to abnormal development and birth defects in lab animals.[2]

Until very recently, my life as a parent and my life as an environmental scientist occupied two very separate psychic realms. On the surface, this seems an odd assertion: my books are autobiographical as well as biological, with my own children appearing as characters and case studies in many of my writings. But, heretofore, the bridge between motherhood and biology carried one-way traffic. While my children's lives have helped inform my work—and certainly my love for them drives me to do better science—my work does not inform them. When Faith and I go searching for salamanders in the creek bed, we don't talk about the ability of the weed-killer atrazine to deform amphibian larvae at levels legally allowable in drinking water, even if that's what I've been studying for the past two weeks. When I sit down to nurse Elijah, I experience our communion as a sacrament—even when I am breastfeeding with one hand and reading a new study about breast milk contamination with the other.

But now, as Faith and Elijah continue grow up and become more aware—and are learning how to read—that's all beginning to change. Here are a few recent episodes from my household.

SCENE ONE

Elijah announces that he wants to be a polar bear for Halloween. It's his *totem animal*, he informs me solemnly. (His older sister has said so, as it turns out.) I agree that a polar bear is a great identity for Halloween and go to work making a costume out of scraps of white flannel and a chenille bedspread. During the costume's construction, to get a better idea of what the ears should look like, we search the house together for books and pictures of polar bears—Elijah calls them "lightning bears"—and come across a file of papers and monographs in my office. Scrawled across the top, in my handwriting, is the bear's Latin name, *Ursus maritimus*. One of the papers inside is entitled "Female Pseudohermaphrodite Polar Bears at Svalbard." It's authored by researchers in Sweden who report increasing numbers of hermaphroditic polar bears, specifically, females with fully functioning penises. Polar bears are thought to be among the most chemically polluted mammals on earth. They have two immutable facts working against them: they live in the Arctic, which is the final repository for persistent organic pollutants that cycle around in the global atmosphere, and they eat high on the food chain. Some of the chemicals known to concentrate in seal blubber, a mainstay of polar bear diets, are known to disrupt sex hormones.[3]

I flip to the next report in the file. This one is about the effect of global climate change on the ice floes where the bears hunt. Some researchers estimate that, if current trends continue, polar bears could become extinct within 50–70 years.[4]

My son may well outlive his totem animal.

I decide to hide the file box from him.

SCENE TWO

To commemorate my daughter's first piano recital, my mother sends a package of my old songbooks and sheet music, which she has scooped from the bench of my own childhood piano where they had undoubtedly sat for more than 30 years. Faith immediately seizes on *The Red Book,* one of my very first lesson books, and begins to sight-read some of the pieces. Her favorite is "Tune of the Tuna Fish" (copyright 1945), which introduces the key of F major. (I must have had trouble remembering to flat the B because that note is circled in pencil throughout the score.) The cartoon drawing accompanying the song depicts a yodeling fish. The lyrics are as follows:

> Tuna fish! Tuna fish! Sing a tune of tuna fish!
> Tuna fish! Tuna fish! It's a favorite dish.
> Everybody likes it so. From New York to Kokomo.
> Tuna fish! Tuna fish! It's a favorite dish.

After we belt the song out a few times together, Faith asks, "Mama, what is a tuna fish? Have I ever eaten one?" In fact, she hasn't. Although tuna salad sandwiches were a mainstay of my own childhood diet, tuna has, during the time period between my childhood and my daughter's, become so contaminated with mercury that I choose not to buy it.

A few weeks later, at a potluck picnic, an elderly woman offers Faith a tuna sandwich. She loves it. She announces that she wants tuna sandwiches for her school lunches. She wants to eat one *every day.* I smile and say, "We'll see." She breaks into song, "Everybody likes it so! From New York to Kokomo. . . ."

A month later, Faith walks up to me with an alarmed look. Is it true, she wants to know, that tuna fish have mercury in them? And mercury poisons children? Will she die from eating that sandwich at the picnic? I'm able to reassure her that she's fine, but I'm left wondering where she's heard all this. Then I notice that I've left out on my office desk a copy of an article about the impact of mercury on fetal brain growth and development. It's one that I myself have authored. Could she have seen it? Can she read enough now to have figured it out?

I decide we should have a mother-daughter talk about mercury in fish.

SCENE THREE

On the way home from an afternoon of running errands with the kids in the backseat, I remember that we are out of shampoo, so I pull into our local food co-op to pick some up. I'm running late, so I tell the kids firmly that we are only here to buy one item, that dinner is imminent, and that no one should ask me for treats. Elijah, nevertheless, shoots right over the deli section, which is featuring his favorite side dish today—steamed kale with sesame seeds and tamari sauce. His eyes light up and he pleads with me to have some. I say no and remind him of our singular task. The frustration of the situation is too much for him, and he throws himself the floor, wailing, "I want kale!" at top volume. I point out that he just had some yesterday, that we did not come to buy treats today, but he is too distressed to recoup.

I suddenly become aware that a crowd is gathering. People are laughing. Everyone wants to see a three-year-old throwing a tantrum over a dark green leafy vegetable.

Let's look at these three scenes more closely. I'll take them in reverse order and start with vegetables.

I have no trouble at all talking to my children about the importance of eating healthy food. In this, I follow dietician Laurine Brown, who believes that children really need only to recognize three food groups: go foods (whole grains and complex starches for energy), grow foods (protein for building body parts), and glow foods (brightly colored fruits and vegetables, full of vitamins). The child's job is to help herself to all three food groups at every meal. Divide your plate into thirds. Fill one third with go food, one with grow food, and one with glow food. Throw in a few glow food snacks, and you've got a great diet. Good advice for a lifetime.

Meal times are relaxed in our household. Children help cook and serve. No one is made to eat anything that looks yucky. Cleaning your plate is not required. Food is never used as bribe or reward. (Thursday night is ice cream night, in case you want to pay us a visit. Otherwise, it's fruit for dessert.) Lots of games are played at the dinner table. Recently, we've been pretending we are the Flopsy Bunnies eating lettuces in Mr. McGregor's garden. ("Very soporific!") I seldom issue nutritional lectures at the table, but I do sometimes try out my ventriloquism skills—as when, for example, Faith's eyes ask me for sweet potatoes so they can see better in the dark or Elijah's skeleton, in very spooky tones, begs for more calcium-rich lentils for strong bones. No foods are forbidden outright, but when we dine at other people's homes—or my children are party guests—they are encouraged to make good choices.

And mostly they do. At Faith's four-year-old birthday party, she chose to serve her guests pea soup, applesauce, apple cider, and apple pie. And then there is Elijah's ongoing obsession with kale.

Recently, my conversations with my children about food have grown to include discussions about why we buy organically grown groceries. I haven't shared with them the results of the 2003 Seattle study that measured pesticide levels in the urine of preschool children. Children with conventional diets had, on average, nine times more organophosphate insecticide residues in their urine than children fed organic produce.[5] But what I do say to Faith and Elijah is that I like to give my food dollars to farmers who sustain the soil, are kind to their animals, and don't use chemicals that poison birds, fish, and toads. I say that I like to buy food that is grown right here in our own county. It tastes better and doesn't require lots of gasoline to bring to our house. (This point is most relevant when we are lugging watermelons, eggs, and potatoes up the hill from the Saturday farmers' market.)

My task is made easier by the fact that organic agriculture is a thriving industry in the Ithaca, New York area. We are surrounded by organic farms, so that my children can see firsthand where their food comes from. Essentially, all the food we eat at home comes from our local food coop, the village farmers' market, or the community-supported farm in which we are share-holders. We also have no television. The result for my two kids is that they have never been advertised to. The images, jingles, and pitches of the food industry have, by and large, never reached them. Their food preferences have, consequently, been entirely shaped by their direct experience with the food itself and the farmers who grow it. No cartoon characters stare at them from boxes of presweetened cereals displayed at pediatric eye level in supermarket aisles. No candy bars wait in the checkout lane, ready to spark a parent-child battle of wills. No television commercials seduce them with pictures of chips and fizzy drinks.[6]

In short, I have a three-year-old who's crazy for kale because my motherly message to him about what foods are good to eat is reinforced by the larger culture in which he lives. This would not be the case if I were raising my children in the same small Illinois town where I grew up. My walking route to my former elementary school, for example, which once led through fields, woods, and neighborhoods, is now a neon strip of fast-food outlets and billboards touting fries, doughnuts, and Big Gulps. In that environment, the contradiction between my food message and the message beamed out from the landscape itself would be so vast as to be overwhelmingly confusing to a small child.

Hence, the challenge for parents—as they imagine a world in which a child's need to develop healthful eating habits is honored—is to transform the food institutions around them. Supporting local, organic farmers is one good starting point. With our own household in order, we can then take on the school lunch program, the church potluck, the PTA bake sale, and the children's menu at the family restaurant.

Now let's consider tuna fish.

There is no "organic" option to buying tuna. No mercury-free tuna exists. When the world's oceans are contaminated with mercury from coal-burning power plants, the ocean's ancient bacteria add a carbon atom to this heavy metal and turn it into a potent brain poison called methylmercury, which is quickly siphoned up the food chain. Tuna, a top-of-the-food-chain predator, inexorably concentrates methylmercury in the flesh of its muscle tissue. There is no special way of cleaning or cooking the tuna that would lower its body burden. Nor is there any way of keeping mercury from trespassing into a child's brain, once the tuna is consumed. Nor is there a way of preventing those molecules of mercury from interfering with brain cell functioning. In that sense, the problem of tuna fish is more akin to the problem of air and water pollution: it is not a problem we can shop our way out of. It is a problem that requires political solutions.

Recognizing the potential for methylmercury to create neurological problems in children, the U.S. Food and Drug Administration has now promulgated advisories and guidelines on how much tuna is safe for pregnant women and children to eat in a month's time.[7] There is debate about whether these current restrictions are protective enough.[8] But even if they are sufficient, I find them highly impractical. Children do not want to eat a food they like once a month, or even once a week. In my experience, when children discover a new food item to their liking, they want it all the time. They want it for breakfast, lunch, and dinner, from here to Sunday. Children's dining habits, are, for mysterious reasons, highly ritualized. Elijah, for example, ate two avocados a day for the better part of his second year. (This was before his kale phase.) I vaguely recall one summer when I, at about age eight, ate liver sausage on saltines as part of every meal.

How, then, do you explain to a young child who likes tuna that she'll have to wait until next month until she can have her favorite dish again? Do you tell her that she's already consumed her monthly quota of a known brain poison, as determined by the federal government? Or do you make up some other excuse?

In my case, I sat down with Faith and showed her the article I had written. I said that I was working hard to stop the mercury contamination of seafood so that she could someday enjoy tuna without needing to worry. I said that keeping mercury out of tuna required generating electricity in some way other than burning coal, which is why her father and I supported solar energy and wind power. And I said that every generation has had problems to solve. When I was little, children were born with brain problems because their mothers were sick with rubella measles when they were pregnant. But now we have vaccines for that. Paint and gasoline once contained lead, which also hurt children's brains. And now we've gotten rid of lead. When Nana was little, she was afraid of polio, but now we've solved that problem, too.

Faith thought hard about all this. Then she herself pointed out that the old stone building overlooking the lake, where she attended nature camp, was once a "preventatorium" where children exposed to tuberculosis were housed because their parents were sick. And that problem has been solved, too, right?

That's right, I said. All problems are solvable when we work together.

As for polar bears, I have not had a conversation with either of my children about the demonstrable threats posed by global climate change. I am planning to wait until they encounter this topic on their own. Perhaps by then, the official response of their government will be something other than denial, obfuscation, and hope-for-the-best paralysis.

Right now, my children take great pleasure in the regular procession of the seasons, with its rhythmical departures and returns of leaves, birds, buds, and flowers. So do we adults, of course. But I've become aware that children also depend on climatic events to mark the passage of time. When one is not yet old to read the calendar or the clock's face, when the difference between "next month" and "tomorrow" still seems a little fuzzy, it is comforting to know that the year's longest day comes when the strawberries appear, that one's birthday falls during apple-picking time, that the geese fly away when the pumpkins are ripe, that the big snows come on Valentine's Day, that the robins come back when the peepers start singing. Right now, I want my children to simply trust in these events, to take them for granted. Meanwhile, I'll be working as hard as I can, outside of their earshot, to push for environmental policies that respect the climatic life support system on which all of us—polar bears and humans—depend. As Raffi informs his young listeners in "Berry Nice News,"

Oh, we have excellent news for you today. What's the good news? What if I tell you that once again this year we will see the four seasons in exactly the same order as last year? Yes! The same order we've come to know and love for so very long. Just think! Once again this year, spring will give way to summer, to be faithfully followed by autumn, and then inevitably by winter. And after that, the circle will bring us forward to another spring and so on. Oh, what a relief! What berry nice news.[9]

May it ever be so.

Chapter 10

The Indigenous Child: The Afrikan Philosophical and Spiritual Basis of Honoring Children

Paulo Wangoola

There comes a time when the best adults can do is to follow their children.

—an African saying

CHILDREN ARE EVERYTHING!

Without children, the individual, family, nation, and, indeed, humanity, has neither a past nor a future; and even the present may be doubtful. Without children, there is no life before birth; and no life after death. Indeed there is no life at all! In Afrikan folklore, children are considered to be more important for species survival than adults; the younger more important than the older. Indeed, sayings abound in Afrikan languages to the effect that "the young trees are the forest." Not surprisingly, the birth of a child occasions incredible joy in the family and in the immediate neighborhood, which responds with an offer of milking cows, to provide free milk to the mother and baby.

In the Afrikan indigenous order of being and relationships, adults and children both have a responsibility to honor one another. Adults, however, have a far greater responsibility, because they know and understand better (or *should* understand better) the critical importance of their duty to the children. The honoring of children by adults is at the very center of the continuation and improvement of humanity. The young trees truly are the forest.

We are human not by biology (God's basic creation), but by culture and built-in reason. By culture, I refer to the communal ordering of the values and rules which govern relationships between and among men, women, and their children; between people and their environment; and between people and the spirit world. A people's culture is consistent with their knowledge, level of technology, and understanding of their Creator—what they believe to be the purpose of life and the place of the individual therein. The values and world outlook that a people articulate, in time and space, undergird their culture, as well as informing and guiding their thought, deed, and action. The peace that a people make with nature usually defines the peace people have: self with self, self with and among others, and peace with other peoples. All these factors combine to determine the place of children (collectively as well as individually) in a community.

A HISTORICAL MOMENT

Today there is worldwide concern with the condition of children: physical, material, spiritual, emotional. This is a new phenomenon. A generation or two ago, it was popularly assumed that as children in the industrialized countries lived in earthly paradise, it was the condition of children in the *Third World* which needed to be attended to. But the tendency among Afrikan elites has been to assume that the condition of children in the West sets the standards to be emulated. For many therefore, it comes as a shock that some of the indicators of a good life for children can be a danger to children's welfare; for example, mountains of food, family cars, television, games and toys, and so forth.

A consumerist logic may cater to the material needs of children, but it ignores their spiritual and emotional needs. Consumerist economics, which is private-profit driven, poses direct dangers to children because it poisons the Earth with effluence and chemicalized agriculture. On a poisoned Earth, children eat poisoned food, the air they breathe is not clean, and rain, rivers, and lakes are befouled. For these reasons, a consumerist economy is not sustainable. It squanders and exhausts Nature, the very basis of its viability, degrades current quality of life, denies children a better life than adults, and spells doom for future children.

In the meantime, the condition of children in the Third World, particularly in Afrika, can be hell on Earth. According to the World Health Organization (WHO), of the 40 million people worldwide living with HIV/AIDS, 28 million (including 2 million children)—70 percent of all victims of this disease—are Afrikans in sub-Saharan Afrika. As less than 1 percent of the millions of Africans who need anti-AIDS drugs ever receive them, the death toll is very high. It is estimated that in sub-Saharan Afrika almost 5,000 men and women (parents), and almost 1,000 of their children, are killed by AIDS every 24 hours! Millions of children who survive are left orphaned, altogether 12 million. Furthermore, about 90 percent of all deaths relating to AIDS and malaria occur in black Afrika.

Black Afrika is the only region of the world that has experienced a substantial increase in the number of malnourished children and adults in the past 30 years. Since the early 1970s the numbers of malnourished children have risen (by more than 75%) to 33 million today, and they are still rising! In the Afrikan Great Lakes Region alone, it is estimated that in the last 10 years, about 10 million people, most of them children and women, have perished in wars and related causes. And thousands are further victimized by child soldiering!

If such is the condition of vast numbers of Afrikan children (and their parents), how can Afrika have a future—without its people?

This seems to be a juncture in the history of humanity when *all* children of the world are under threat. This means *humanity* is under threat, both in the Majority (Third) World, and in the minority (industrialized) countries. In other words, the majority of peoples of the world who eke out a living on their sweat and resources of their ancestral lands, and a small minority of peoples in a handful of countries who fatten themselves on the toil of others, *both* face a bleak future due to the growing threats posed to their children.

Through the agency of religion, corporations, militarism, conquest, occupation, annexation, and empire building, a small network of people based largely in the north has (through centuries) established unparalleled power over the peoples of the world and their resources. Never in the history of humankind have the peoples and resources of the entire world been controlled by so few. Never before have so few benefited by the overall damnation of so many. Big Business and Big Government have developed an overbearing ideology and a global intelligentsia to justify suicidal consumerist economics of infinite growth, for infinite profit by a few.

BACK TO ROOTS: OLD WAYS TO THE FUTURE

In solving problems, we draw lessons not from the unknown or from the future, but by learning from history. This is why we need to go to our history to look for guidance in building a new world, a world whose foundation and centerpiece are the children. Such undertaking can be driven sustainably only by a people's ideas, ideals, and values as captured in their world outlook and spirituality, and/or their religious and theological beliefs and teachings. Let me share with you some strategic aspects of the Afrikan world outlook and spirituality which are part of the sources and foundations of honoring the Afrikan indigenous child.

Creation Story

From the multiplicity of Afrikan creation stories, there is the tale of Ssewamala, the Son of God, and Namala, his wife. According to this story, the Creator, *Kyetonda Tonda Namugereka,* is Pure Living Spirit, with two essential attributes, male and female. Indeed, the Creator's full names attest to this duality: Kyetonda Tonda is the male, and Namugereka, the female. In the same duality, the Creator sent to Earth his son Ssewamala and his wife Namala; they comprised the first Holy Matrimony and begot and delivered the first twins, Musoke, a boy and Namusoke, a girl. Thus, the Creator set in motion and gave an order to all living things to reproduce themselves into pairs and sets of male and female, in perpetuity. Moreover, the Creator gave instructions for life everlasting.

This story is of tremendous importance to relationships of honor: self with self, self with and among others, people with nature, and people with their Creator. With this story, Afrikans see themselves to be the direct offspring of the Creator, as Pure Living Spirit. In this sense we are made in our Creator's image. We are born good and great, but infinitely greater is the Creator whom we worship. We are like him/her, but s(he) is infinitely greater. Further, Kyetonda Ttonda Nnamugereka simultaneously created female and male aspects, and created them equal. Female did not come out of male, nor did male come out of female.

In Afrikan spirituality, therefore, this is the divine basis of the equality between female and male, woman and man, boy-child and girl-child. The Creator is male-female; and so on Earth, we have woman and man, boy and girl. On Earth, Kyetonda is like Ssalongo (father of twins), while Nnamugereka becomes Nnalongo (mother of twins). Indeed, every now and then humans show their Creator-likeness when they too have twins.

When the Creator ordered all living things to reproduce themselves in pairs and sets of male and female, this became possible because the Creator allocated part of his/her pure living spirit to each of the species and individual plants and animals. In that sense, all living and nonliving things are also made in the image of their Creator. In Afrikan spirituality this explains why men, women, and children are raised to respect and honor the whole of nature. In this order of things, men, women, and their children are not apart from or above nature; they are an integral part of it.

Because the living and nonliving everywhere have part of the Pure Living Spirit of the Creator as originally inherited, everything is sacred. Indeed, it is on this basis that in Afrikan spirituality we know that Kyetonda Ttonda Nnamugereka (God) is everywhere. Thus, everything has a divine spirit force on the basis of equality. The whole of Earth is alive and sacred.

War: A Threat to Child Honoring

A big threat to the wholesome growth, development, and maturation of children comes from war—its planning and prosecution. It diverts community, family, and individual resources which could otherwise be deployed for the welfare of children; destroys existing resources and infrastructure necessary for their welfare; kills millions of children and their parents; destroys homes, inflicts emotional and psychological trauma; forces millions of children worldwide into child-soldiering; and poisons the Earth and its atmosphere. Most wars between countries, people, cultures, and civilizations are directly or indirectly over land, natural resources, and religion.

Today, the world is mired in wars (and the threat of yet more wars) which arise from the belligerence of a handful of governments led by the United States. These few governments claim some divine right to their national interest and national security. They feel entitled to control all the world's resources, even if it means the suffering of the vast majority of the rest of the world.

According to Afrikan spirituality, this type of articulation and justification of disharmony can only be the result of departing from the Creator's original instructions—that each of the peoples of the world inherited color, language, land, and culture; and that each one of them was to worship and praise their Creator in their language, consistent with their culture; that each culture had to be in harmony with the Creator's laws of nature, of harmonious coexistence, in perpetuity.

Kyetonda Ttonda Nnamugereka (God) was simultaneously revealed to all peoples of the world. In this way, the Creator instituted a horizontal ordering of peoples (their culture, language, spirituality, and rights) such that there is no heathen or infidel people, no civilized and no barbarians. For that reason, therefore, there cannot be a chosen or a civilizing people, with the divine mandate to civilize others. Equally, no language or culture is superior to another; and no one people or nation has rights over others; and no people can have preeminent rights over resources located in the ancestral territories of other peoples.

THE AFRIKAN PHILOSOPHY OF LIFE

This Afrikan philosophy of life is summed up by the Ubuntu philosophy, which is popularly summed up as "I Am Because You Are; And Because We Are, Therefore I Am." In other words, I am an extension of you, and you are of me. Any harm to you is harm to me, and harm to all. For that reason, caring for your well-being is not an act of charity on my part, but the enlightened pursuit of my own interest. Accordingly, I can only have abundant and everlasting life *with* you. And not only you as a person, but with *all* of you as plants, animals, water, air, the earth—everything.

The Ubuntu philosophy and its concept of universal brotherhood and sisterhood has been symbolically captured in the totem system. Afrikan peoples are organized in clans, each with a totem of an animal, a plant, or some natural phenomena. For millions of years the Earth was covered by plants; animals appeared much later on. Human beings appeared only recently, maybe a mere couple of a million years ago! All animals directly survive on plants for their food; even carnivorous animals eat animals that eat grass.

Plants and animals lived on earth for millions of years without people; they did not need human beings to live on Earth and still do not. Indeed, humans have extinguished thousands of plant and animal species, and constitute a growing threat to an increasing number of plants and animals. The reverence of plants and animals through the totem system enables humans to pay homage to their senior brothers and sisters—in fact, patrons—of the plant and animal kingdoms, on whom they utterly depend.

Still, some contemporary scientists, particularly those who have internalized the propaganda to discredit Afrika as a source of classical knowledge (knowledge that has passed the test of time, and on which subsequent knowledge can be constructed), may insist that the universal brotherhood enshrined in Ubuntu philosophy and expressed in the totem system is mythical and superstitious. The truth of the matter is that every science, in this case Afrikan indigenous environmental science (and also Western environmental science), has its myths.

On close scrutiny, we find that most myths in indigenous science are designed to enforce unquestioning general community and individual compliance with prudent practices for survival.

On the whole, indigenous myths have a basis in science. Their mythical presentation is the packaging for a lay public, for purposes of enlisting compliance through an understanding of relationships rooted in Afrikan spirituality and thought processes.

Children: A Source of Knowledge

An examination of Afrikan folklore relating to children reveals that on observation adults came to the conclusion that their children can be as intelligent, resourceful, creative, imaginative, and brave as adults; and often even more so. Our families, communities, nations, countries, and the world as a whole would be the poorer if they organized themselves in a manner which does not take into full account the children's potential to contribute to society's progress.

To illustrate this, here is one Afrikan story. Once upon a time there was an old man who wanted to have a monopoly of knowledge. He collected all the valuable knowledge, skills, and wisdom in the village, put them in a calabash (gourd), and tightly corked it. Using a string he hung the big calabash around his neck and started to climb the tallest tree in the village. His plan was to put all the knowledge and wisdom beyond the reach of everyone; henceforth, the only way to access this knowledge and wisdom was to be through him. However, the old man found climbing the tree with the calabash hanging in front of him extremely difficult. Then a small boy who had been watching the old man's clumsy efforts shouted to him and advised that for easy climbing he should hang the calabash on his back, not in front of himself. On hearing this, the old man realized he had not, after all, collected all knowledge. In anger and frustration, the old man threw the calabash to the ground. The calabash broke into pieces and scattered the knowledge which he had collected in all directions! This is why, as many proverbs attest, nobody has a monopoly on wisdom.

In Uganda, for example, there are several proverbs and sayings that translate as follows: "An old man is not automatically knowledgeable or wise"; "No single person knows everything while the rest know nothing"; "A person is wise on account of what he or she has learnt from others"; and finally, "There comes a time when the best adults can do is to follow their children."

THE WAY FORWARD TO CHILD HONORING

The Science of Dishonoring Everything and Everybody

The widespread global awareness of the precarious predicament of all children of the world is an indication that the problem is cancerous, and requires radical surgery. At the core of the problem is the dominant Western science and culture of death and destruction, denial, misinformation, and outright lies. It is a science whose bottom line is to justify monopoly private profit. In that sense it is not science; it is scienticism—that is the science of proving predetermined positions and conclusions.

Probably nothing illustrates better the science of death in practice than the pharmaceutical and agrochemical industries. The pharmaceutical industry seems not to be interested in curing diseases. Most drugs are developed primarily to relieve symptoms, as a basis for sustainable profits. Ronald and Emile Lewis have reported that:

> In Canada and the US, as in other Western European countries, we are bombarded with chemicals from the cradle to the grave, and at all times in between . . . Our food is chemically flavoured and enriched with artificial additives, wrapped and stored in synthetic plastics . . . The air we breathe, the water we drink, the soil in which we grow our plants, the feed that we feed our animals, the animals, the plants and fish we consume, all are showing the effects of toxic environmental pollution.
>
> As in the case of stockpiles of diseases, the industrialized countries continue to manufacture and stockpile hazardous chemicals and drugs (banned in their countries) for export to the third world, often by deception or by force. In keeping with the Science of Death, the pharmaceutical, chemical and biological warfare industries withhold public information about the effects and risks of prescription drugs, vaccines, chemicals, the stockpiles of diseases and disease manufacturing laboratories. The life-threatening side effects are either put in small print, misrepresented, omitted or openly denied.

The Science of Honoring Everything and Everybody

Honoring is indivisible. This means that a world organized around the long-term future interests of the children, and therefore society as a whole, can only be possible if all elements (and subsets) in securing the long-term needs and interests of children are well taken care of. This necessarily includes adults (particularly the women), plants, animals, and the earth. To turn the tide of the science of death or dishonoring, we need to give prime space to the science of life, the science of honoring everything and everybody, as summed up in the Afrikan Ubuntu philosophy. The point is to turn the tide *not* by dismissing or being blind or hostile to Western scientific gains and achievements; but rather by breathing Ubuntu (life) into Western science. This way, Western science and technology can be transformed into an instrument and vehicle of honoring and advancing the wholesome well-being of nature and people. Because science and technology would thus serve the needs of communal survival, the honoring of children would be automatically engaged. In fact, consideration of children would necessarily be at the center of science and technology and, indeed, all human endeavors, as sustainability can only be based on children—not only human children, but also the children of the plant and animal kingdoms.

For the science of life, we must look to indigenous science, a science developed under the hegemony of values and a world outlook that put a premium on relations of mutual adoration and solidarity between and among men, women, and their children, on the one hand; and on the other, between people and nature. According to indigenous science, the earth, plants, and animals are not factors of production for private profit, but God's sacred bounty for human sustenance—a sustenance that regards the Earth and nature as a fixed deposit account out of which only part of accrued interest may be withdrawn for consumption. This is in sharp contrast with the adversarial values, world outlook, and relationships that inform Western, private-profit driven economics.

It is imperative to identify and locate communities that still embrace indigenous science, and recognize them to be sacred sites of human heritage. Against all odds imposed by the rogue scientism of death, these communities have done humanity, nature, and the gods proud by holding on to the science of life, for posterity. Fortunately, the science of life is to be found among indigenous peoples in all continents of the world. Indeed, even in Western Europe and the cultural satellites of North America and Australia, Western science is only a recent development, hardly 300 years old. This means that in historical terms, indigenous science lies below the skins of the different peoples of the world. A little scratch, and we can all be there! With the general revival of indigenous science, it will become possible to breathe considerable life into Western science, worldwide. And as it will not be a one-way traffic, Western science can also be the basis for the updating of indigenous science. Then we can truly have a people's science!

These momentous developments can only take root with a new international consciousness that recognizes and assures every community, language, culture, and civilization a future, with each culture and civilization open to learning from others. Central to all this is the need for each community to be educated on the history of humanity, and the contributions of different peoples and cultures to human development, progress, civilization. Out of all this, a Global Manifesto for Child Honoring, focused on cross-cutting values and best practices, can be articulated as a Global Resource for Humanity, to be drawn on by the different communities as they reconstruct and construct their communities of abundant and everlasting life—a life that can be possible only if focused around the child.

Chapter 11

Lily's Chickens [1]

BARBARA KINGSOLVER

My daughter is in love. She's only five years old, but this is real. Her beau is shorter than she is, by a wide margin, and she couldn't care less. He has dark eyes, a loud voice, and a tendency to crow. He also has five girlfriends, and Lily doesn't care about that, either. She loves them all: Mr. Doodle, Jess, Bess, Mrs. Zebra, Pixie, and Kiwi. They're chickens. Lily likes to sit on an overturned bucket and sing to them in the afternoons. She has them eating out of her hand.

It began with coveting our neighbor's chickens. Lily would volunteer to collect the eggs, and then she offered to move in with them. Not the neighbors, the chickens. She said if she could have some of her own, she would be the happiest girl on earth. What parent could resist this bait? Our lifestyle could accommodate a laying flock; my husband and I had kept poultry before so we knew it was a project we could manage, and a responsibility Lily could largely handle by herself. I understood how much that meant to her when I heard her tell her grandmother, "They're going to be just *my* chickens, grandma. Not even one of them will be my sister's." To be five years old and have some other life form entirely under one's own control—not counting goldfish or parents—is a majestic state of affairs.

So her dutiful father built a smart little coop right next to our large garden enclosure, and I called a teenaged friend who might, I suspected, have some excess baggage in the chicken department. She raises championship show chickens, if you can imagine that, and she culls her flock tightly. At this time of year she'd be eyeing her young birds through their juvenile molt to be sure every feather conformed to the gospel according to the chicken-breeds handbook that is titled, I swear, "The Standard of Perfection." I asked if she had a few feather-challenged children that wanted adoption, and she happily obliged. She even had an adorable little bantam rooster that would have caused any respectable chicken-show judge to keel over—he was the love child of a Rose-comb and a Wyandotte. I didn't ask how it happened.

In Lily's eyes *this* guy, whom she named Mr. Doodle, was the standard of perfection. We collected him and a motley harem of sweet little hens in a crate and brought them home. They began to scratch around contentedly right away, and Lily could hardly bear to close her eyes at night on the pride she felt at poultry ownership. Every day after feeding them she would sit on her overturned bucket and chat with them about the important things. She could do this for an hour, easily, while I worked nearby in the garden. We discovered they loved to eat the weeds I pulled, and the grasshoppers I caught red-handed eating my peppers. We wondered, would they even eat the nasty green hornworms that are the bane of my tomato plants? *Darling,* replied Mrs. Zebra, licking her non-lips, *that was to die for.*

I soon became so invested in pleasing the hens, along with Lily, I would let a fresh green pigweed grow an extra day or two to get some size on before pulling it. And now, instead of carefully dusting my tomato plants with *Bacillus* spores (a handy bacterium that gives caterpillars a fatal bellyache), I allow the hornworms to reach heroic sizes, just for the fun of throwing the chickens into conniptions. Growing hens alongside my vegetables, and hornworms and pigweeds as part of the plan, has drawn me more deeply into the organic cycle of my gardening that is its own fascinating reward.

Watching Mr. Doodle's emergent maturity has also given me, for the first time in my life, an appreciation for machismo. At first he didn't know what to do with all these girls; they were just competition for food. Whenever I'd toss them a juicy bug he would display the manners of a teenage boy on a first date at a hamburger joint—rushing to scarf down the whole thing, then looking up a little sheepishly to ask, "Oh, did you want some?" But as hormones nudged him toward his rooster imperatives he began to strut with a new eye toward his coop-mates. Now he rushes up to the caterpillar with a valiant air, picking it up in his beak and flogging it repeatedly against the ground until the clear and present danger of caterpillar attack has passed. Then he cocks his head and gently approaches Jess or Bess with a throaty little pick-up line, dropping the defeated morsel at her feet. He doles out the food equitably, herds his dizzy-headed girls to the roost when it's time for bed, and uses an impressive vocabulary for addressing their specific needs: a low, monotonous cluck calls them to the grub; a higher-pitched chatter tells them a fierce terrestrial carnivore (our dog) is staring balefully through the chicken-wire pen; a quiet, descending croak says "Heads up!" when the ominous shadow of an owl or hawk passes overhead. Or a dove, or a bumblebee—okay, this isn't rocket science. But he does his job. There is something very touching about Mr. Doodle when he stretches up onto his toes, shimmies his golden feather shawl, throws back his little head and cries—as Alexander Haig did in that brief moment when he thought he was President—"As of now, I *am* in control!"

With the coop built and chickens installed, all we had to do now was wait for our flock to pass through puberty and begin to give us our daily eggs. We were warned it might take awhile because they would be upset by the move and need time for emotional adjustment. I was skeptical about this putative pain and suffering; it is hard to put much stock in the emotional life of a creature with the I.Q. of an eggplant. Seems to me, you put a chicken in a box and she looks around and says, "Gee, life is a box." You take her out, she looks around and says "Gee, it's sunny here." But sure enough, they took their time. Lily began each day with high hopes, marching out to the coop with cup of corn in one hand and my 20-year-old wire egg basket in the other. She insisted that her dad build five nest boxes in case they all suddenly got the urge at once. She fluffed up the straw in all five nests, nervous as a bride preparing her boudoir.

I was looking forward to the eggs, too. For anyone who has eaten an egg just a few hours' remove from the hen, those white ones in the store have the charisma of day-old bread. I looked forward to organizing my family's meals around the pleasures of quiches, Spanish tortillas, and soufflés, with a cupboard that never goes bare. We don't go to the grocery very often; our garden produces a good deal of what we eat, and in some seasons nearly all of it. This is not exactly a hobby. It's more along the lines of religion, something we believe in the way families believe in patriotism and loving thy neighbor as thyself. If our food ethic seems an unusual orthodoxy to set alongside those other two, it probably shouldn't. We consider them to be connected.

Globally speaking, I belong to the twenty percent of the world's population—and chances are, you do too—that uses two-thirds of its resources and generates 75% of its pollution and waste. This doesn't make me proud. U.S. citizens by ourselves, comprising 5% of the world's people, use a quarter of its fuels. An average American gobbles up the goods that would support thirty citizens of India. I am a critic of wasteful consumption, and since it's nonsensical, plus embarrassing, to be an outspoken critic of things you do yourself, I set myself long ago to the task of consuming less. I never got to India but in various stages of my free-wheeling youth I tried out living in a tent, in a commune, in Europe, and eventually determined I could only ever hope to dent the salacious appetites of my homeland and make us a more perfect union by living *inside* this amazing beast, poking at its belly from the inside with my one little life and the small, pointed sword of my pen. So this is where I feed my family and try to live lightly on the land.

For years I've grown much of what my family eats, and tried to attend to the sources of the rest. As I began to understand the energy crime of food transportation I tried to attend even harder, eliminating any foods grown on the dark side of the moon. I began asking after the processes that brought each item to my door: what people had worked where, for slave wages and with deadly pesticides, what places had been deforested, what species were driven extinct for my cup of coffee or banana bread. It doesn't taste so good when you think about what died going into it.

Responsible eating is not so impossible as it seems. I was encouraged in my quest by *This Organic Life,* a compelling book by Joan Dye Gussow that tells how, and more importantly why, she aspired to and won vegetable self-sufficiency. She does it in her small backyard in upstate New York, challenging me to make better use of my luxuries of larger space and milder clime. Sure enough, she was right. In the year since then, I've found I need never put a vegetable on my table that has traveled more than an hour from its home ground to ours.

Nearly every vegetable we consume, we can grow ourselves. Most of what-ever else I need comes from the local growers I meet at farmers' markets. Our family has arrived, as any sentient people would, at a strong preference for the breads and pasta we make ourselves, so I'm always searching out proximate sources of organic flour. Just by reading labels I discovered I can buy milk that comes from organic dairies only a few counties away, and I've become captivated by the alchemy of creating our own cheese and butter. (Butter is a sport; cheese is an art.) Winemaking remains well beyond my powers, but fortunately good wine is made in Virginia. I am especially glad to support some neighbors in a crashing tobacco-based economy who are trying to keep their farms by converting to vineyards. Somewhere near you, I'm sure, is a farmer who desperately needs your support, for one of a thousand reasons that are pulling the wool out of the proud but unraveling traditions of family farming.

I am trying to learn about this complicated web as I go, and I'm in no position to judge anyone else's personal habits, believe me. My life is riddled with energy-inconsistencies: we try hard to conserve, but I've found no way to rear and support my family without a car, a computer, the occasional airplane flight, a teenager with a hair dryer, et cetera. I'm no Henry D. Thoreau. (And just for the record, for all his glorification of his bean patch, Henry is known to have habitually walked next door to eat Mrs. Ralph W. Emerson's cooking). Occasional infusions of root beer are apparently necessary to my family's continued life, along with a brand of vegetable chips made in Uniondale, NY. And there's no use my trying to fib about it either, for it's always when I have just these things in the grocery cart, and my hair up in the wackiest of slap-dash ponytails, that some kind person in the checkout line will declare, "Oh, Ms. Kingsolver, I just love your work!"

Our quest is only to be thoughtful, and simplify our needs, step by step. As imported goods go, I try to stick to non-perishables that are less fuel-costly to ship: rice, flour, and coffee are good examples. Just as simply as I could buy coffee and spices from the grocery, I can order them through a collective in Fort Wayne, Indiana, that gives my money directly to cooperative farmers in Africa and Central America who are growing these crops without damaging their tropical habitat. We struggled with the prospect of giving up coffee altogether, until learning from ornithologist friends who study migratory birds being lost to habitat destruction, there is a coffee cultivation practice that helps rather than hurts. Any coffee labeled "shade grown"—now found in most North American markets—was grown under rainforest canopy on a farm that is holding a piece of jungle intact, providing subsistence for its human inhabitants and its birds.

I understand the power implicit in these choices. That I have such choice about food at all is a phenomenal privilege in a world where so many go hungry, and our nation uses as a political weapon the withholding of grain shipments from places like Nicaragua and Iraq. I find both security and humility in feeding myself as best I can, learning to live within the constraints of my climate and seasons. I like the challenge of organizing our meals as my grandmothers did, starting with the question of season and what cup is at the moment running over. I love to trade recipes with gardening friends, cheerfully joining the competition of how many ways one can conceal the i.d. of a zucchini squash.

And it does feel like a moral and political matter to me. There has never been a more important time to think about where our food comes from. We could make for ourselves a safer nation, overnight, simply by giving more support to our local food economies and learning this way of eating and living around a table that reflects the calendar.

I struggle—along with most parents I know—to raise children with a clear distinction between love and indulgence. I honestly believe material glut can rob a child of certain kinds of satisfaction, although deprivation is no picnic either. And so our family indulges in exotic treats on big occasions. A box of Portuguese Clementines one Christmas is still on Lily's catalogue of favorite memories, and a wild turkey from Canada one Thanksgiving remains on my own. We enjoy these kinds of things spectacularly because at our house they're rare.

There are good reasons that compel me most toward a vegetable-based diet—the ones revealed by simple math. A pound of cow or hog flesh costs about ten pounds of plant matter to produce. So a field of grain that would feed one hundred people, when fed instead to cows or pigs which are *then* fed to people, fills the bellies of only ten of them while the other ninety I guess will just have to go hungry. That, in a nutshell, is how it's presently shaking down with the world, the world's arable land, and the world's hamburger-eaters.

Some years ago our family took a trip across the Midwest to visit relatives in Iowa, and for thousands of miles along the way we saw virtually no animal life except feedlots of cattle—surely the most unappetizing sight and smell I've encountered in my life (and my life includes some years of intimacy with diaper pails). And we saw almost no plant life but the endless fields of corn and soybeans required to feed those pathetic penned beasts. Our kids kept asking, mile after mile, "What used to be here?" It led to long discussions of America's vanished prairie, Mexico's vanished forests, and the diversity of species in South American rainforests now being extinguished to make way for more cattle graze. We also talked about a vanishing American culture; during the last half-century or so, each passing year has seen about half a million more people move away from farms (including all of my children's grandparents or great-grandparents). The lively web of farmhouses, schoolhouses, pasture lands, woodlots, livestock, poultry and tilled fields that once constituted America's breadbasket has been replaced with a meat-fattening monoculture. When we got home our daughter announced firmly, "I'm never going to eat a cow again."

When your ten-year-old calls your conscience to order, you show up; she *hasn't* eaten a cow again and neither have we. It's an industry I no longer want to get tangled up in, even at the level of the 99-cent exchange. Each and every quarter-pound of hamburger is handed across the counter after these productions costs, which I've searched out precisely: 100 gallons of water, 1.2 pounds of grain, a cup of gasoline, greenhouse gas emissions equivalent to a six-mile drive in your average car, and the loss of 1.25 pounds of topsoil, every inch of which took 500 years for the microbes and earthworms to build. How can all this cost less than a dollar, and who is supposed to pay for the rest of it? If I were a cow, right here is where I'd go mad.

Thus our family parted ways with all animal flesh wrought from feedlots. But for some farmers on certain land, assuming they don't have the option of turning it into a national park (and that people will keep wanting to eat), the most ecologically sound use of the place is to let free-range animals turn grass and weeds into edible flesh, rather than turning it every year under the plow. We also have neighbors who raise organic beef for their family on nothing more than the by-products of other things they grow. It's quite possible to raise animals sustainably, and we support the grass-based farmers around us by purchasing their chickens and eggs.

Or we did, until Lily got her chickens. The next time a roasted bird showed up on our table she grew wide-eyed, set down her fork and asked, "Mama . . . is that . . . Mr. Doodle?"

I reassured her a dozen times that I would *never* cook Mr. Doodle, this was just some chicken *we didn't know.* But a lesson had come home to, well, roost. All of us sooner or later must learn to look our food in the face. If we're willing to eat an animal, it's probably only responsible to accept the truth of its living provenance rather than pretending it's a "product" from a frozen-foods shelf with its gizzard in a paper envelope. I've been straight with my kids ever since the first one leveled me with her eye and said, "Mom, no offense but I think *you're* the tooth fairy." So at dinner that night we talked about the biology, ethics, and occasional heartbreaks of eating food. I told Lily that when I was a girl growing up among creatures I would someday have to eat, my mother promised we would never butcher anything that had a first name. I was always told from the outset which animals I could name. I promised Lily the same deal.

So she made her peace with the consumption of her beloved's nameless relatives. But we weren't sure how we'd fare with the issue of eating their direct descendents. We'd allowed that next spring she might let a hen incubate and hatch out a few new chicks (Lily quickly decided on the number she wanted and, significantly, their names) but we weren't in this business to raise ten thousand pets. Understood, said Lily. So we waited a week, then two, while Jess, Bess, and company worked through their putative emotional trauma and settled in to laying. We wondered, how will it go? When my darling five-year-old pantheist, who believes even stuffed animals have souls, goes out there with the egg basket one day and comes back with eggs, how do we explain she can't name those babes because we're going to scramble them?

Here is how it went. She returned triumphantly that morning with one unbelievably small brown egg in her basket, planted her feet on the kitchen tile, and shouted at the top of her lungs: "Attention everybody, I have an announcement: FREE BREAKFAST."

We agreed the first one was hers. I cooked it to her very exact specifications and she ate it with gusto. We admired the deep red-orange color of the yolk, from the beta-carotenes in those tasty green weeds. Lily could hardly wait for the day when all of us would sit down to a free breakfast, courtesy of her friends. I wish every child could feel so proud, and that every family could share the grace of our table.

I think a lot about those thirty citizens of India who, it's said, could live on the average American's stuff. I wonder if I could build a life of contentment on their material lot, and I look around my house, wondering what they'd make of mine. My closet would clothe more than half of them, and my books—good Lord—could open a library branch in New Delhi. Our family's musical instruments would outfit an entire (very weird) village band, including electric guitars, violin, eclectic percussion section and a really dusty clarinet. We have more stuff than we need, there is no question of our being perfect. I'm not even sure what "perfect" means in this discussion. I approach our efforts at simplicity as a novice approaches her order, aspiring to a lifetime of deepening understanding, discipline, serenity, and joy. To liken voluntary simplicity to a religion is not hyperbole or sacrilege. Some people look around and declare the root of all evil to be sex or blasphemy, and so they aspire to be pious and chaste. Where I look for evil I'm more likely to see degradations of human and natural life, an immoral gap between rich and poor, a ravaged earth. At the root of these I see greed and overconsumption by the powerful minority. I was born to that caste but I can aspire to waste not, and want less.

Consider this: the average food item set before a U.S. consumer traveled 1,300 miles to get there. If Mr. Average eats ten or so items a day (most of us eat more), in a year's time his food has conquered five million miles by land, sea and air. Picture a truck loaded with apples and oranges and iceberg lettuce rumbling to the moon and back ten times a year, all just for you. Multiply that by the number of Americans who like to eat—picture that *flotilla* of 285 million trucks on their way to the moon—and tell me you don't think it's time to revise this scenario.

Obviously if you live in Manhattan, your child can't have chickens. But I'll wager you're within walking distance of a farmer's market where it's possible to make the acquaintance of some farmers and buy what's in season. (I have friends in Manhattan who actually garden—on rooftops, and in neighborhood community plots.) Nearly 3,000 green markets have sprung up across the country, in which more than 100,000 farmers sell their freshly harvested, usually organic produce to a regular customer base. Also, in some 700 communities, both rural and urban (including inner-city New York), thousands of Americans support their local food economy by subscribing to Community-Supported Agriculture, in which farmers are paid at planting time and deliver produce weekly to their subscribers until year's end. Thousands of communities have food co-operatives that specialize at least in organic goods, if not local ones, and promote commodities (such as bulk flours, cereals, oils, and spices) that minimize energy costs of packaging and shipping. Wherever you are, if you have a grocery store, you'll find something in there that's in season and hasn't spent half its life in a boxcar. The way to find out is to ask. If every U.S. consumer would dedicate ten dollars a month to local items, the consequences would be huge.

Before anyone rules out eating locally and organically because it seems expensive, I'd ask them to bargain in the costs paid outside the store. The health costs, the land costs, the big environmental VISA bill that sooner or later comes due. It's easy to notice that organic vegetables cost more than their chemically-reared equivalents, but that difference is rarely the one consumers take home. A meal prepared at home from whole, chemical-free ingredients costs just pennies on the dollar paid for the highly processed agribusiness products most Americans eat at restaurants or heat up at home, nearly all the time. For every dollar we send to a farmer, fisherman or rancher, we send three to the shippers, processors, packagers, retailers, and advertisers. And there are countless other costs to that kind of food. Our history of overtaking the autonomy and economies of small countries with large corporations, our wars and campaigns that maintain our fossil fuel dependency—these have finally brought us costs beyond our wildest fears. Cancer is expensive too; so are topsoil loss, and species extinction. The costs of global warming will bring us eventually to our knees. When I have to tell my kids someday that, yes, back at the turn of the century we *knew* we were starting to cause catastrophic changes in the earth's climate that might end their lives prematurely, do I have to tell them we just couldn't be bothered to change our convenience-food habits?

Like many busy families, we cook in quantity on the weekends and freeze portions for easy mid-week dinners. And we've befriended some fascinating microbes that will stay up all night in our kitchen making yogurt, feta, neufchatel, and sourdough bread without adult supervision. (I think copulation is involved, but we're open-minded.) Gardening is the best way I know to stay fit and trim, so during garden season when it's up to me to make the earth move, I don't waste hours at the gym. Eating this way requires organization and skills more than time. Our great-grandmas did all this, and they may not have had other employment but they did have to skin hogs for shoe leather, cut stove wood, sew everybody's clothes, and make the soap to wash them. Sheesh. My kitchen's on Easy Street.

Now that I've gotten into local eating I can't quit, because I've inadvertently raised children who are horrified by the taste of a store-bought tomato. Health is an issue too—my growing girls don't need the hormones and toxins that lace American food in regulated quantities (the allowable doses are more about economic feasibility than proven safety). But that is only part of the picture. Objecting to irresponsible agriculture for reasons of your personal health is a bit like objecting to a nuclear power plant in your backyard for reasons of your view. My own two children are the smallest part of the iceberg. Millions of children in sub-Saharan Africa and other places now facing famine and historically unprecedented climatic extremes because of global warming—they are the other part of the iceberg.

Developing an intimate relationship with the processes that feed my family has brought me surprising personal rewards. I've tasted flavors of heirloom vegetables with poetic names—Mortgage Lifter Tomato, Moon and Stars Watermelon—that most may never know because they turn to pulp and vinegar in a boxcar. I've learned how to look a doe-goat right in the weird horizontal pupil of her big brown eye, sit down and extract her milk, and make feta cheese. (Step 1 is the hardest.) I've discovered a kind of citrus tree that withstands below-zero temperatures, almost extinct today but commonly grown by farm wives a hundred years ago. I've learned the best-tasting vegetables on God's green earth are the ones our garden-wise foremothers bred for consumption, not hard travel. And best of all, I'm raising kids who like healthy food. When Lily streaks through the crowd at the farmers' market shouting, "Mama, look, they have *broccoli,* let's get a *lot!*"—well, heads do turn. Women have asked me, "How do you get one like that?"

I'm not going to tell you it's a done deal. If my cupboards were full of junk food, it would vanish, with no help from mice. We have our moments of abandon—Halloween, I've learned is inescapable without a religious conversion—but most of the time my kids get other treats they've come to love. Few delicacies compare with a yellow-pear tomato, delicately sun-warmed and sugary, right off the vine. When I send the kids out to pick berries or fruit, I have to specify that at least *some* are supposed to go in the bucket. My younger daughter adores eating small, raw green beans straight off the garden trellis; I thought she was nuts until I tried them myself.

The soreness in my hamstrings at the end of a hard day of planting or hoeing feels so good, I can hardly explain it except to another gardener, who knows exactly the sweet ache I mean. My children seem to know it too, and sleep best on those nights. I've found the deepest kind of physical satisfaction in giving my body's muscles, senses and attentiveness over to the purpose for which these things were originally designed—the industry of feeding itself and remaining alive. I suspect that most human bodies have fallen into such remove from that original effort, we've precipitated an existential crisis that requires things like shopping, overeating, and adrenalin-rush movies to sate that particular body hunger.

And so I hope our family's efforts at self-provision will not just improve the health and habitat of my children, but will offer a life that's good for them, and knowledge they need. I wish all children could be taught the basics of agriculture in school along with math and English literature, because it's surely as important a subject as these. Most adults my age couldn't pass a simple test on what foods are grown in their home counties and what month they come into maturity. In just two generations we've passed from a time when people almost never ate a fruit out of season, to a near-universal ignorance of what seasons mean.

I want to protect my kids against a dangerous ignorance of what sustains them. When they help me dig and hoe the garden, plant corn and beans, later on pick them, and later still, preserve the harvest's end, compost our scraps, then turn that compost back into the garden plot the following spring, they are learning important skills for living and maintaining life. I have also observed they appreciate feeling useful. In fact, nearly all kids I've ever worked with in gardening projects get passionate about putting seeds in the ground, to the point of earnest territoriality.

"Now," I ask them when we're finished, "what will you do if you see somebody over here tromping around or riding a bike over your seedbeds?"

"*We'll tell them to get outta our vegables!*" shouted my most recent batch of five-year-old recruits to this plot of mine for improving the world one *vegable* at a time.

Maria Montessori was one of the first child advocates to preach the wisdom of allowing children to help themselves and others, thereby learning to feel competent and self-assured. Most teachers and parents I know agree, and organize classrooms and homes to promote it. But in modern times it's not easy to construct opportunities for kids to feel very useful. They can pick up their toys or take out the trash or walk the dog, but these things have an abstract utility. How useful is it to help take care of the dog whose main purpose, as far as they can see, is to be taken care of?

Growing food for the family's table is concretely useful. Nobody needs to explain how a potato helps the family. Bringing in a basket of eggs and announcing, "Attention everybody: FREE BREAKFAST" is a taste of breadwinning that most kids can only attain in make-believe. I'm lucky I could help make my littlest daughter's dream come true. My own wish is for world enough and time that every child might have this—the chance to count some chickens before they hatch.

Part II

Reclaiming Our Future

Section II A

Templates for Change

Chapter 12

Our Most Vulnerable

Philip J. Landrigan

Children are our most valuable players, and also our most vulnerable. They are extremely sensitive to toxic chemicals released by industrial pollution in environments all around them: in their homes, schools, and playgrounds, and in the very air they breathe. When infants are exposed to the minutest amounts of these poisons, their health can be damaged, their development disrupted, their intelligence reduced, and their capacity to grow into strong, productive, and loving members of society forever diminished. Child Honoring's focus on the very young recognizes this critical developmental issue.

All children have a right to live and grow up toxic free. The toxic threats to the very young are tragically real, but they can be reversed if we care enough and take action. We can honor our children by recognizing and understanding their unique vulnerability, and by taking steps in our own lives as well as in the broader society to protect them from environmental hazards of our own making. Indeed, if we were to apply this understanding to other hazards infants face, we would have the basis for a fundamental change in how we view the world.

CHILDREN'S UNIQUE VULNERABILITY

Although all children are highly vulnerable to chemical toxicants, the period of greatest sensitivity is prenatally and in the early years. This vulnerability arises from several sources, primarily the fact that young children have exceptionally heavy exposures to environmental toxins. Pound for pound of body weight, infants drink more water, eat more food, and breathe more air than adults. In the first six months of life, babies drink seven times as much water as the average adult. One- to five-year-olds eat three to four times as much as an adult; they also spend a lot of time on the floor or on the ground, and often put their fingers in their mouths. That's why the very young have far greater exposure than adults to the toxic chemicals that are present in water, food, or air.

In addition, because their metabolic pathways—especially in the first months after birth—are not sufficiently developed, children are less able than adults to metabolize, detoxify, and excrete many toxicants, such as lead and organophosphate pesticides. They do not yet have the enzymes necessary to metabolize these toxins and thus are far more vulnerable to them.

Another source of children's unique vulnerability is their rapid growth and development. Prenatally, organ systems undergo very rapid and extraordinarily complex change from one cell at conception to billions of organized, differentiated, and constantly intercommunicating cells at birth. These fast-developing systems are very delicate and are not well able to repair damage caused by environmental toxicants. When chemicals such as lead, mercury, or solvents destroy cells in an infant's brain or send false signals to the developing reproductive organs during critical periods of early development, there is a high risk that the resulting dysfunction will be permanent and irreversible.

Because the young have more future years of life than most adults, they have more time to develop chronic diseases triggered by early exposures. Many of those diseases, including cancer and neurodegenerative diseases, are now thought to arise through a series of stages that require years or even decades to evolve from earliest initiation to actual manifestation. Carcinogenic and toxic exposures sustained in early life, including prenatal exposures, can more likely lead to disease than similar exposures encountered later.

ENVIRONMENTAL EXPOSURES AND CHRONIC DISEASE

The natural environment in which our children live today is markedly different from that of 50 years ago. Presently, more than 80,000 chemicals are registered with the EPA for commercial use. More than 2,800 of these are high-production volume chemicals (HPVs) produced in quantities of more than 1 million pounds per year.[1] These HPV chemicals are widely distributed in air, food, water, and also in consumer products. They include endocrine-disrupting phthalates used widely as plastic softeners in such products as pacifiers and baby bottle nipples; carcinogenic formaldehyde found in pressed wood furniture and in wall-to-wall carpeting; and carcinogenic perfluorinated compounds, the basic building block of Teflon. Young children are thus extensively exposed to toxicants which enter their bodies by ingestion, inhalation, or absorption through the skin.

Of great concern to those of us who care about the impacts of chemicals on children's health is the fact that only 43 percent of the HPV chemicals have been even minimally tested for their potential to cause toxicity, and fewer than 20 percent have been tested for their capacity to interfere with fetal and infant development.[2] This lack of testing means that every day our young are exposed to hundreds of chemicals of unknown hazard. Many of these chemicals are now commonly found in young children's bloodstreams.

Over the last century, patterns of illness have changed dramatically among children in the industrially developed nations. The classic infectious diseases have been greatly reduced and many of them controlled. Infant mortality has been lowered and life expectancy at birth has increased by more than 20 years. Children's environmental health, however, has become a growing concern.

Today, the most serious diseases confronting children in so-called developed nations are a group of chronic, disabling, and sometimes life-threatening conditions termed the "new pediatric morbidity." Evidence is growing steadily that industry's toxic chemicals—air pollutants, water pollutants, pesticides, solvents, and metals—are in great part causing these illnesses.

Examples of chronic diseases that are becoming increasingly prevalent in American children are:

- Asthma, for which incidence and mortality have more than doubled in the past decade. We now know that asthma is caused by automotive air pollution (especially diesel exhaust), second-hand cigarette smoke, house dust, cockroaches, and mold and mildew. Control of these exposures can sharply reduce asthma incidence in children and the frequency of acute, life-threatening attacks.
- Childhood cancer, for which incidence of the two most common types, leukemia and primary brain cancer (glioma), has increased substantially in the past 30 years. Although the death rate from childhood cancer has declined as the result of great gains in treatment, the incidence of leukemia has increased by 25 percent and the incidence of glioma by 40 percent since the early 1970s.

- Testicular cancer in adolescent boys, which has increased by 65 percent over the past 25 years.
- Congenital defects of the reproductive organs such as hypospadias.
- Neurodevelopmental and behavioral disorders such as dyslexia, attention deficit/hyperactivity disorder (ADHD), mental retardation, cerebral palsy, and autism, which all together affect 5–10 percent of all babies born each year in the United States. Prenatal and early life exposures of babies to lead, polychlorinated biphenyls (PCBs), methyl mercury, and arsenic are known risk factors for these conditions.

A major impediment to preventing the diseases that are caused in children by toxic chemicals is our current legalistic approach to their regulation. It presumes that chemicals are "innocent" until they are proven hazardous beyond even the remotest shadow of a doubt. This approach results in long delays, often of years and even decades, between the first recognition of the hazardnous nature of a chemical and its eventual control. The result of these delays is that under current law children can be exposed to toxic chemicals for many years after their danger is first recognized.

The existing regulatory framework puts the burden where it cannot belong, on our children. *We must reverse the onus: it must be on the manufacturer,* to scientifically prove beyond a reasonable doubt that a proposed new chemical is safe for use. When we can't know that a given compound is safe for children, we must not approve its use; the same precaution ought to be applied to existing toxicants. Because the current approach to chemical regulation fails to give our children the same protection that it gives to chemicals, we clearly need a prudent and precautionary way of regulating chemicals that serves our children well—by recognizing their unique vulnerability.

To protect children from exposure to environmental toxins, strong, protective governmental policies are essential that first require the testing of chemicals to learn of their toxicity *before* they are approved for commercial use, and that control and phase out known chemical hazards.

A CHILD-HONORING ENVIRONMENTAL PROTECTION LAW

In 1988, an event of great importance made U.S. policy makers aware of young children's unique vulnerability to environmental toxicants. Stimulated by growing concern at that time about environmental hazards to children's health, the Senate Committee on Agriculture called on the National Academy of Sciences (NAS) to conduct a study of the unique vulnerabilities of children to environmental toxins. This resulted in the formation of the NAS Committee on Pesticides in the Diets of Infants and Children. The congressional charge to this landmark committee was threefold:

1. To explore differences in levels of exposure to pesticides between children and adults and the implications of those differences in risk assessment
2. To explore differences in susceptibility to pesticides between children and adults and their implications for risk assessment
3. To analyze federal laws and regulations regarding food use pesticides to determine whether those rules adequately protected the health of infants and children

I had the privilege of being invited by the National Academy of Sciences to chair this committee, a responsibility that I accepted and fulfilled to the best of my ability over the next five years.

The committee's main finding, which was reached by unanimous vote and published in 1993 in the NAS report, *Pesticides in the Diets of Infants and Children,* was that "children are not little adults." In reaching this conclusion and thus in scientifically affirming the unique vulnerability of the very young, the committee ratified for policy makers what was already well established in pediatric and child development circles. In this way, the NAS report moved knowledge of children's vulnerability from the realm of science to the arena of policy and regulation. The report called for expanding toxicological testing protocols to assess threats to reproduction and development, and for reframing risk assessment in order to better safeguard young children from environmental threats to their health.

The NAS Committee's most far-reaching conclusion was that existing federal laws and regulations governing the use of agricultural pesticides *were not strict enough to protect the health of children.* The committee found that those laws and regulations were targeted toward protecting the health of adults and accounted for neither the unique exposures nor the special susceptibilities of children. The committee recommended, therefore, that federal policies for regulating agricultural pesticides be fundamentally changed to recognize those most vulnerable—the very young.

The major recommendations of the NAS report were incorporated into federal law in 1996 when both houses of Congress unanimously passed the Food Quality Protection Act (FQPA), the principal statute regulating the use of pesticides in the nation's agriculture. FQPA was the first environmental law in the United States to clearly affirm the unique vulnerability of children and to require explicit consideration of children in risk assessment and regulation. *It is thus the first explicitly child-honoring environmental law ever passed.*

Embodying all the major recommendations of the NAS Committee, FQPA requires that pesticide exposure standards be based primarily on the protection of health and that they be set at levels that protect the health of infants and children. It requires that an extra margin of safety be incorporated into pesticide risk assessment when (1) data show that a particular pesticide is especially toxic to infants and children or (2) data on the toxicity of a pesticide to infants and children are lacking. This requirement of a child-specific safety factor is an excellent example of applying a precautionary approach in chemical regulatory policy. The FQPA also requires consideration of the interactive effects among pesticides. And finally, it requires that pesticides be assessed systematically for possible endocrine-disrupting effects.

Passage of the FQPA was a watershed event for children's environmental health. It marked a paradigm shift in federal policy: the FQPA is the first environmental statute anywhere to call for the protection of children's health specifically against environmental hazards. The consequences of the FQPA extend far beyond the regulation of agricultural pesticides. For example, just a few weeks after the passage of the act, Carol Browner, then administrator of the U.S. Environmental Protection Agency (EPA), established a new EPA Office of Children's Health Protection. This office was given a broad charter to examine the impact of environmental factors on the health of children in all EPA programs of research and regulation.

In April 1997, President Clinton and Vice President Gore signed an Executive Order on Children's Environmental Health and Safety, declaring that the protection of children's environmental health would be a high priority across all federal agencies of their administration. A cabinet-level oversight committee on children's environmental health was established and cochaired by the EPA Administrator and Secretary of the Department of Health and Human Services. This committee was given broad responsibility to review the programs of all cabinet agencies to ensure that they were protective of children's health. Also in 1997,at a meeting of the environmental ministers of the G-8 nations, led by EPA Administrator Carol Browner of the United States, the Children's Health Declaration was released, which affirmed "the right of children worldwide to live in a world free of toxic hazards."

Later in 1997, the EPA, the National Institute of Environmental Health Sciences (NIEHS), and the Centers for Disease Control and Prevention (CDC) jointly established a new national network of 8 centers in children's environmental health and disease prevention research. (Never before had children's environmental health had such a high profile within the federal government.) The establishment of these centers, now 11 in number, marked the largest federal research investment to date in children's environmental health. It is hoped that as the existing centers grow in size and number, they will a achieve a much-needed, critical mass of researchers and clinicians trained in understanding the impact of environmental factors on children's health and development.

THE FUTURE

Protecting prenatal, infant, and child development is of utmost importance to the health and wealth of nations. To fathom the gravity of even a small assault on children's early brain development, consider the impact of a neurotoxin such as lead (or mercury) that is capable of producing an average drop of 5 IQ points across a wide population. This in fact happened in the United States in the 1960s and 1970s, when the entire population was exposed to over 200,000 tons of lead emitted each year to the atmosphere in particulate form as the result of burning leaded gasoline.

The resulting 5-point average drop in IQ across the U.S. population produced a downward shift in the IQ of the entire nation: a 50 percent decline in the number of gifted children with IQs above 130 (on a 200-point scale) and a 50 percent increase in the number of children with low IQ—below 70. According to a Harvard University estimate, the costs of this widespread decline in IQ are truly staggering: $200 billion in lost economic productivity for each year's lead-exposed newborns. (The overall opportunity cost to society is far greater, and lead's impact on the well-being of children, though known, is hard to fully quantify.)

Fortunately, by removing lead from gasoline over the past 20 years we have reversed this trend in the United States and in many other nations. But with our current absence of knowledge about the toxic properties of so many of the chemicals to which our children are exposed, can we be sure there aren't other hazards as bad as or worse than lead still lurking? Will we summon the will to recognize the similar threat mercury and so many other known toxicants pose to developmental health and act to curb its hazards in every feasible way?

There is an enormous need for adequately funded comprehensive testing of individual and cumulative effects of chemicals on the health of children (as well as the overall population). It deserves priority attention. But research alone is not enough. Scientific data must be translated into medical practice, and used to produce evidence-based state and federal policies that protect children from harmful exposures.

Until now, scientific progress in outlining the role of environmental factors in chronic childhood disease has been slow and incremental. Nearly all studies have examined relatively small populations of children; have considered only one toxicant at a time; have had little statistical power to examine interactions among chemical, social, and behavioral factors in our lives; have had limited ability to examine gene-environment interactions; and have suffered from brief duration of follow-up.

In a development of critical importance for children's health, the U.S. National Institutes of Health proposes next year to launch the National Children's Study—a multiyear epidemiological study to examine how early exposures to environmental factors influence health, disease, and development in children. It will address critical research questions such as the contribution of indoor and ambient air pollution to the origins of asthma, environmental causes of developmental disabilities, effects of endocrine disruption, and the causes of rising incidence of certain pediatric cancers.

The National Children's Study will follow a representative sample of 100,000 American children from early pregnancy through age 21; a subset sample will be recruited before conception. Exposure histories and biological samples will be obtained during pregnancy and from newborns as they grow. The large sample size will facilitate simultaneous examination of the effects of multiple chemical exposures, of interactions among them, and of interactions among biologic, chemical, behavioral, and social factors.

When completed, the National Children's Study will make a unique and significant contribution to our understanding of how behavioral, social, and environmental factors in early life may cause or predispose individuals to certain chronic diseases or conditions. This study will be the richest information resource for questions related to child health in the United States and will form the basis of child health guidance and policy for generations to come. It may become one of the most important ways in which our generation safeguards its children.

CONCLUSION

Honoring our children requires all of our intellect and all of our love. Through the conduct of scientific research that identifies hazards to children and through the development of strong, scientifically based policies that protect children's health, we can do our best for all children—the children of today and the children of generations yet to come.

It is our responsibility to learn as much as we can through testing and research about the chemical threats to the health of our very young, for there is much we still do not know. *But we have a solemn responsibility to act on the great deal we do know.* To adequately protect our children, we urgently need to change the way in which we regulate the chemicals that confront them. We need to reverse the onus of their body burden.

In my work, I come face-to-face with the suffering of children and with the data that overwhelmingly confirms the link to industrial pollution. The overriding goal of chemical regulation must be the prudent, precautionary protection of the health of young children and thus of our world. Humanity's children cannot remain the unwitting research animals in a vast toxicological experiment that nobody wants. We must move heaven and earth to correct this injustice.

Chapter 13

The Power of Empathy

MARY GORDON

Nine-year-old Sylvie came to school wearing running shoes that did up with a Velcro strap. Some of the other children taunted her, saying she wore baby shoes, geeky shoes. She was the target of a double-barreled criticism—her shoes were not only cheap and unfashionable, they were immature. This is the kind of humiliation that would shrivel the spirit of any nine-year-old. But then something happened. When the class headed outside for recess, Sylvie's best friend June swapped one shoe with her. The empathic insight and quick thinking of this child gives us hope. Her actions said, "I'm your friend and I'm proud to wear your shoes and be just like you." She turned a mean, exclusionary attack into something playful, without saying a word. Every other child in the class got the message: "This is my friend—make fun of her and you are making fun of me. Keep it up and you may find yourself outnumbered by kids who care.

While the courage of this little girl's action is exclusively her own, her capacity not only to empathize with her friend but to turn empathy into effective action has been encouraged through the perspective-taking skills acquired in her Roots of Empathy class. Through this program, children like her come to see that it is not just a matter of what you stand for but what you stand up for. They are taught that to witness unkindness and cruelty and do nothing is to condone injustice. They are encouraged to be "chang-ers." At nine years of age June has become a social activist, standing up for justice.

EMPATHY: AN ESSENTIAL HUMAN TRAIT

The empathic relationship between parent and child is a template for all future relationships. Lessons in empathy begin in infancy when our parents respond lovingly to our needs as they arise, and understand our feelings even when we are not yet able to articulate them. What we say to young children is important, but more crucial still is *how we say it* and what we are conveying about our respect for them as individuals. Brazelton and Greenspan express it well:

> Empathy is taught not by telling children to be nice to others or to try to understand others, but by parents' having the patience to listen to children and children's feeling understood. Once they understand what empathy feels like, they can create it in their relationships.[1]

Empathy is at the very core of civil society, whether that society is the classroom, the school, the community, the country or our "global village." It is therefore of vital importance to instill in children a sense of themselves as strong and caring individuals, and to inspire in them a vision of citizenship that can indeed change the world.

Empathic Ethics

Bill Drayton, the Founder of Ashoka, coined the term *empathic ethics.* The Oxford English Dictionary defines *ethics* as "a set of moral principles." Accordingly, it defines *principle* as "a fundamental truth or proposition serv-ing as the foundation for belief or action," and *morals* as "standards of behav-iour, or principles of right and wrong."

By weaving empathy and ethics together, we can create moral principles that bridge the gap between *us* and *them,* so that it becomes natural to identify with and understand the feelings of others. In doing so, we redefine identity by seeing ourselves with multiple memberships in a pluralistic and interde-pendent world. So if justice is an ethic, empathic ethics imply that we need to understand the situation of those who are treated unjustly and we are *com-pelled* to care about injustice. Justice then is not just an idea but a discussion about the core of what it is to be human.

We have many examples of communities, groups, and cultures that are based not on empathic ethics but on *common* ethics, bound and constrained by narrow self-identification. While we may have tribal or communal affiliations that give us our sense of identity, empathic ethics moves us to connect with something greater—with our shared humanity. Those outside our social spheres are not outside our consciousness.

Empathy In Action

In *Truth and Ethics in School Reform,* T. E. McCullough writes

> Moral imagination is the capacity to empathize with others, i.e., not just to feel for oneself, but to feel with and for others. This is something that education ought to cultivate and that citizens ought to bring to politics.[2]

Empathy is frequently defined as the ability to identify with the feelings and perspectives of others. I would add, *and to respond appropriately.* Perhaps it is only when we reflect on what happens when empathy is absent that we begin to grasp the profound, complex, and fundamental role it plays in healthy human relations and in the creation of caring, peaceful, and civil societies.

When we think of the Holocaust or South Africa under apartheid we are horrified at the scale of cruelty perpetrated on an entire group of human beings. We might try to distance ourselves from the atrocity by focusing on the fact it was far away or long ago and couldn't happen here, couldn't happen now. But were the people who participated in these atrocities, or stood by and watched them happen, fundamentally different from us? And if they weren't, what force was at work that drew them into a situation that we find unconscionable?

In both cases, a relentless campaign of propaganda, indoctrination, and intimidation was mounted to convince the dominant population that Jews and black South Africans were alien, threatening, or something less than human. And yet, a significant minority resisted the propaganda and actively engaged in the struggle for justice. Why? Their capacity for empathy, their ability to identify with the feelings and perspectives of others made it impossible for them to do otherwise. Failure of empathy at best leads to apathy and complicity; at worst, it leads to cruelty and violence.

The same forces are at work on a smaller scale in the bullying that plagues our schools and communities. The victim is singled out on any number of grounds—perhaps because she is smaller, weaker, has poor social skills and few friends, or is a new immigrant and talks or looks differently. Whatever the factors, they are used to marginalize the victim, to define her as different and inferior to the dominant group. She then becomes not only the victim of the bully, but also—to a lesser, but still hurtful, degree—the victim of the onlookers. When we do not actively work to give children the skills and the courage to act on behalf of the victim, we are failing to give our children the tools to form healthy, respectful relationships—we are failing to show them that aggression is destructive. And we are failing to give them a sense of their role as valued members of a civil society. Empathy is at the root of conflict resolution, altruism, and peace.

THE ROOTS OF EMPATHY PROGRAM

Roots of Empathy was born out of a real need, both in our culture and in our educational system. Early in my career, I spent over two decades working with young parents, many of whom (scarcely beyond childhood themselves) were physically abusive towards their children. It became clear to me that these parents were not monsters (as the public thought), but people desperately in search of acceptance, recognition, and love, whose own life experiences had left them unable to create healthy relationships or to relate empathically to their own children. A majority of these abusive parents had themselves been abused at the hands of their own parents. Witnessing the devastating impact of the cycle of neglect and violence set me on a path to find a way to help break this cycle. Raising parents' empathic awareness lay at the heart of my parenting programs. I came to feel that lessons in empathy were best *not* left until parenthood, but integrated into the school curriculum.

Ideally, public education should meaningfully engage both the mind *and* the heart. Classrooms can serve as a microcosm of a model society by providing children with the opportunity to find the self-confidence to ask questions freely and to find their own voice. This sense of voice is central if they are to become citizens in a democratic society. Unfortunately, the average public school curriculum does not give lessons in empathic development. In addition, bullying and exclusive social hierarchies are increasingly common in the classroom and the schoolyard.

I began to envision a school program that would not only offer children a window on loving and responsive parenting, but on an entire spectrum of social and emotional learning—a program that would strengthen children's capacity to build a positive sense of self, to form caring relationships, and to see themselves as people who could make a difference in the world. This vision culminated in the development of the Roots of Empathy program.[3]

Roots of Empathy is an evidence-based program for school-aged children from kindergarten through eighth grade that takes place right in their own classrooms during the school day. Once a month, over a period of nine months, beginning when the infant is two months old, a parent and infant visit the classroom for about half an hour, accompanied by a Roots of Empathy instructor.

Through observation of the infant's remarkable physical, cognitive, and emotional growth during the first year of life, and the attuned responsiveness of the parent, children learn about empathy through their spontaneous identification with the infant and the parent's modeling. The baby serves as the "textbook" as the children, through discussion and labeling of the baby's feelings. The instructors follow up on the experiential learning of the nine family visits to the classroom with an additional 18 classes without the baby. Through guided discussion, music, drama, art, literature, and writing, the children learn skills in self-awareness, problem solving, and consensus building.

Launched as a pilot project in 1996, as of 2005, Roots of Empathy programs are now in every Canadian province except for Saskatchewan and the Territories, including French, English, and Aboriginal communities, for a total of more than 1,800 programs, reaching more than 45,000 children. The program is currently being implemented in Australia and will begin in New Zealand in 2006. We are also developing Seeds of Empathy, which will serve preschool children in a variety of settings.

Roots of Empathy: Success Stories

Social Inclusion and Responsibility: David was nine years old and suffered from an autistic spectrum disorder. His parents shared that David had never been invited to a birthday party by any of his classmates until the year that Roots of Empathy came into his classroom. During that year, David was invited to three birthday parties and his feelings about himself and his attitude towards school took a 180-degree turn. No medicine ever affected his life as much as the inclusive response of his classmates. These remarkable achievements came from the children's heightened understanding of the pain of exclusion and the importance of including someone who is different.

Every human being has a deep need to be heard, to be seen, to belong. That's why a fundamental value in Roots of Empathy is inclusion. We create an environment where everyone has a voice, where every contribution has meaning. We work with children to break down barriers, encourage communication and acceptance, and create in the classroom a microcosm of democracy and collaboration. The lessons—on respect for individual temperament, responsiveness to the feelings of others, seeing the world from another person's perspective—come together to build a community of social trust within the classroom. Inclusion means that when problems arise, everyone in the class takes responsibility for solving them; and when conflict emerges, respect for one another is the framework for resolving the conflict.

It may seem like a cliché to point out that so much of the strife in our communities and in our world today can be linked to an intolerance for any person or group or religion or nation that is felt to be different and thus a threat. A focus on empathy is a focus on our common experiences, on what unites us rather than what divides us. Recognizing our shared humanity frees us to see our differences in a new light: as interwoven threads that together create a rich tapestry, leading to more tolerant and meaningful relationships and worldviews.

Decrease in Bullying: During a Roots of Empathy session, the instructor was encouraging children to talk about a time when they were bullied or someone they knew was bullied. Nine-year-old Sam spoke up: "Is it okay to talk about it if you were the bully?" What ensued was a story not unlike South Africa's Truth and Reconciliation Commission in the wake of the end of apartheid. Sam told the class that he'd been threatening a kid in grade 1 and taking his lunch money from him. The response from the class? "That's a very hard thing to own up to." Sam was commended by his classmates for his courage in confessing to his bullying behavior and the discussion moved on to what he needed to do to make amends. It was agreed that Sam should apologize to the grade 1 student and give him back the money he took. When it emerged that the now ex-bully didn't have enough money, the rest of the children chipped in pennies and dimes to make up the amount. Intent on collaborating on doing the right thing, these children ensured that self-respect and social justice triumphed over humiliation, shame, and damaging isolation.

Research tells us that students who have completed the Roots of Empathy program exhibit an increase in prosocial behavior and a decrease in bullying, aggression, and violence.[4] The program reduces bullying when children gain insight into the impact of their overt or covert actions. Rather than targeting bullies, the children are mobilized to challenge the cruelty of bullying. It works.

At school, so much administrative time is spent controlling problems rather than preventing them. Control, as opposed to prevention, also reigns in our penal systems—we build jails and boot camps instead of family support systems and child care. Similarly, in our medical systems we invest in cures rather than prevention. Prevention is seen as "soft" and intervention is seen as "hard." If you think about it, which would you rather have?

Intrinsic Motivation: We foster intrinsic motivation when instructors thank the children for their contribution to discussion, instead of giving them evaluative praise. Adult praise, in group settings like the classroom, spawns competition and praise junkies, who make contributions for the impressions they might make. Every child's questions and observations are welcomed and respected and even the shyest in the group participate. When children are given the opportunity to take charge of their own problem solving, they develop the inner motivation needed to become confident, contributing adults. They acquire a sense of pride that has nothing to do with vanity and everything to do with conviction. They become true givers, because they don't give to get praise or recognition, but rather because they have a sense that their contribution is worthwhile.

Authentic Communication: Authentic communication is an important principle in Roots of Empathy. Real communication happens at an emotional level. When we share our feelings, opinions, values, and deeply held beliefs with each other, we are able to relate fully as human beings. This means that adults don't hide behind a persona of grown-up experts, but honestly reveal their feelings when the context requires it and when to do otherwise is disrespectful to the child. It means that adults don't ask children manipulative questions. It means that our questions provoke reflection and encourage a child to express their own thoughts and feelings. Authentic communication is the foundation for the growth of social and emotional competence and the basis for developing empathy.

Children love to hear stories of their parents' lives and experiences, as long as the stories are not of the "I had to walk six miles to school, uphill both ways" genre. They want to hear the stories that make us human. We need to tell our stories as honestly as we can, making the feelings they contain come alive. Children like to know about life's challenges and tough times; it makes their own challenges a little easier to face. Admitting to a child that there are times when we have been afraid, far from unsettling the child, inspires confidence that everyone can be afraid and everyone can overcome it.

Authentic communication helps the child build a foundation of sustainable self-esteem, an inner moral sense that will stand up to the challenges that are an inevitable part of growing into adulthood. If children have a learned method for deciding, for making judgments, if they have internalized principles to live by and learned to be true to themselves, they develop the courage to say no to things that make them feel uncomfortable or strike them as wrong.

Our research shows that children who have completed the Roots of Empathy program include *nearly all* class members as "friends," as compared to far fewer in the comparison group of children who have not been a part of the program.[5] One particular grade 4 program included a hearing-impaired boy. In the safe bully-free environment that had developed in the classroom, a child asked the little boy what it would feel like if he took off his hearing aids. The boy responded, "First, my life goes grey and then I get angry because I feel left out and frustrated that I don't understand." This empathic exchange helped every child in the class get closer to their classmate. So often, a child with hearing aids or other visible disability is punished by exclusion. In our program, children's differences are recognized, accepted, and understood.

CHANGING THE WORLD CLASSROOM BY CLASSROOM

Roots of Empathy's magic is understanding the whole through the part, humanity through the baby. Through the baby, children also learn to understand the *other*—someone who doesn't speak their language, who cannot walk, who is completely dependent on others. The children become advocates for the baby; they make huge efforts to understand her and try to meet her needs. The experience allows them to imagine and extend this caring for all babies in the world. This learning also fosters caring for their classmates and even for people they don't know.

The first year that the program was offered in Manitoba, the local media ran a story about a baby who had died after being shaken by his father. The grade 5 students in the program started to talk about it with their teacher during a current affairs discussion. The teacher had been concerned about what the students' reactions would be to the media story. Would they be ready with the "should haves" and "could haves"? Would they vent their anger at this father whose child had just died?

Although very upset and sad that a child had died, the students' first reaction was "Can you imagine how bad this dad must feel?" "How scared and alone he must feel in jail? If only he had known what to do." "If only he had put the baby in a safe place until he was calm." The feelings expressed by the students demonstrated an all-encompassing level of empathy that included sadness at a preventable infant death and insights into the horror the parent would feel in the aftermath of an explosive moment. When the teacher later shared this discussion with her colleagues in the staff room, they were stunned—not only by the mature, compassionate response of the students but by their handling of the complexity of moral issues involved.

This story illustrates the power of empathy. Empathic ethics learned in childhood will reach far into the adult years. Roots of Empathy children learn to become "changers," challenging injustice and cruelty where they see it. They can grow up to build peace in their own families and pass on this learning to their children. Building peace in the family by supporting parenting capacity is a foundation for building peace in the world.

Imagine a generation of children across the world growing into adulthood, citizenship, and parenthood with self-esteem, a reciprocal understanding of emotions, a sense of community, a commitment to peaceful resolution of conflict, and values of social inclusion. Imagine the world this would call into being if we all believed we shared the same lifeboat.

Imagine every child raised on love in a society where new parents are supported (not penalized, in terms of income, opportunity. or self-development); every school a center of collaborative learning that trains the heart as well as the mind, where character and intelligence are equally valued and nourished, where we measure helpfulness, cooperation, and kindness as well as math; every community a place of human connection, where social trust abounds, where no one is left to struggle in poverty or neglect or isolation; every nation a peaceful member of an interdependent global family in which supporting optimal infant development and restoring our planetary home are the yardsticks by which all decisions are measured.

These are not new values or ideals. What is new is identifying children as indispensable change makers. As a society, we have identified the limitless power of the sun, water, and wind, but we haven't begun to tap the untold power hidden in the hearts and minds of children. In Roots of Empathy, children see that the common experience of being human unites us beyond any other affiliations, and that with this understanding comes a responsibility beyond borders. They are changing the world classroom by classroom. Let us honor them and follow their lead.

Chapter 14

What Matters Most

MEASURING GENUINE PROGRESS BY
RONALD COLMAN

MEASURING WHAT MATTERS MOST BY
MARK ANIELSKI

MEASURING GENUINE PROGRESS[1] BY RONALD COLMAN

Too much and too long, we seem to have surrendered community
excellence and community values in the mere accumulation of material
things. . . . The GNP [GDP] measures neither our wit nor our courage,
neither our wisdom nor our learning, neither our compassion nor our
devotion to our country. It measures everything, in short, except that
which makes life worthwhile.

—Robert F. Kennedy, 1968

There is growing evidence that the doctrine of blind economic growth
must give way to new ways to count what matters in our lives. Economists
and social scientists around the globe are responding to the basic human need
to know how well we are doing, and whether or not we as a society are making progress. We want to know: "Are we better off or worse off than we were
20, 30, or 50 years ago? What kind of world are we leaving our children? Are
we leaving it in better or worse shape than we found it?"

I have a 13-year-old daughter, and like many parents I take these questions quite personally. I wonder, often, what kind of world my daughter is

inheriting. In terms of material comforts, my daughter and her friends are certainly better off than when I was her age. Back then, my family had no car, no home videos, no CD player, and we lived in a tiny apartment. These days, we generally have larger homes than our parents did, often two cars in a family (almost unheard of 45 years ago), and living rooms filled with entertainment equipment. There is no doubt that—materially—we have made progress.

But in other aspects of our lives, I am not so sure we are making genuine progress. We are much more likely to lock our homes and our cars than in the past, and my wife and I worry more about our daughter coming home late at night than our parents had to worry about us. We are less likely to know our neighbors, and our communities often don't feel as safe as they did a generation ago. We have more stuff, but we are more secure economically? Our young people graduate into debts that were unheard of a generation ago, debts that will take years to pay off. And they worry much more than we did about whether they'll have a decent job when they graduate. They are more likely to graduate into categories of work that were virtually unheard of then—"on-call" work, and temporary, part-time jobs with no benefits.

We are living somewhat longer lives and we have medical interventions that are more likely to save us if we have clogged arteries and other problems. But are we really healthier? It's a mixed picture. We are still afflicted by a range of preventable chronic illnesses. We are smoking less, but rates of diabetes and obesity—with a wide range of attendant health consequences—have increased exponentially. Childhood asthma and environmental illnesses are on the rise. And we have been living in such a toxic soup of chemicals that our immune systems are compromised.

And if we look at our natural world, we know that we are certainly losing ground. There are far fewer fish in the oceans than when I was my daughter's age. In Nova Scotia, where we live, nearly all our remaining old forests in the last 50 years have vanished. Scientists tell us that we are killing off species worldwide at 1,000 times the natural rate—largely through loss of habitat. So it's a different experience for my daughter to take a walk in the woods than when I was her age; she'll see far fewer old trees and hear fewer songbirds. In my day, we used to think of pollution as a local problem—a mess that had to be cleaned up, something dumped where it should not have been. But we did not conceive (nor could the public or scientists imagine) that human activity could actually change the climate of our planet. There's no doubt that ours is a degraded natural world, one that is considerably more threatening to our lives. And yet, as an intelligent species, we must ask: do we really lack the collective ability to create a better world for our children when, surely, we all *aspire* to do so?

ENGINES OF GROWTH

What's intriguing is that there is a remarkable consensus that crosses all political divisions on the fundamental principles of a decent society and on the benchmarks that would signify genuine progress. We all want to live in a peaceful and safe society without crime. We all value a clean environment with healthy forests, soils, lakes, and oceans. We all want good health and education, strong and caring communities, and free time to relax and develop our potential. We want economic security and less poverty. No political party officially favors greater national insecurity, a degraded environment, or more stress, crime, poverty, and inequality. Why then do we see policies that promote those very outcomes? Why is there such a gap between the will of the people and government policy? Why are we unable to create the kind of society we genuinely want? Why do we not order our policy priorities to accord with our shared values and human needs?

One reason is that we have been getting the wrong message from our current measures of progress. All of us—politicians, economists, journalists, and the general public—have been hooked on the illusion that economic growth equals well-being and prosperity. *Indeed, there is probably no more pervasive and dangerous myth in our society than the materialist assumption that "more is better."*

Look at the language we use: When our economy is growing rapidly, it is called "robust," "dynamic," and "healthy." When people spend more money, "consumer confidence" is "strong." By contrast, "weak" or "anemic" growth signals "recession" and even "depression." Increased car sales signal a "buoyant recovery." "Free" trade actually means "more" trade. The more we produce, trade, and spend, the more the Gross Domestic Product (GDP) grows and, by implication, the "better off" we are. But this was not the intention of those who created the GDP. Simon Kuznets, its principal architect, warned 40 years ago: "The welfare of a nation can scarcely be inferred from a measurement of national income. . . . Goals for 'more' growth should specify of what and for what."

Here's the key thing to remember: Our growth statistics were never meant to be used as a measure of progress as they are today, when activities that degrade our quality of life, like crime, pollution, and addictive gambling, all make the economy grow. The more fish we sell and the more trees we cut down, the more the economy grows. Working longer hours makes the economy grow. And the economy can grow even if inequality and poverty increase. For decades, we have made a tragic error—confusing economic growth with well-being.

In the American economy, one of the fastest-growing sectors is imprisonment, at an annual growth rate of 6.2 percent per year throughout the 1990s. One in every 140 Americans is now behind bars, the highest rate in the world, compared to one in 900 Canadians and one in 1,600 Nova Scotians. The O.J. Simpson trial alone added $100 million to the U.S. economy, and the Oklahoma City explosion, Columbine High School massacre, and attacks on the World Trade Centre and Pentagon fueled the booming U.S. security industry, which now adds $40 billion a year to the economy. Are these the indicators of a desired "robust" and "healthy" economy? Gambling is growing rapidly—a $50 billion-a-year business in the United States. Divorce adds $20 billion a year to the U.S. economy. Car crashes add another $57 billion. Prozac sales have quadrupled since 1990 to more than $4 billion—are these sign of progress?

Monetary economic growth is fed by many undesirable factors such as overeating, starting with the value of the excess food consumed and the advertising needed to sell it. Then the diet and weight-loss industries add $32 billion a year more to the U.S. economy, and obesity-related health problems another $50 billion, at the same time that 20 million people, mostly children, die every year from hunger and malnutrition in the world. Similarly, toxic pollution, sickness, stress, and war all make the economy grow. The more rapidly we deplete our natural resources and the more fossil fuels we burn, the faster the economy grows. Because we assign no value to "natural capital," we actually count its loss as economic gain.

Economic growth statistics make no distinction between beneficial economic activity and that which causes harm. What family could live by such a code? The Exxon *Valdez* contributed far more to the Alaska economy by spilling its oil than if it had brought it safely to port, because all the cleanup costs, lawsuits, and media coverage added to the growth statistics. In the 1990s, the Yugoslav war stimulated the economies of the NATO countries by $60 million a day, just as the wars in Afghanistan and Iraq are stimulating the U.S. economy today. Our economies benefit even more by rebuilding what we destroy! In fact, so long as we are spending money (it doesn't matter on what), the economy grows, even if that growth comes from a decline in well-being. Try explaining the logic of this to a child.

HAS GROWTH MADE US "BETTER OFF"?

Are we "better off" as a result of decades of continuous economic growth? Are we happier? A recent U.S. poll found that 72 percent of Americans had more possessions than their parents, but only 47 percent said they were happier. We are more time stressed. Our jobs are often more insecure. Our debt levels are higher. The gap between rich and poor is ever widening. Economists predict that, for the first time since the Industrial Revolution, the next generation may be worse off than the present one. Blind growth has undermined our natural resource base, produced massive pollution, destroyed plant and animal species at an unprecedented rate, and changed the climate in a way that now threatens the entire planet.

Ironically, while counting all the money that is spent, we assign no value to vital unpaid activities that really do contribute to our well-being. Voluntary community service, the backbone of civil society, is not counted or valued in our measures of progress because no money is exchanged. If we did measure it, we would know that volunteer services to the elderly, sick, disabled, children, and other vulnerable groups have declined throughout Canada—by a remarkable 12.3 percent since the early 1990s—at the same time that government cut many vital social services, leading to a cumulative 30 percent erosion in the social safety net during the 1990s.

Even though household work and raising children are essential to basic quality of life, they have no value in the GDP. We value Canada's booming child care industry, but we do not count unpaid child care, and so we may not notice that parents spend less time with their children than ever before. If we did count voluntary and household work, we would know that they add $325 billion a year of valuable services to the Canadian economy.

A steady increase in both paid and unpaid work has led to an overall loss of free personal time. In 1900, a single-earner male breadwinner worked a 59-hour week in Canada, while a full-time female homemaker put in an average 56-hour week of household work, for a total household work week of 115 hours. Today the average Canadian dual earner couple puts in 79 hours of paid work and 56 hours of unpaid household work a week, for a total family work week of 135 hours—an increase of 20 hours a week! What is the cost to children of all this extra work and stress? This question needs to be high on the policy agenda and discussed in our legislatures.

Aristotle recognized 2,400 years ago that leisure was a prerequisite for contemplation, informed discussion, participation in political life, and genuine freedom. It is also essential for relaxation and health, for spiritual growth, and for a decent quality of life that truly honors our children and gives them what they often need most: our precious time, loving care, and attention.

In policy making, what we measure and count as a society quite literally tell us what we value. If we don't count our nonmonetary and nonmaterial assets, we effectively devalue them. And what we don't measure and value in our central accounting system will be overlooked by policy makers. If, for example, a teacher tells students that a term paper is very important but worth nothing in the final grade, the real message conveyed is that the paper has no value, and the students will devote their attention to the final exam, which counts for something.

Similarly, we may pay pious public homage to environmental quality, and to social, human, and spiritual values. But if our growth markers count nature's degradation as progress, we will continue to send misleading signals to policy makers and public alike—blunting effective remedial action and distorting policy priorities. We will continue to focus on the wrong things.

A BETTER WAY TO MEASURE PROGRESS

We desperately need measures of well-being and true prosperity that explicitly value the nonmaterial relationships and assets that are the real basis of our wealth, including the strength of our communities, our free time, our environmental quality, the health of our natural resources, our concern for others, and the care and attention we give our children. Here's the good news: we have the means to do so.

After three California researchers developed a Genuine Progress Indicator in 1995, incorporating 26 social, economic, and environmental variables, 400 leading economists, including Nobel laureates, jointly stated:

> Since the GDP measures only the quantity of market activity without accounting for the social and ecological costs involved, it is both inadequate and misleading as a measure of true prosperity. Policy-makers, economists, the media, and international agencies should cease using the GDP as a measure of progress and publicly acknowledge its shortcomings. New indicators of progress are urgently needed to guide our society . . . The GPI is an important step in this direction.

In Nova Scotia, GPI Atlantic, a nonprofit research group, has worked for eight years to develop a Genuine Progress Index (GPI) as a pilot project for Canada. GPI Atlantic has now joined with indicator practitioners from across the country to develop a new Canadian Index of Well-being (CIW), and with experts in New Zealand, Australia, the United Kingdom, and elsewhere to develop internationally comparable measures that can accurately measure genuine progress and sustainable development.

The new indices assign explicit value to our natural resources, including our soils, forests, fisheries, and nonrenewable energy sources, and they assess the sustainability of our harvesting practices, consumption habits, and transportation systems. They measure and value our living standards and our unpaid voluntary and household work, and they count crime, pollution, greenhouse gas emissions, road accidents, and other liabilities as economic costs, not gains as at present.

These common-sense indicators rise or fall according to whether the overall quality of life improves or declines; they correspond with the realities of our daily lives as we actually experience them. They measure our health, leisure time, educational attainment, and true economic security. They attempt, in short, to measure "that which makes life worthwhile." The new measures are essential to creating a society that genuinely honors its children, one that would leave them a liveable world to inherit.

Costs and Benefits

Unlike the GDP, the new measures distinguish economic activities that provide benefit from those that cause harm. By incorporating social and environmental costs directly into the economic accounting structure, "full cost accounting" mechanisms can help policy makers identify activities that cause benefit or harm to society. Gambling, clear-cutting of forests, and coal-fired power plants would receive less government support if social costs were measured and counted, and sustainable practices would receive the subsidies they deserve.

For example, GPI Atlantic found that a modest 10 percent shift from truck to rail freight would save Nova Scotian taxpayers $11 million a year when the costs of greenhouse gas emissions, road accidents, and road maintenance costs are included. Telecommuting two days per week would save $2,200 annually per employee when travel time, fuel, parking, accident, air pollution, and other environmental and social costs are included. Canadians currently spend $102 billion a year on their cars, $11 billion more on highways, $500 million on car advertisements, and billions more on hospital beds, and police, court, and funeral costs for the 3,000 killed and 25,000 seriously injured car crash victims every year. All this spending currently counts as "progress" and "consumer confidence." (Carpooling *slows* GDP growth.) By contrast, full cost-benefit accounting would favor taxation policies and subsidy shifts that support mass transit alternatives and other sustainable practices.

Valuing Natural Resources

An accounting framework that gives value to both natural resources and personal time recognizes inherent limits to economic activity and values balance and human equilibrium; it values natural resources as finite capital stocks, subject to depreciation like financial capital. Genuine progress is measured by our ability to live off the income (or interest) generated by natural resources without depleting the capital stock that is the basis of ongoing prosperity both for ourselves and our children.

The GPI forestry account, for example, counts not only timber production, but also the value of forests in protecting watersheds, habitat, and biodiversity; guarding against soil erosion; regulating climate and sequestering carbon; and providing for recreation and spiritual enjoyment. Healthy soils and the maintenance of multi-species, multi-aged forests in turn provide multiple economic benefits, by enhancing timber productivity, increasing the economic value of forest products, protecting against fire, disease, and insects, and supporting the burgeoning eco-tourism industry. This is holistic measurement that takes the whole relational picture into account.

Valuing Time

Like natural resources, time is also finite and similarly limits economic activity. We all have 24 hours a day and a limited life span. How we pass that time, and how we balance our paid and unpaid work, our voluntary service, and our free time, is a measure of our well-being, quality of life, and contribution to society. The GPI and the new Canadian Index of Well-being use time surveys to measure a full 24-hour period and to do a cost-benefit assessment between its various uses.

According to current accounting methods, the more hours we work for pay, the more the GDP grows, and the more we "progress." In a recent interview, a Fortune 500 Chief Executive Officer stated that he works from 6:00 A.M. to 10:00 P.M. every day and has no time for anything else except sleep. While his $4 million annual income (before bonuses and stock options) makes him appear rich, according to the GPI (where family time, voluntary service, and personal well-being are all measured and valued) his life seems quite impoverished.

What happens when we start valuing time? The policy implications are profound. For example, GPI Atlantic found that Nova Scotians give 140 million hours of volunteer time a year, the equivalent of 81,000 jobs, or $1.9 billion worth of services, equal to 10 percent of our GDP—a reservoir of generosity invisible in our conventional accounts.

Measuring unpaid household work shines the spotlight on the time stress of working parents struggling to juggle job and household responsibilities, and on the need for family-friendly work arrangements and flexible work hours. The workplace has not yet adjusted to the reality that women have doubled their rate of participation in the paid work force. Working mothers put in an average of 11 hours a day of paid and unpaid work on weekdays, and 15 hours more of unpaid work on weekends. What are the consequences for children? A child-honoring society would ask that vital question, and would have good measuring tools to answer it.

Measuring housework also raises important pay equity issues. Work traditionally performed by women in the household and regarded as "free" has been devalued in the market economy, resulting in significant gender pay inequities. Though skilled child care professionals are extremely important to our children, child care workers in Canada generally earn less than $10 an hour—barely above minimum wage. Single mothers put in an average of 50 hours a week of productive household work. If valued for pay in the market economy, this work would be worth $450 a week. Because it is invisible and unvalued, most single mothers in Nova Scotia live below the low-income cut-off, the major cause of child poverty in the province. From the GPI perspective, social supports for single mothers are not welfare. They are seen as essential social support for the household economy.

Equity and Job Creation

Millions of Americans have been left behind by the country's growth economy. The U.S. Census Bureau reports that income inequality has risen dramatically since 1968, by 18 percent for all U.S. households and by over 23 percent for families. The richest 1 percent of American households owns more than 40 percent of the national wealth, while the net worth of middle-class families has fallen or stagnated due to rising indebtedness. Bill Gates alone owns more wealth than the bottom 45 percent of U.S. households combined.

In 1989 the Canadian House of Commons unanimously vowed to eliminate child poverty by the year 2000. But child poverty rates were higher in

2000 than they were in 1989. In other words, a robust economic tide (as in the 1990s) does not necessarily "lift all boats." The evidence indicates that the opposite is frequently the case. For this reason the Genuine Progress Index and the Canadian Index of Well-Being explicitly value increased equity and job security as benchmarks of genuine progress. Indeed, Statistics Canada recently recognized that concern for equity is inherent to any measure of sustainable development. *Once limits to growth are accepted, the issue is equitable distribution rather than increased production.* If everyone in the world consumed resources at the Canadian level, we would require four additional planets like Earth!

Statistics Canada points to a growing "polarization of hours" as the main cause of increased earnings inequality. The growth of insecure, temporary, and marginal employment—the engine of employment growth in the 1990s—means that more Canadians cannot get the work hours they need to support themselves. At the same time, due to downsizing and declining real incomes, more Canadians are working longer hours.

In North America we are conditioned to believe that jobs are contingent on economic growth, forgetting that to work and earn a decent livelihood is a fundamental human right, enshrined in Articles 23 and 25 of the Universal Declaration of Human Rights. "If" we bring in casinos, "if" we cut a new deal with China, "if" we entice another corporation with a tax break or subsidy, it is said, "then" perhaps we can create or save jobs. Instead, we might learn from some European countries that have created more jobs by reducing and redistributing the existing workload. The Netherlands, for example, has a 3.5 percent unemployment rate and also the lowest annual work hours of any industrialized country, and part-time work is legally protected, with equal hourly wages and prorated benefits. Sweden has generous parental and educational leave provisions that create job openings for new workers. Phased retirement options gradually reduce the work hours of older workers, who can pass on their skills and expertise to younger workers taking their place. One creative experiment gave parents the option of taking the summer months off to be with their children, with guaranteed reentry to the work force in September, thus providing much-needed summer jobs for university students and cost savings to employers.

Reducing and redistributing work hours can also improve the quality of life by creating more free time. Family time currently has no value in our market statistics, and its loss appears nowhere in our existing measures of progress. But we know of a number of good practices that do contribute to well-being. By counting underemployment and overwork as economic costs, and by giving explicit value to equity and free time, the GPI can point to a range of intelligent job creation strategies.

SHIFTING THE LENS

At the Rethinking Development conference in Nova Scotia in June of 2005, leading sustainability practitioners from around the world (leading practitioners of socially and environmentally responsible development) met to chart pathways towards what the government of Bhutan refers to as "gross national happiness." A keynote with a unique perspective that had us listening and clapping (and ultimately dancing!) was Raffi's word-and-song delivery of his Child Honoring philosophy. After his passionate call for a society that honors its young, Raffi sang several songs he's recently written to express his vision musically. Among them was the world premiere of *Count With Me*—his brilliant pitch for replacing the GDP with an index of well-being—backed by a chorus of economists appropriately dubbed "The Indicators" (including Marilyn Waring of New Zealand, Mike Salvaris of Australia, John Helliwell of Vancouver, and Hans Messenger of Statistics Canada in Ottawa). In an emotionally engaging way, Raffi's dynamic presentation offered a lens for connecting all that matters most in our lives.

Quickly, we as a society need to shift our attention to the work that is needed. We need intelligent development, not the blind growth as measured by GDP. There is vital work to be done: raising children, caring for those in need, restoring our ecosystems, securing adequate food and shelter for all, providing a wide range of useful services, pursuing scientific knowledge, deploying sustainable energy systems, and strengthening our communities.

To create a genuinely child-honoring society requires that we escape from the materialist illusion that has trapped us for so long. Clearly, we can no longer measure our well-being according to the GDP and economic growth numbers. More accurate and comprehensive measures of well-being may point to different economic structures—like more self-reliant and self-sufficient forms of *local* economy—which may provide alternatives to the effects of the globalized economy: a chance for communities to reclaim their destinies from the hands of forces beyond their control.

We have reached a moment in history where new measures of societal progress can provide the knowledge necessary to overcome our habitual short-term preoccupations. It is a moment that invites us to consider our legacy, and to lay the foundations of a genuinely humane society that truly honors our children and all the world's inhabitants.

MEASURING WHAT MATTERS MOST BY MARK ANIELSKI

The *Covenant for Honouring Children* states that certain joys and truths about children are self-evident. As parents of two young girls, my wife and I try to nurture and guide our children so that, in Raffi's words, they are able to "sing their own song." We believe that each of us, not only parents, must nurture the next generation and also act as a steward of our planet.

As senior policy advisor to the Alberta Government from 1984 to 1998, I provided guidance on how to measure the performance of governments. I learned that we might be great at measuring the monetary value of things, but we're not good at accounting for the value of intangibles like joy, happiness, or well-being.

Robert F. Kennedy's 1968 critique of the GNP, as a measure of progress, had been my credo in measuring what matters. Kennedy summed it up well by saying that the GNP measures everything "except that which makes life worthwhile." Kennedy's stinging critique of the GNP or GDP (in essence identical) was accurate. I describe the GDP tool as like a calculator that knows only how to add but can't subtract. The GDP adds up all expenditures in a country's economy (by households, governments, and businesses) without considering whether they improve the overall quality of life. Thus, the GDP of a nation actually rises with every environmental disaster, every divorce, every auto crash, and every nuclear weapon produced. Moreover, the value of some of the important things in life, like clean air, safe neighborhoods, and the quality time we spend with our children, counts for nothing if no money has changed hands. Next time you hear economic reports on the latest rise in the GDP or economic growth, ask yourself: What actually contributed to this year's growth? Was it a genuine contribution to our well-being or a regrettable cost?

Are we measuring what really counts or what really matters in defining our happiness or quality of life? What about what matters to our children? What matters most, my daughters tell me, is time spent playing with their parents or hearing nighttime stories. For them, it's love and attention that matters, but this is not what economists count when they measure and report on the GDP for any given year. An economy might be growing rapidly while quality time with our kids, our grandparents, or our life partner is shrinking. How should we measure the value of loving relationships compared with time in building things and consuming stuff? These are questions that a more enlightened society needs to be asking itself, questions that Raffi has been asking for some time.

I came to meet Raffi through his interest in the Atkinson Foundation's work to develop an alternative measure to the GDP, and I was immediately intrigued with Child Honoring as a novel lens for societal change. Moved by his Covenant and Principles, in October of 2003 I invited Raffi to open the Canadian Society for Ecological Economics (CANSEE) conference I convened at Jasper National Park, Alberta. Raffi began by asking us to remember that the child is sustainability's premiere client—to remember the child in all our deliberations—and then, as if to emphasize his message, he sang two of his recent inspirational songs. The room full of economists—including two of the "fathers" of ecological economics, Herman Daly and John Cobb, Jr.—loved it!

During the conference, Raffi joined me in a dialogue with the kids present about what mattered most to them. Their responses were, as you can imagine, spontaneous and wonderful. When asked, "What makes you happy inside?" the kids (who ranged from 3 to 15 years) responded: the sun, kindness, good food, dogs, spending time with my family, dancing, singing, bugs, and chocolate. When we asked them, "What is the strongest thing in the world?" they told us: God, a tree, love, and honesty. When we asked, "What kind of world do you want to live in?" they said, "I wish our world was safe; I wish there were no more wars, and I wish no animals got killed." When we presented the kids' session results to the plenary audience, we all realized that our kids were challenging us to remember (and count) the things that make life worthwhile.

Shortly after the conference, I visited Raffi at his Troubadour Centre on Mayne Island, where we worked on a "Monday morning framework" for a change in how the economic and financial news of the day would be reported. If what is measured counts for policy decisions and gets our attention, Raffi and I reasoned, why not begin to report on what really matters to most peoples' families? Imagine asking our citizens what measures of well-being and progress would matter most to them and then having our economists, policy analysts, and politicians report regularly on *these* indicators of our communal well-being. Imagine people hearing about an up or down change in the communal happiness indicators that mean something to them—whether they live in Edmonton, Houston, or Mayne Island.

For example, instead of reporting on the percentage change in the Gross Domestic Product (GDP), imagine hearing about a change in the Index of Well-Being (IWB), a broader measure of societal and ecological well-being that takes into account the full costs (social and environmental) and benefits associated with producing goods and services in the economy. Such a shift in measuring what makes life worthwhile would change the conversations at the breakfast table, in the coffee shops of our communities, and in our workplaces.

Despite Kennedy's 1968 lament about the GNP, it is only in the last 10 to 15 years that any serious efforts were made to develop new approaches to measuring progress that would serve as a practical alternative to the GNP/ GDP and national income accounting. It was theologian John Cobb, Jr., and ecological economist Herman Daly who, in their 1989 book *For the Common Good,* proposed an Index of Sustainable Economic Welfare (ISEW) as a measure that attempted to identify the regrettable costs of social and environmental depreciation (degradation) that they felt should intuitively be deducted from the U.S. GDP figures. Their pioneering work showed that while the U.S. GDP continued to rise since after World War II, the new ISEW rose along with the GDP only until the mid-1970s, when it began a steady downward slide, suggesting (from then on) an erosion of overall well-being in the United States.

The ISEW eventually emerged as the Genuine Progress Indictor (GPI), developed and refined by Cliff Cobb (the son of John Cobb, Jr.) who, with the economic think-tank Redefining Progress in San Francisco, released the 1995 U.S. GPI estimates. They made the front pages of the October 1995 issue of *Atlantic Monthly* with a provocative article titled, "If the GDP Is Up, Why Is America Down?" The hope was that the GPI might be the best chance of dethroning the GDP as the dominant measure of progress used by virtually every nation. Yet despite many replications of the GPI and ISEW by various scholars in other countries, no government has yet to adopt this well-being accounting method. It's high time they did.

It was the U.S. GPI work combined with Kennedy's challenge that motivated me over the last five years to envision and develop practical measures of economic progress. The 2001 Alberta GPI that I designed examined not only the regrettable social and environmental costs of economic growth of the province from 1960 to 1999, but also the trends in over 50 indicators of economic, social, human, and environmental health. The results showed that while Alberta's hot economy showed steady GDP growth, the overall quality of life of many Albertans and the well-being of their natural environment had declined over the past 40 years.

This work eventually led me to create a new system of well-being measurement which I call Genuine Wealth accounting. To be genuine, of course, means to be authentic or true to one's values, and *wealth* actually originates from the Old English and means "the conditions of well-being." Wealth is thus much more than simply material possessions or property or riches.

The word *economy* comes from the Greek (*oikonomia*), meaning the management or stewardship (*nomia*) of the household (*oikos*). The word ecology is a very close cousin of economics, combining the words *oikos* (household) with *logia* (logic or knowledge). The more I thought about the origins of these words, the more I realized that for most people economics has become disconnected from its true meaning, which is really about the health and stewardship of human households and nature's household.

To me, the Genuine Wealth accounting or measurement system is a synthesis of the best existing tools and systems. It is a way of engaging people in a dialogue about the selection of well-being indicators. When citizen input on values and well-being is combined with genuine indicators that account for the current and past quality-of-life factors, a kind of Genuine Wealth Balance Sheet can show both the strengths (assets) and weaknesses (liabilities) of well-being for a community. I believe such a balance sheet can better serve decision making by both city or town councils, and by organizations (like the United Way) and businesses, in assessing where to invest time and other resources to sustain or improve quality of life.

The Genuine Wealth model has been tested and improved in different settings from Nunavut, in the high eastern Arctic, to Santa Monica, California, and my own neighboring community of Leduc, Alberta. What these communities have in common is that they know that the conventional measures of economic progress, like the GDP, are no longer sufficient and are seeking more meaningful measurements.

China's high-level Communist Planning Commission is currently seeking advice on how to develop a suite of environmental and social indicators that would create a more balanced and harmonious approach to development than their current torrid (and unsustainable) economic growth. Its ambitious goal is to introduce "green GDP accounting" that incorporates environmental depreciation costs. In May of 2005 I presented my Genuine Wealth model as a holistic measurement system for achieving China's goal of a harmonious society.

In Canada, a group of measurement experts are developing the Canadian Index of Well-being (CIW) under the leadership of Ron Colman of GPI Atlantic, and with the support of the Atkinson Foundation. This is an initiative to create the world's first measure of genuine well-being that aligns with the values of its citizens. In the United Kingdom in 2005, the New Economics Foundation (NEF) has developed "a well-being manifesto for a flourishing society." The NEF showed that quality of life in the United Kingdom had not regained its 1976 peak (similar to the U.S. GPI results) and has called upon the U.K. Labour government to consider adopting the well-being manifesto to help U.K. citizens be not richer and more depressed, but happier and more fulfilled.

These are all signs that we are in the midst of a campaign to end the mismeasurement of societal worth, so that we can create societies that have more of what matters most and less of what harms us. I am confident that we are indeed on the verge of a renaissance in the world of economics and politics where what gets measured and reported as progress will actually matter to us and to our children, and will thus serve all that makes life truly worthwhile.

Section II B

Turn This World Around: Policy and Practice

Chapter 15

State of the Child

GLOBAL CITIZENSHIP BY THE HONORABLE LLOYD AXWORTHY

FROM RHETORIC TO ACTION BY GRAÇA MACHEL

GLOBAL CITIZENSHIP BY THE HONORABLE LLOYD AXWORTHY

One of the most basic human instincts is to protect one's child from harm and suffering. Children represent our global future, and the desire to guard them from the many forces that can destroy their hope and innocence is universal. Doing so is an essential part of our broader aspiration to promote human security and to create stable, peaceful societies.
—Lloyd Axworthy, Canada's Foreign Affairs Minister,
Accra, Ghana, April 2000

Ours is a time of global citizenship. In our increasingly interconnected world, the insecurity of others sooner or later becomes a matter of our own insecurity. This new global context has forged common interest and common humanity into a powerful impetus for common action. To this end, we need to adapt international relations to make the security of people—their rights, safety, and lives—a collective priority, especially the rights of children. This means rewiring global machinery to fit the needs of this new century, not the last one.

For Canada, this has meant putting people first. It was the inspiration behind the Anti-Personnel Mines Ban Convention, the impetus for the creation of the International Criminal Court, and the motive for our efforts to address the proliferation of small arms and the needs of war-affected children.

Children, the most innocent of the world's citizens, are often the ones most gravely affected by the decisions and actions of the adults around them. They are orphaned by AIDS or armed conflict. They are abducted from their homes and forced into a life of servitude as child soldiers. They are sold into slavery and prostitution. Millions of children worldwide are continually denied the basic human rights (to shelter, clean water, and food, to live in freedom from fear and suffering) that so many of us take for granted.

The victimization of civilians in war is as old as time, but never more prevalent than in our century. The more recent and disturbing phenomenon of the "civilianization" of conflict has provided the global community with a compelling reason for engagement today. More than ever, noncombatants— especially the most vulnerable—are the principal targets, the instruments, and overwhelmingly the victims of modern armed conflict. The number of casualties from armed conflict has almost doubled since the 1980s to about one million a year; and of those, 80 percent are civilians.

I suggest to you that the narrative of public life today is increasingly centered on the human story, not a soliloquy of the state. During my years at the Canadian foreign ministry I had the chance to come across quite an interesting galaxy of people and attended more than my share of state events featuring world-renowned individuals. But the one person who sticks out in my mind is a 13-year-old Uganda girl named Emma who sat across from me five years ago during a conference in Winnipeg on war-affected children. She told a story of being abducted from her village in Northern Uganda at the age of 9, abused daily as a bride of one of the leaders of the rebel group, The Lord's Resistance Army, asking to become a warrior to escape her violation and being told that she would have to kill a relative to prove her courage, which she did.

As far as we can determine, presently, Emma is free of her captors, and with her 2-year-old child is trying to find a new life in a refugee camp. But this isn't a trouble-free existence. A report on Northern Uganda done for Canada's Development Agency stated that life there is harsh and uncertain: "The escalating violence in Acholiland has resulted in approximately 400,000 people being internally displaced in 25 to 35 camps. The largest of these, Pabbo, contains 45,000 people within a one square kilometer area. Conditions are severe, with food shortages, infectious diseases (HIV/AIDS), rape and other violence and continuing threats of LRA abductions and killings."

This is Emma's world—a world that she had left to travel briefly to Canada to make her case for help from all those ministers, officials, and notables at the conference. Hers is a tragic story, one repeated daily around the globe.

I would like to tell you about another Emma, one whose story is just beginning. She is my granddaughter, born in the summer of 2001, a member of the millennium generation. Still innocent of the ways of the world, still cradled in the cocoon of her parents' love and protection in a small house in the apparent safety and security of the Beaches area of Toronto. Yet within days of her birth the universe shifted its moorings.

Terrorism came to North America with a terrible crash just seven hundred kilometers from Emma's home. As the World Trade Center crumbled, there was a similar shock to the very meaning of security: global politics received a jolt and the world agenda became dominated by the crusade of anti-terrorism. A Manichean struggle pitting the mighty hegemonic power of the United States against the covert, hidden, deadly network of Al Qaeda has created a seismic shift in the world order. Caught in the undertow, Canada has faced renewed pressures both from within and without to become even more in step with our southern neighbor. As Emma grows up, it's conceivable she may never know that at one time we had an independent foreign policy and played a defining role in the world.

The political space that gives Canadians the freedom to choose our own course is being squeezed. How to protect that space against further erosion is very much in the hands of this generation of Canadians. In fact we should be striving within this new security environment to *expand* our political space and extend our capacity and range to make independent decisions for the global good; we should be seeking to enhance our role as a global player "with attitude."

Canada was the first country to decide not to develop nuclear weapons, despite having the capacity to do so. That does set us apart and gives us, in my opinion, a special vocation. As a middle power, with a demonstrated history of being at the forefront of human rights initiatives, we are in a position to advocate for global citizenship, a concept that stretches far beyond our own continent.

This shift of consciousness towards global citizenship must encompass a realization that the threats to human security faced today are not limited to national concerns and cannot be addressed by the government of any one nation, even the world's most powerful one. Issues of climate change, of infectious disease, of nuclear arms proliferation, of an increasingly more sophisticated underworld, are *global* threats that require a broader awareness and international cooperation. If there is one truth that will dominate the lives of the millennium generation, it is that they will be affected by people, events, and actions around the globe. Wherever one resides, a sense of calamity will prevail unless there is a radical change in the way we do business globally.

Over a billion people are currently at the bottom of the rung, entrapped in a web of failed states, either embroiled in warfare or recovering from its ravages, and who simply don't have the capacity to be part of the global economy; trade and investment are not their solutions. They can only be rescued by massive assistance from richer countries to build basic health, education, and public works—public goods their present governments simply can't or won't provide. But it does not have to be a doomsday scenario. If we're aware of the shoals, we can alter our course.

The World Bank forecasts a world population rise to nine billion and a global GDP of the United States of $140 trillion by 2022—staggering numbers, and ones that will lead to widespread environmental disasters and social breakdown unless policies are dramatically changed to manage this growth in a responsible, sustainable way. Unattended, these pressures will lead to a dysfunctional global society with enormous demand on basic resources, not to mention widespread suffering and devastation.

For the children born of this new century, there is a story not yet written, a work in progress, a chance for today's political playwrights to create a new plot and prescribe directions for which the world's children might be thankful, or at least not hold us to blame. In the case of Emma from Uganda she must live with how the past 50 years has impacted her young life. For Emma in Toronto it is the present that will shape her future. Where she will be in 50 years, and the state of the world she will share, is what's at stake. This is hard to grasp as we dance to the daily drumbeat. The rush and volume of events are overwhelming in variety and pace, their meaning and significance often drowned by the flood of information, commentary, and opinion pouring out from our mass media. But we should not be driven by the headlines or the talking heads on CNN. There needs to be a longer view.

A monumental task of our time is to counter a return to a might-makes-right society and to control the supply and use of weapons. The huge international weapons trade fuels global unrest and insecurity. Small-arms proliferation has a devastating impact on the efforts of developing nations to bring the basics of life to their populations. For the sake of the children who are most likely to fall victim to the weapons of war, we must be more vigilant in our efforts to curb the practice of aiding and profiting from violence in all its forms.

This is a message of intergenerational responsibility. The broad notion of human security with its emphasis on the protection for children must be seen through the dimension of time. The past offers lessons on how to govern the present. Equally, the present is the cradle of the future: today's decisions will shape the landscape for a long time to come. Any draft prospectus for the next 50 years must accept the responsibility to protect individuals from threat not just here and now, but for the future. Any hope for a *viable* future for our children must accept their status as most vulnerable to our decisions.

Canada is undergoing sweeping changes in its social and economic makeup. The increasing diversity of our urban cultural mix can be of significant benefit: it adds a dynamic quality to those centers that are the gateways for new arrivals that not only gives greater texture to our cultural mosaic, but also further strengthens the pattern of "group rights" that is so much a Canadian trademark. It also increases our contact with and understanding of so many other places on the globe.

This increased cultural diversity also means that many of the war-affected children that Canada has been involved in trying to protect are now here living among us. In short, the issue of children traumatized by conflict is no longer a concern of foreign relations. In recent conversation with representatives of the Winnipeg downtown school division, it was brought to my attention that as many as four thousand war-affected children are now in the Winnipeg school system alone. These are children who have seen and often lost more than we can imagine, being asked to fit into an elementary school classroom. Are we living up to our responsibility to these children and to others like them around the world? Are we living up to our responsibility to protect? Will we teach them by example the principles of global citizenship so essential to this age and to their future?

We are only as secure as the children we raise. So for Emma's sake, and all those like her, I would say emphatically that the welfare and security of children is a responsibility shared among all global citizens. It is adults who wage war and children who pay the greatest price. It's high time we took responsibility to protect the world's children. Our future depends on it.

FROM RHETORIC TO ACTION BY GRAÇA MACHEL

We stand here at the beginning of the twenty-first century: a time filled with great promise, and yet, great misery for children. This is an era of amazing technological innovation, when we have greatly advanced our global interaction and communication abilities. It is an era during which the world has accumulated huge amounts of knowledge, even if we do not always use it with wisdom.

It is a time of extraordinary scientific advances, where illness and diseases that were once fatal are now preventable. It is also a time of enormous wealth within and among nations. The global economy generates 30 trillion dollars. Truly then, our world and times should be full of hope and promise for our children.

Yet in these amazing times, 600 million children in the world live in absolute poverty, on less than one dollar a day. Ten million children die each year from preventable disease; 60 million girls and 40 million boys do not have access to basic schooling. Indeed, it is estimated that from 50 to 60 million children, instead of being in a classroom, are forced to undertake intolerable forms of labor. Millions of children have died as a result of armed conflict in the last decade alone, while countless millions more have been left physically and emotionally disabled by armed conflicts where children have been deliberate targets.

In sub-Saharan Africa, it is estimated that 13 million children have lost their mothers or both parents to AIDS. Every five minutes, an African youngster between the age of 15 to 25 is infected with HIV. And the epidemic is spreading with frightening rapidity in many parts of Asia, Eastern Europe, and the Caribbean with devastating impacts on families, communities, and nations throughout the world.

These are only a few of the statistics that paint a terrible picture of the lives that millions of children live. But they are statistics that I believe should motivate all of us, statistics that make me impatient for change, and frustrated with the lack of progress we have made in improving the lives of children despite the many promises made by adults and leaders of all kinds.

From Copenhagen to the Social Summit, from the Summit of Children and the Millennium Session, millions of promises have been made to children. We have the knowledge, we have the resources, and we have the capacity. And so, it is totally unacceptable that we allow millions of children to suffer so cruelly.

In the 1990s, despite promises of increased aid and investment in children, at the World Summit on Children and at the Education for All conferences, official development assistance plummeted. The Netherlands, Sweden, Norway, and Denmark are the only four industrialized countries that have consistently met the target of 0.7 percent of national GNP, a target that was set and agreed upon by industrialized countries themselves. However, the list of countries that are nowhere near meeting this target is long and includes Canada and the United States. We must work to eliminate the contradictions and gaps that lie between the commitments that the international community makes and the actions taken to fulfill those commitments.

In Africa, our own national budgets do not prioritize the basic rights of children. Yet, increasing budget allocations for health, education, water, and sanitation would help overcome poverty, improve human development, and help promote peace and security. It is a sad fact that many African countries, particularly those in conflict, spend more on defense budgets than on basic social services.

Why is it that we can mobilize vast resources to fund wars, but we do not mobilize adequate funds to protect children throughout the world? The future of our children lies in many ways in leadership, and the choices that leaders make. Governments must be held accountable for their leadership in putting the well-being of children at the center of all national and international agendas and decision making. But commitment and action cannot be left to government leaders alone.

Each of us, in our professional capacities and in our personal lives, must take action. We must embrace a number of social, economic, and political measures that promote the rights and well-being of children, and break down the linkages between poverty, discrimination, and violence. As individuals, organizations, governments, and societies, we must ensure that resources are available to address inequities within nations and internationally. We must promote and build partnerships between industrialized and developing countries, and between governments and peoples.

Using their strengths as academic institutions, universities can change the nature of the discourse on implementing child rights and child protection internationally. They can promote research that enables government and civil society to better target their development efforts. They can use their experience in training to strengthen the capacity of civil society groups to develop strategies and programs more effectively. They can mold their curricula to promote true leadership in their student body. They can use their research skills to monitor and evaluate the promises that governments and international institutions have made to improve the lives of children, and use such information in advocacy. And they can share their information, knowledge, and capacity with institutions in the south that are struggling to provide similar services.

The challenge for each of us is to move from rhetoric to action. We must realize that behind every statistic is the face and the life of a child: someone's daughter or brother, or grandchild. We all have opportunities to effect change in the lives of children—in Canada, in Mozambique, in South Africa, in Somalia, and throughout the world. When we see and treat all of the world's children the way we see and treat our own children, maybe then we will act with the urgency that they so desperately need.

Chapter 16

Kids and the Corporation

Joel Bakan

Recently I gave a speech to a gathering of chief executive officers (CEOs) from the food and beverage industries. The idea I presented to them—that corporations are inherently self-serving, and that stringent and strongly-enforced regulatory standards are needed to stop their companies from plying junk food to kids—was, I thought, unlikely to generate a very positive response. To my surprise, the CEOs seemed to like the speech, and as I mingled and chatted with them afterwards I got a sense of why: many of them told me that they too, as parents, worried about the ill effects of junk food on their children, that it was a real concern for them. We were thus united enough, at least at that personal level, to prevent them from booing me off the stage.

Still, I had no illusions about how much I might have changed their thinking. These were, after all, the same men and women who, in their roles as CEOs, supervised the development and production of unhealthy foods and drinks for kids, and targeted them with blatantly manipulative advertising campaigns. Apparently, when acting as CEOs, they were able to defer their personal and human concerns about children to the often inhuman demands of their corporations. The ability to do this, to live what was in effect a split moral life, was, I realized, the very thing that made them good CEOs.

What worries me today is that this same socially undesirable trait—unremarkable for and expected of CEOs—is coming to mark society as a whole. We seem to be evolving into a culture that normalizes the routine sacrifice of our most important human concerns to the imperatives of corporations. And this tendency, I argue below, is putting at risk what we hold to be most precious—our children. We need to turn things around, to change our social, political, and legal cultures fundamentally, to ensure that children are protected from those who callously exploit them. The situation is serious, and urgently in need of redress.

We cherish children; we believe they must be nurtured, protected, and constantly cared for and loved. We demand compassion, altruism, sacrifice, and generosity in the ways we as adults relate to them. These beliefs about children are core parts of who we are, and of what makes us human. They are embraced by all of us. Yet they hold no meaning or value for the institution that most dominates our lives today—the large, publicly traded corporation.

Corporations, as I have elaborated in my book and film, *The Corporation,* are required, by law, to make decisions and take actions, including ones that may destroy nature and exploit people, solely on the basis of what is in their (and their shareholders') best interests. From this pathologically self-serving vantage point, children are either *invisible*—their unique vulnerabilities ignored (unless strategic concerns, such as public relations or potential legal liabilities, make it necessary to consider them, or at least to pretend to)—or *exploitable,* as potential consumers or cheap workers.

Despite the corporation's dangerous character, we as a society are granting it ever greater powers and freedoms. By the mid-1990s the wheels of economic globalization had been in motion for about a decade, and it was becoming increasingly clear that transnational corporations were poised to enter an unprecedented phase of power and influence in the world. New technologies, along with policies of deregulation and privatization, liberalized international trade, and relaxation of merger and acquisition laws, combined to expand the size, the power, and the scope of operations of corporations—to the point where they were, and now are, able to dominate the very governments that created them. Along the way, important democratic and public interests have been, and continue to be, sacrificed—including, most notably, the health of children.

Epidemic levels of obesity and diabetes, my main concern when addressing the food industry executives, result, in part, from the ability of corporations to operate largely free of regulatory constraints on the production and marketing of junk foods. Another and equally tragic set of children's health issues is the range of developmental disabilities—such as autism, dyslexia, depression, anxiety, and learning problems—that now afflict children in record numbers. The U.S. National Research Council estimates that 28 percent of these disabilities result directly or indirectly from exposure to neurotoxins, chemicals that are pumped into our air, water, and food by various corporations. Autism has been linked to mercury emissions (of which coal-burning plants are a major source); and learning difficulties and behavioral and emotional problems have been linked to lead exposure, ingestion of artificial additives, and dyes that are common in processed foods.[1] These are just a few examples of children's unique vulnerability to neurotoxins, and how children they bear the brunt of ill effects caused by them.[2]

Yet the main concern of corporations that produce, use, and dispose of toxic chemicals is to ensure that governments do not redress harmful effects by imposing costly restrictions on them. That is why these corporations spend millions of dollars every year lobbying to stop governments from creating new environmental protection laws, and trying to persuade governments to roll back or weaken existing laws. It is also why they pour money into political campaigns to help elect industry-friendly politicians, and wage public relations campaigns to try to convince citizens and politicians that regulations are unnecessary.

These strategies have kept the production and emission of toxic chemicals virtually unregulated in the United States (and either unregulated or underregulated in other industrialized nations) thereby ensuring that children's unique sensitivity to such chemicals remains well below the political radar. The Bush administration in the United States, to take a particularly worrisome example, has been openly hostile to environmental protection laws. Over the last three years, it has launched over 300 rollbacks of such laws—rollbacks that, according to environmental lawyer and activist Robert F. Kennedy, "are weakening the protection of our country's air, water, public lands and wildlife."[3]

Hundreds of synthetic chemicals have been found in human breast milk and in umbilical cord blood, some known to be extremely toxic to humans. New York House Representative Louise Slaughter has stated that "if ever we had proof that our nation's pollution laws aren't working, it's reading the list of industrial chemicals in the bodies of babies who have not yet lived outside the womb." "Today," New Jersey Sen. Frank Lautenberg adds, "chemicals are being used to make baby bottles, food packing and other products that have never been fully evaluated for their health effects on children—and some of these chemicals are turning up in our blood." The Government Accountability Office, the investigative arm of Congress, has acknowledged that the

Environmental Protection Agency lacks sufficient powers to assess the safety of new chemicals and of those already on the market.[4]

Underregulation and the dangers it presents to children are not, however, unique to *chemical* toxins. Other kinds, including what might best be described as *mental toxins,* also threaten children's health. The average child in the United States watches 30,000 television advertisements a year—most of which pitch products directly to them (since a legal ban on direct advertising to kids was lifted in the early 1980s), and all conveying a series of subtle, and corrosive, messages: that they will find happiness through their relationships with products—with things, not people; that to be cool and accepted by peers, they need to buy certain products; that fast food and toy companies, not parents and teachers, know what is best for them; that corporate brands are the true bases of their social worth and identities. Children also receive these messages when they are away from their screens: in school, visiting libraries or museums, at sports and cultural events, all of which have become venues for corporate marketing and advertising as cash-strapped administrators accept financial support from corporations.

Branding and consumerism are not the only toxic influences on children's minds, however. Children are also routinely exposed by mass media to graphic and inappropriate violence and sex as corporations aim to boost sales and ratings. Television is becoming more violent—"Graphic violence against women is fall TV's most disturbing trend" with "plots that reach distressing levels of brutality against women,"[5] according to *Entertainment Weekly,* to cite just one example—and movies made for children regularly feature gory and graphic violence, a ubiquitous presence in computer and video games as well; books featuring pornographic themes are peddled to young teens,[6] and young girls are being sold an increasingly sexualized image by the cosmetic, fashion, and entertainment industries.

More generally, children are spending more and more time in isolated interaction with machines—television, DVDs, video and computer games, and the Internet—rather than with human beings, an unhealthy trend regardless of what they are watching. Research on child development has consistently shown that contact with parents and other caregivers is essential for healthy emotional and cognitive development, yet today "screen time" is often replacing such contact. This is a product not only of the relentless marketing of electronic gadgetry to children, but also the fact that parents are less available to children because they are working longer hours, for less pay and with less security, as employers, again driven by profit, shed permanent staff and rely more on part-time and temporary employees, and overtime. There is a vicious circle here that poses a direct threat to the well-being of children, by alienating them from parents and other adults with whom they may have close bonds.

With all these factors in play—chemical toxins in children's physical environments, violence and sex in their mental environments, rampant consumerism, and overworked parents—is it any wonder that children are suffering from near-epidemic levels of emotional and learning disorders? To make matters worse, the devastating effects of these disorders are, for corporations, just further opportunities to be exploited for profit. "How can we make money out of children's problems?" is the fundamental question corporations ask, not "How can we solve those problems?" While the latter question might point towards strengthening laws and policies designed to reduce mental and physical stressors, the former necessarily points to producing and marketing profitable goods and services.

The dynamic is well illustrated by the pharmaceutical industry's response to children with learning and emotional disorders, the anxious parents of whom are ready-made markets for an array of products that pharmaceutical companies produce.[7] Just a decade and a half ago, psychotropic drugs were seldom prescribed for children's emotional and learning problems. Today, they are often a treatment of first resort, with almost 11 million prescriptions for antidepressants written for children between the ages of 1 and 17 in the United states in 2002 (2.7 million of these for children between 1 and 11), and over 4 million children diagnosed with ADHD being treated with stimulants. Many children who suffer from developmental disorders are being prescribed drugs that may have dangerous side effects, and that fail to address the social and environmental roots of their problems. Not only does this cheat individual children of appropriate responses to their problems, but also, at a broader societal level, it serves to mask, and thus perpetuate, the social and environmental dysfunctions that cause these problems in the first place.[8]

Cellular phone companies, like pharmaceutical companies, are also seeking to cash in on parents' fears—especially their fear that, because of the chaotic pace of contemporary life, they are losing touch with their kids. "Firefly phones keep kids connected to the people who matter most," according to Firefly Mobile's marketing campaign for a cell phone designed for children between the ages of 8 and 12.[9] "Kids feel greater self confidence when they are able to communicate whenever they need to, with important people in their lives," quotes the company from a physician's statement supporting its product.[10] Similarly, the new Barbie brand mobile phone, marketed by Mattel alongside its Barbie My Scene toy line, and aimed at girls between the ages of 8 and 14, is being pitched as a tool for parents to communicate with their children—parents are invited to draw up a list of their children's responsibilities (making their bed, doing homework, not fighting with their siblings, and so on) at a Web site, MySceneMobile.com, and to reward their children by buying them extra call minutes for completing prescribed tasks.[11]

For cell phone providers, as for pharmaceutical companies, children are a growth area in a competitive industry where many markets are already saturated. David Bottoms, vice president of strategic partnerships for Sprint, has stated that preteens—children between the ages of 8 and 12—are "a segment of the market that's under-penetrated."[12] In other words, underexploited. The industry plans to go deep into that market by making products that are popular with children. Cellular phone companies have created partnerships with Disney, Mattel, and Sesame Street, and associated their products with the likes of Elmo, Daffy Duck, Big Bird, and Hillary Duff, as well as Barbie. Parents, who are unlikely to get too excited about Barbie or Big Bird, are lured instead with promises that children will be safer, and easier to monitor, with cell phones in their hands.

The latter claim, questionable on its own terms, rings especially hollow when made by an industry that often ignores, dismisses, and downplays the safety *risks* to children of using cellular phones. Some phones have Internet capacity, which can be used by kids to access inappropriate sexual and violent content, and by advertisers, not to mention cyber harassers, bullies, and predators, to access children.[13] Cellular phones are particularly dangerous in these ways because, unlike home computers and television sets, they are mobile, and thus capable of being used by children without adult supervision.

Cell phones also have potentially harmful physical effects for children. According to some scientists, children are uniquely at risk for ear and brain tumors from cellular phone use because they have thinner skulls and underdeveloped nervous systems. Public health authorities in Canada, the United Kingdom, and Europe, as well as the World Health Organization, have urged a precautionary approach to children's use of cellular phones due to these possible health hazards. Norway's ombudsman for children, Trond Waage, has gone so far as to recommend that parents should not give children their own cell phones until they become teenagers ("We know too little about what radiation from ever more powerful mobile telephones can do to children under the age of 13," he says, "we must not use them as guinea pigs"). None of this has had any impact on the industry's zeal to peddle cellular phones to children.[14]

"Disney is considered safe and trusted," according to David Bottoms, and that, he says, is why the company is so well positioned to tap into the kid cell phone market.[15] The perception of corporations as safe and trusted—not just Disney, but many other major transnational corporations as well—explains a lot more, I believe, than Disney's ability to attract child cell phone users.

This chapter has noted a fundamental contradiction: While we individually and collectively believe in and espouse the principle that children's health and welfare is paramount, we continue through our social and economic policies to grant ever-greater powers and freedoms to corporations—businesses which, because of their institutional makeup, cannot help but ignore or exploit the vulnerabilities of children. The current explosion of emotional and learning disorders among children is, I have suggested, at least in part the result of corporate-made toxins—physical, social, and mental—that combine to create a profoundly unhealthy society for children.

Over the last decade and a half, large publicly traded corporations have been working hard to cultivate an image of themselves as "safe and trusted," capable of genuine concern for social and environmental interests. Under the banner of corporate social responsibility many have succeeded in shifting their public image from greedy and money-hungry to benevolent and socially concerned. They have persuaded governments to roll back laws designed to protect important public interests (including those relating to children) on the grounds that they are now socially responsible and can be trusted to regulate themselves.[16]

We have been duped into underestimating just how dangerous an institution the publicly traded corporation can be, how far such corporations will go to fulfill their self-obsessed missions, and how profoundly uncaring and predatory they can be when it comes to the most vulnerable among us—our children. That is, I believe, a large part of the explanation for why we have put up with their harmful and exploitative behavior.

There is no single solution for making things right. But, there is much that can and should be done. As a first step, we must become more realistic, and more alert, about the pathological character of corporations and their brazen ambitions. This is the point worth stressing: There is nothing in the institutional make-up of large publicly traded corporations that *enables* them to be concerned about the public interest. To the contrary, their unblinking self-interest compels them to lie, suppress and manipulate information, pressure governments, break the law, and ride roughshod over all values and interests that are not their own. From what we've seen of Enron and a host of supposedly respectable companies gone wrong, not to mention the routine exploitation and harm inflicted by corporations on people and the environment, it is clear that corporations are unable to constrain their own bad behavior, and that the marketplace is an insufficient instrument for inducing good behavior. The sooner we recognize this and translate that recognition into political action, the better it will be for our children (and everyone else).

What it takes to protect children from corporate harms and exploitation will always depend on context. Some of the problems facing children and their families that I have addressed in this chapter—such as direct marketing of products such as cell phones to children, the dramatic increase in the use psychiatric drugs, and obesity—are wealthy country concerns. They have little relevance in developing countries where poverty, starvation, and an absence of medical facilities and clean water are the most pressing issues, and where children tend not to be consumers, but consumed—as child laborers, or by disease and hunger. Other problems, such as the ill health effects of toxic chemicals, can take far more pernicious forms in those countries than in ours—a point painfully illustrated by the Bhopal tragedy.[17]

The possible strategies offered here for combating the corporate poisoning of our children's minds and bodies are most applicable to countries such as Canada, the United States, and others in the developed industrialized world. In all of these places, in different ways and to different degrees, the last few decades have seen a shift towards political ideologies and practices that weaken the role of government in protecting public interests from corporate harms and exploitation. Trust the market, we have been told, trust corporations—roll back regulations, open public domains to commercial exploitation. The results of doing so have been, and continue to be, disastrous for children. For, as I have argued above, the market and corporations do not—cannot—care about them.

Governments and public agencies are the only institutions with sufficient authority, legitimacy, and mandate to set and enforce standards, and provide necessary services to protect children. Regulatory laws, and effective enforcement of them, are the only political and democratic mechanisms we, the people, have to control how corporations behave. The principle underlying the regulatory system—that democratic institutions should set public interest standards for corporate actors—is worth fighting for and should guide our efforts to restore the system's integrity and effectiveness. That means, at a minimum, freeing our lawmakers and regulatory agencies from corporate influence; funding and staffing enforcement agencies at effective levels; and relegitimating the principles and practices of regulation at a time when they are under attack.

It also means embracing the precautionary principle, which commands regulatory action where good reasons exist to believe an activity is harmful even if harm has not been definitively proven. In light of evidence that currently exists, strong precautionary arguments could be made to justify regulation of toxic chemicals (especially in products and places where children are likely to come into contact with them), and regulation of cell phone use by children.[18]

Even with the precautionary principle in place, however, and certainly without it, effective regulation of products and production—not to mention political momentum to motivate lawmakers to act—requires reliable scientific information. Today, the priorities, questions, methodologies, and results of scientific research are increasingly dictated by the needs of corporations, as public funding of research is withdrawn and replaced by self-interested corporate support. We have to turn this around, and dedicate public institutional and financial support to scientific research that creates genuine understanding of children's susceptibility to various toxicants and their harmful effects, and of the best means to prevent exposure. In addition to reaching lawmakers with such information, other sectors of civil society must also be informed. Health practitioners should be taught, in their initial degree programs and subsequent professional training, the basics of children's environmental health issues. Teachers should be encouraged and helped to develop curricula that transmit this information to students of appropriate age. Media and advertising campaigns should be mounted by governments and public health authorities to create widespread public awareness around these issues.

These are realistic goals, not utopian dreams. But their realization depends upon commitment to, and struggle for, a deeper set of principles about how our society and polity should be ordered. Today, the word *public,* and the social and political practices it connotes (including solutions, such as those proposed above, that rely on a robust conception of the public sphere), have been discredited. They have become unfashionable, pushed aside by the glorification of everything private and commercial. We need to change that.

We have a choice. We can either continue to weaken our public regulatory system, keep privatizing, and depend more and more on corporations to regulate themselves, or we can revitalize our regulatory system and the public sphere, to make them better able to protect the public interests they are meant to protect. I believe we must emphatically choose the latter.

Our children deserve no less.

Chapter 17

Honoring Children in Dishonorable Times: Reclaiming Childhood from Commercialized Media Culture

Susan Linn

I was lucky enough to be visiting a friend at the moment his seven-month-old daughter made an astounding discovery—her knees. Squealing with glee, she extended her arms to her father, letting him know in no uncertain terms her desire to stand up. As her tiny fists gripped tightly to a finger she pushed up from her toes, and straightened to a standing position. After a few wobbly, upright moments she began to squat, bending her legs slowly. Then, like an inebriated ballet dancer rising from a plié, she teetered up once more. Beaming with pride she repeated the sequence again—and again and again and again.

Eventually she noticed a favorite stuffed kitten on the floor. Holding on with only one hand, wobbling even more ferociously, she began to reach for the kitten only to find that (a) it was too far away to grab and (b) it was at ground level. With great deliberation, she extended her free hand toward the cat. Tottering precariously, completely focused on her mission, she began the glorious process of bending—and was saved from an undignified tumble by her father's protective arm. She allowed herself a brief rest on the floor and, with joyful determination, began the process anew.

Babies are born with an innate drive to love, to learn, to actively engage in the world, and to move over time from total dependence toward independence. An impressive body of research has established that in the first months and years of life, optimal intellectual, social, and emotional development requires direct engagement with the world. Yet, for over two decades, pro-corporate, anti-regulatory government policy has enabled the media and marketing industries to penetrate virtually all aspects of childhood, removing children further and further from the very experiences that are essential for healthy development.

Although in the late 1970s laws were passed that made it illegal to create television programming for children for the clear purpose of selling them products, in 1984 these laws were struck down, leaving children's media largely unregulated. The deregulation of children's television—combined with the proliferation of screen technologies and growing numbers of "latch-key kids," who are home alone with their TVs, game systems, computers, and cell phones—has had a profound impact on children's lives. Today, children between the ages of 2 and 18 years spend about 40 hours a week engaged with electronic screen media, most of which is commercially based.[1]

Even though they already spend more time with media than any activity other than sleeping, children are the targets of an unchecked and relentless push to expand its reach. Not satisfied with targeting children while they are home, media executives now want to reach them during the "interstitial" moments of their lives—when they are between places.[2] Screens in the back seats of minivans and in cell phones, on portable DVD players for preschoolers, in airports, and even on public transportation—to say nothing of restaurants and pediatricians' offices—mean that many children are exposed to screen media, and the products they market, almost all of their waking hours.

Given the current confluence of sophisticated electronic media technology and the glorification of free-market consumerism, it is becoming difficult to provide children with an environment that encourages healthy development. They are assaulted with the noise from commercialized media and the things it sells from the moment they wake up until bedtime. The time, space, and silence available for their own ideas and their own images, for unhurried interactions with people, print, or pictures shrinks with every blockbuster children's film or television program—inevitably accompanied by a flood of "tie-in" food, toys, books, videos, and clothing.[3]

Before I go any further, I should explain that I'm neither a Luddite nor a technophobe. Nor do I see media as inherently harmful. I had the good fortune to be mentored by the late Fred Rogers, appearing occasionally on *Mister Rogers Neighborhood* and working with his production company to develop video teaching materials about topics such as racism and mental illness. I spent a significant portion of my adult life creating children's television and video programs designed to help children talk about difficult issues. However, in recent years, the *business* of children's media and the marketing that drives virtually all of its production has become a serious threat to the health and well-being of children. So over the past decade I have moved from being primarily a performer and a clinician to being an advocate for children who are targeted, mainly through media, with an unprecedented barrage of corporate marketing.

In 2000, I co-founded the Campaign for a Commercial-Free Childhood (CCFC), a national coalition of health care professionals, educators, parents, activists, and advocacy groups working to stem the tide of advertising and marketing aimed at children. CCFC has about 24 organizational members, and over 4,000 people subscribe to our newsletter.[4] In the pages that follow I will describe the extent to which commercialized screen media infiltrates children's lives, why it undermines their healthy development, and what we can do about it.

HOW COMMERCIALIZED MEDIA OVERRUN CHILDHOOD

In 1983, corporations spent $100 million annually in direct advertising to children. Now they spend $15 billion.[5] Today, huge corporate conglomerates own television, radio stations, web businesses, and film studios. One of the outcomes of the consolidation of media ownership is that it has become even easier for marketers to sell products directly to children. Giant media companies partner with giant food and toy companies to produce icons for children, such as *Dora the Explorer* or *SpongeBob SquarePants,* that become colossal money-making franchises. In response to public funding cuts—both actual and threatened—public television increasingly relies on the private sector for funding. Much of the children's programming on PBS is dependent on commercial sponsorship and product tie-ins for funding and is not even remotely commercial-free.

At this point in time, we can no longer even think about children's media without confronting the unprecedented escalation of child-targeted marketing during the past two decades. As I discuss in my book, *Consuming Kids,* the efforts of this gargantuan and ever-expanding industry are linked to a myriad of childhood ills including the erosion of children's creative play, youth violence, precocious and irresponsible sexuality, childhood obesity, eating disorders, rampant materialism, and family stress.[6] Even thoughtful media programming for children is now problematic. However positive its content, it's hard to see how a media program is good for children if it promotes junk food or toys that inhibit rather than promote creative play.

Television is still the primary venue for advertising to children, but marketing on the Internet is escalating. Nickelodeon's web site, nick.com, took in $9.6 million between July 2004 and July 2005—more advertising revenue than any other site.[7] In fact, as digital technology becomes more sophisticated, TV and the Internet are merging to become a whole new interactive media and marketing experience for children. Although children see thousands of commercials each year on television alone, modern marketing methods extend well beyond the traditional 30-second ads.

Product Placement: Inserting products into the content of media programs—called "product placement"—is technically illegal in TV programs created specifically for children.[8] However, it is prominent in programs that they like to watch. *American Idol,* for instance, which is often rated among the top 10 most popular programs for 2- to 11-year-olds, is rife with Coca-Cola product placement.[9] Products are also routinely inserted into the content of web sites, movies, songs, books, video games, and other media for children. At its most extreme, product placement has morphed into "advergaming," in which entire web-based games revolve around a product. For instance, visit www.candystand.com and go bowling with Life Savers, or visit www.kidztown.com and play follow-the-leader with Hershey's Peppermint Patty and animated Hershey Kisses.

Brand Licensing: Probably the most popular method for marketing to young children is brand licensing, when a media image is sold to other companies in order to market toys, food, clothing, and accessories. Most children's media characters have become tools for marketing other products. About 97 percent of American children age 6 and under own something—such as a doll, stuffed animal, action figure, bedding, or clothing—that features the image of a character from the media.[10] It is increasingly difficult to find any products for children—from food to toys—that are unadorned by media characters and logos. Today, even children's books are often media-linked. As a result, children's play, reading, art, and music are primarily shaped by pre-created characters, plots, and themes. What were once tools for self-expression are now designed to remind children constantly of media programs and their products. If young children experience the world only as it is molded by consumer culture—if they have little or no opportunity for alternative experience—how will they develop the values or the sense of self necessary to resist commercial messages?

Sex and Violence Sells Media: Of course, products are not all that a commercialized media sells to children. They also market attitudes and values—including values about sex as a commodity and the glorification of violence.

Myriad studies show that viewing media violence can have an impact on children's behavior as well as their attitudes toward violence.[11] There is mounting evidence that teenagers turn to the media for information about sex[12] and that viewing media sex can affect their attitudes about it as well as their sexual behavior.[13]

Media producers rely on sex and violence because they sell. To keep viewers engaged, marketers and media producers employ the concept of "jolts per minute" as a means to keep us interested in their products. The goal is to keep us in state of arousal, and both violence and sex are effective means of doing that. Studies of media violence show that we can become habituated to it and that it takes increasingly graphic and extreme images to give us the rush of adrenalin we might have initially experienced viewing milder scenes.[14] This phenomenon is of utmost concern when we consider that, particularly in video games, graphic sex and violence are being marketed to younger and younger children. In 2003, *Grand Theft Auto: Vice City*—in which players can have screen sex with a prostitute and then kill her—was the top-selling video game *among preteens*.[15]

The Baby Media Market

While screen media has been a mainstay in children's lives for several decades, it is only in recent years that media has been designed and marketed explicitly for infants and toddlers. In 1998, American public television imported *Teletubbies* from Britain and marketed the series as educational for children as young as 12 months of age. This was a landmark event in that it set the stage for a huge business[16] aiming to convince parents that intellectual development is impossible—even for babies—without the intervention of screen media.[17] As a result, we have witnessed a floodgate of media programs that target babies and toddlers. And now, handheld media devices, such as personalized DVD players for toddlers and even cell phones, are becoming popular. In 2005, Sesame Workshop partnered with Verizon to announce a new plan for parents to download *Sesame Street* content on cell phones to hand to babies for soothing during travel. According to a recent article in the *New York Times,* cell phones are the new rattle.[18]

In 2005, my colleagues and I identified more than 200 videos and DVDs aimed at babies, including newborns. Adorned with titles such as *Baby Einstein, Brainy Baby, Baby Genius, Baby Mozart, Baby Baseball,* and *The Bee Smart Baby Vocabulary Builder,* the programs make dubious claims about their educational value, including alleged benefit for babies' brain development.

At least one video series makes the patently false claim that it teaches babies to read. More than a few of these base their educational claims on a study published in 1993 claiming that listening to Mozart improved college students' performance on a standardized test.[19] In spite of the fact that the study was never replicated, and that—in any case—it was done with college students and not babies, the so-called "Mozart Effect" is still reverberating in the baby and toddler media market.[20] Meanwhile, parents are bombarded with messages that what they might normally do with their babies—cuddle, play, sing, talk, and read to them, exactly what babies do need—is not good enough. Instead, they are urged to prop them in front of the television.

As if this weren't hard enough for parents to contend with, children's computer software industry has also infiltrated the baby market. *Baby Einstein,* which was recently sold to Disney Interactive, now also comes as "lap ware," that is, computer software designed for babies and toddlers who sit on their parents' laps in order to use the computer. In addition to "brain building" software, babies are also targets for software derived from television programs or movies, including such offerings as *Sesame Street Baby* (for ages 1 to 3 years) and Disney's *Winnie the Pooh Baby* (ages 9 to 14 months). Whether it's spent with television, computers, DVDs, or cell phones, time with screens takes young children away from play and the active, multisensory exploration of the three-dimensional world so critical for their healthy development[21] and deprives them of the silence so essential to creativity. The baby media industry continues to flourish despite the findings of a recent review that found that infants and toddlers learn more effectively from real life.[22]

HOW THE PROLIFERATION OF SCREENS UNDERMINES HEALTHY DEVELOPMENT

Psychologists and early childhood educators have garnered impressive evidence that all aspects of children's development—cognitive, emotional, social, educational, moral, and spiritual[23]—need to be nurtured through active engagement with the real world and through sensitive mentoring by parents and other caregivers. Our brains are immature at birth and are shaped by these early experiences of empathy, social engagement, problem-solving, and imaginative play.

The American Academy of Pediatrics (AAP) recommends that children under 2 have no screen experience and that screen time for older children be limited to one to two hours per day. This information is essential knowledge for parents, educators, and health care providers. A growing body of evidence demonstrates that, especially for young children, hours spent watching television can be harmful to healthy growth and development. A preschooler's risk for obesity increases by 6 percent for every hour of TV watched per day. If there's a TV in the child's bedroom, the odds jump an additional 31 percent for every hour watched.[24] Obesity rates are highest among children who watch more than four or more hours of television a day and lowest among children who watch an hour or less a day.[25] For children age 3 and under, research suggests that the more TV they watch, the more likely they are to have attention problems—when they become grade school students,[26] score lower on IQ and academic tests,[27] and engage in bullying behavior.[28]

Unfortunately, only 6 percent of American parents even know about the AAP recommendation and 7 percent of these falsely assume that the AAP recommends that young children under age 2 limit their daily viewing to 1 to 2 hours of educational television.[29] And so, on average, children from birth through 6 years of age spend 4.5 hours each day in front of computers, video games, and television.[30] About 26 percent of American children under the age of 2 have a television in their bedrooms,[31] as do 32 percent of children ages 2 to 7[32] and 68 percent of children ages 8–18.[33]

The expanding role of screen time in children's lives constitutes a developmental hazard. The commercialization of media has led not only to all kinds of products being marketed to children, but to increasingly graphic violent and sexual content with which to capture its audience share. Media programs are intensely marketed to children which, coupled with media's inherently seductive nature, means that they are lured into spending more and more time engaged with it. Meanwhile, the very process of engaging with screens for hours each day undermines healthy brain development. Screen time robs children of the very activities that *do* build the brain, such as physical activity, time for quiet and imaginative reflection, conversation, and hands-on exploration. Arguably, in early childhood, the most important of these activities is creative play.

In addition to serving as the foundation of intellectual exploration, creative play stimulates two wondrous and uniquely human characteristics: imagination and the capacity to imbue our experiences with meaning. Through play, we are able to gain a sense of mastery over new information and events, design the future, grapple with the past, and sort out powerful feelings. But, as media consumes more and more of children's leisure time, pretend play is disappearing from the landscape of childhood. In 2002, on average, children ages 6 to 8 spent only 16 minutes engaged in pretend play. For children ages 9 to 12, pretend play occupied only 1 minute of their time each day.[34]

I feel an increasing sense of urgency about preserving creative play in children's lives—much the same way that environmentalists feel about saving the redwoods or the rain forests. Next to love and friendship, imagination and meaningful experience constitute what I value most about being human, yet they are devalued to the point of endangerment by a modern life characterized by commercial culture and rapid-fire bombardment of electronic sounds and images.

WORKING FOR CHANGE

I've come to believe that honoring children has to involve a commitment to do what we can to change the commercial culture that is permeating childhood. In twenty-first-century America, being a parent, or working for the well-being of children, are countercultural activities.[35] Given the amount of time children spend in front of screens and the power that media and marketing have to shape children's attitudes and behaviors, providing opportunities for children to engage in active, creative, unbranded activities has become a political act—because in doing so we allow them to acquire the cognitive, social, and emotional tools to rebel against a commercialized media culture that promotes passivity, conformity, and unthinking brand loyalty not just to products, but to politicians as well.

When I urge people to take action, I often hear two objections: But the media industry is too powerful! Commercialism is too ingrained in our culture! Both of these statements are true, yet it's important to remember that social change usually begins when groups of people—even small groups—gather together to take a stand against prevailing social norms. In eighteenth-century England, for instance, 12 Quakers made a commitment to end slavery that was ultimately successful in Britain and the United States even though slavery was viewed as the bedrock upon which the economies of both nations were resting.[36] There are steps that we can take within our families, our places of work, our communities, and the larger society to limit young children's exposure to exploitive media and commercial culture.

AT HOME AND AT SCHOOL

Before we can help our children, we need to understand our own vulnerabilities to media and marketing. We can serve as positive role models by curbing our own tendencies to seek gratification from purchasing more and more stuff and by curtailing our own media consumption. If we are constantly on the computer or zoning out in front of the television, how can we expect kids to curtail their media use?

We can limit the number of hours children are allowed to watch TV or use their computers in accordance with the AAP guidelines. We can significantly decrease the number of televisions and computers we have in our homes and keep our children's bedrooms free from electronic media.

As we limit exposure to commercial culture, we also need to encourage media- and commercial-free activities that promote prosocial values. The omnipresence of electronic media generates nonstop noise. Choosing to ensure children's access to silence away from electronic bells and whistles affords them a chance to listen to their own thoughts, to act on their own ideas, and to play creatively, and helps them experience life's pleasures that can't be quantified, bought, or sold. So does fostering the development of children's spiritual life, which can encompass a range of experiences, from organized religion to reveling in the wonders of nature. Depending on our inclinations and opportunities, we can spend time with our children in nature, doing art projects, in community service, working for social causes, or in places of worship. We can read, play, cook, and make music together.

Altruism is a good antidote to the me-first, acquisitive values promoted by commercialism, and so is the endangered value of the common, or public, good. We can establish family traditions that involve giving and/or participating in community or civic activism. These can be as simple as an annual shopping trip for a holiday meal to donate to a food bank, engaging children in decisions about the family's charitable giving, or participating in community gardening and neighborhood cleanups.

Electronic media and commercialism are also more prevalent in schools. Day care providers and preschool teachers frequently rely on movies and television to keep children engaged. In recent years, media companies have been aggressively targeting preschools with "educational" curricula based on media characters. For example, Scholastic, Inc. is selling preschool teachers a *Clifford's Kit for Personal and Social Development.* According to Scholastic's website, Clifford the Big Red Dog inspires "Children to become Great Big People."[37] Scholastic recently began partnering with Cartoon Network to market a new block of commercial programming in preschools. In addition to letting principals and school boards know that we want children's time in school to be free of commercialized media, we can let the media and marketing industries know that we want them to stop targeting children in school.[38]

But merely providing alternative experiences for children, limiting media use, and setting a good example aren't enough to prevent children from absorbing predominant societal norms like consumerism. Taking into account where our children are in their social, emotional, and cognitive development, we also need to make a conscious effort to talk with them about commercial values. Very young children can't distinguish between commercials and programming, and until the age of about 8, children can't understand persuasive intent—the fundamental basis of advertising. Not only that, they tend to believe what they see, have a harder time delaying gratification, and are held sway to their emotions more than older children. Although their capacity to reason is more mature than that of their younger brothers and sisters, preteens and teens are vulnerable to peer pressure, riotous hormones, and the often urgent need to establish an identity separate from their parents—all of which can impede their judgment and make them susceptible to manipulation by marketers.

While we certainly can't have the kind of in-depth, intellectual discussion with preschoolers that we can have with teenagers, young children are often quite sensitive to the nuances of feelings expressed by important adults in their lives. By talking with them about the media images and commercial messages they encounter, we can at least provide them with the important tradition of engaging in dialogue about the world around them.

PROMOTING THE COMMON GOOD

Media and marketing executives often point to parents as the sole gatekeepers for this commercial assault on children. It is true that individuals can model positive values and limit their children's exposure to electronic media. But it is unfair for parents to be forced to spend so much time, resource, and energy protecting children from a pervasive, well-funded, commercialized culture that undermines our best intentions as well as our children's health and well-being. Nor can parents control societal influences. Marketing to children and the pervasive role that media play in their lives are problems rooted in society. We need to work together for societal change.

There's no getting around the fact that government policies, or lack of them, have contributed to the fact that we are raising children in the middle of a marketing maelstrom aimed directly at them. Around the world, policies created and policies defeated by conservatives, progressives, and centrists have enabled marketers to target children, as have policies endorsed and condemned by the extreme right and left. These issues cut across the traditional political divide.

Marketing to children and the pervasive presence of electronic media assaults the sanctity of the family, undermines family and religious values, and targets children with ads for provocative clothing and sexually explicit media—issues traditionally associated with conservatives. Commercialized media culture also undermines democratic values by encouraging passivity and conformity, threatens the quality of public education, and inhibits free expression—issues traditionally associated with progressives. It also contributes to public health problems such childhood obesity, tobacco addiction, and underage drinking—issues of concern to all sides of the political spectrum.

Given what we know about its damaging effects, we should stop using media as a tool for marketing to children. In fact, we should stop marketing to them at all. Short of that, there are policies that governments can—and have—put in place to significantly limit commercial access to children and, as a result, reduce the amount of time they spend in front of screens.

Prohibiting marketing to children may seem extreme. It isn't— *but marketing to children is.* The United States regulates marketing to children less than most other industrial democracies. There are a number of restrictions in other countries which could bring welcome relief to American families. Sweden and Norway ban television marketing to children under the age of 12.[39] The Province of Quebec, in Canada, bans marketing to children under 13.[40] Greece prohibits ads for toys on television between 7:00 A.M. and 10:00 P.M.; ads for toy guns and tanks are not allowed at any time.[41] In the Flemish-speaking areas of Belgium, no advertising is allowed within five minutes of a children's television program shown on a local station.[42] Advertising regulations proposed by the European Union would ban commercials suggesting that children's acceptance by peers is dependent on their use of a product.[43] Finland bans advertisements that are delivered by children or by familiar cartoon characters.[44] The French government recently banned all vending machines in middle and secondary schools.[45] And, in 2004, the British Broadcasting Corporation severed marketing ties between their children's programs and junk food companies.[46]

Children have a basic right to live in environments that promote their social, emotional, and intellectual well-being. They have the right to grow up, and parents have the right to raise them, without being undermined by greed. People from all political and religious persuasions have a vested interest in keeping commercial culture—and the media dependence it fosters—in check. While parents have a role to play, they need help from health care professionals, educators, businesses, concerned citizens, and legislators. Let's honor children by honoring childhood, and by standing up to those who subvert it for the bottom line.

Chapter 18

A World Fit for Children

Varda Burstyn

For people who care about the environmental health and safety of children, three different campaigns in 2005 modeled intelligent, effective strategies for using public institutions—in this case, schools—to bring about change. In September, newspaper headlines announced that England had banned junk food in its schools.[1] In the United States, the State of New York, following in the State of Washington's footsteps, banned the use of toxic cleaning products in schools.[2] And, in a number of other states including California and Minnesota, yet another crucial initiative—the "Safe Schools Project"—has been gaining ground.[3] School board by school board, and state by state, the school-yard use of toxic pesticides especially harmful to children has been banned.[4]

These three campaigns show that we *can* use our political institutions and public agencies to say no to harmful products and technologies—and that schools can be very valuable in this process. Even more promising, these examples also contain within them some of the potential seeds of a future child-honoring economy, because they create big markets for producers of environmentally benign technologies to provide Earth- and child-friendly products.

A world fit for children is what all our children deserve: a world where they may grow and live toxic-free, free of the harmful human-made threats to their well-being. Safeguarding children begins with an identification of harms posed by toxic substances early in life, and in utero, where many toxic compounds impact.[5] When Theo Colborn and her colleagues Dianne Dumanoski and John Peterson Myers published the groundbreaking book *Our Stolen Future: Are We Threatening Our Fertility, Intelligence, and Survival? A Scientific Detective Story* in 1996, documenting the special vulnerability of children to chemicals found in everyday pesticides, plastics, solvents, and cleaning materials, most of us got our first look at the profound damage that our chemically dependent economy has been doing to the delicate but all-important inner space of developing cells, tissues, and organ systems in our smallest people. Since then, people like Colborn, as well as Philip Landrigan (represented in this volume) and many others have been working hard to get governments to recognize children's special vulnerability to environmental harms, and to legislate and enforce on the basis of this knowledge.

Creating a world fit for children means acknowledging that we are a species in crisis and we must act quickly. The degree to which our air, soil, and water pollution has reached into the very flesh and blood of our children is itself cause for grave concern. Every day brings new reports of ecological decline so great as to indicate that we have already reached the tipping point on a number of fronts. Estimates from scientists tell us we have 5 to 25 years to deal with the big problems. Global warming, melting glaciers, droughts, destructive hurricanes, hurricanes where there have never been any before—extreme climate change is now believed to be accelerating much more rapidly than was thought even two years ago.[6] Authoritative studies show that we are tapping most of our natural resource systems beyond sustainability or renewal.[7] The longer it takes us to reverse the ratio of positive change to encroaching harm, the harder—and costlier—it will be in the long run.

Addressing the imperiled state of our biosphere and the dangers this poses to children requires systemic change on a massive scale. Tinkering with how we provide health care or how we package and manufacture goods, or driving hybrid cars—while necessary—won't be enough. We do have the *technical* means—the technologies and processes that can reduce our pollution and reverse our use of natural capital to sustainable levels. We will, however, require broad *social* changes to (re)organize the ways we live: how we work (and what work we do), how we grow and prepare food, how we use energy, how we educate and care for ourselves, how we make and use everyday products.

The real key to achieving the rapid and systemic change required is for a large majority of us to become "eco-citizens."[8] It is my conviction that only a massive "greening" of how we all understand and practice citizenship, parenting, economics, and politics can actually produce the government leadership and public participation we'll need for these transformations. Only such widespread awareness can create the weight and momentum required to undertake the major programs that can green the harmful technologies that now threaten both our children and our biosphere. Here, I would like to offer two types of suggestions for sociopolitical action geared to safeguarding our children in their natural and constructed worlds. The first are suggestions for crucial health strategies that are generally applicable in almost all countries and cultures. The second are elements of a global, systemic plan—universally applicable at all levels and in all countries—for making the massive transitions in production that Nature requires of us.

IDENTIFYING THE HARMS, SUPPORTING THE HARMED

Both the acceleration of biospheric decline and the related dangers to our children demand that we take aggressive initiatives, from local to global levels, to identify and support those injured by toxic exposures and to accelerate the cleanup of identified toxic sources. Here are a number of proposals—a platform of health action, if you will—that we need to undertake:

1. Ensure that governments adequately fund research in the public interest that identifies the substances harming children, their extent, and their effects. Numerous scientists and medical clinicians are working to identify and to heal where possible the harms to children from environmental exposures. Names such as Philip Landrigan, Herbert Needleman, Theo Colborn, Shanna Swan, and David Schindler, to mention just a few North Americans, are becoming more and more familiar to people outside specialized circles. But the pace at which their work can get funding and move ahead still lags far behind the need for their wisdom.

2. Promote environmental health care education. The curricula of medical doctors, nurses, and allied health professions need to include new programs to help practitioners identify and treat environmentally induced health problems. In particular, learning how to identify the effects of endocrine-disrupting and neurologically harmful chemicals, heavy metals, food additives and agricultural hormones, and air pollution—ubiquitous problems—need to become their regular curricula. Far too many children with such problems are being ignored or wrongly diagnosed and treated. Professional and government certification of health education facilities and programs should require such education.

3. Public health agencies and programs must become community guardians of environmental health. Since environmental health issues are so profoundly population health issues and public health agencies are the only organizations structurally placed to address these as such, we need much stronger and more powerful public health agencies, with funding commensurate with their duties, than we have today. Their mandates must be changed to include the active monitoring and identification of the symptoms and consequences of environmental harms among their populations. They also need the legal clout and funding to be able to halt the production of toxic materials or the circulation of toxic goods in their jurisdictions, just as they are empowered to address epidemics of infectious diseases.

4. Hospitals, community clinics, and individual health practitioners need to provide environmental health services. Environmental health services must be incorporated rapidly into pediatric services, given what we now know about the special vulnerability of children. Such services presuppose education, understanding, diagnostic capacities, and knowledge of treatment, as well as coordination with other health and social services. And they must be provided to whoever needs them, regardless of ability to pay.

5. Put the school system to work in serving children's environmental health. School boards, school administrators, and teachers all need to be educated about the issues involved in environmental harm and safety for children. With such information, they can become pivotal organizations for children's environmental health at the local level. They can reach parents more directly than any public institution; they have buildings in which to house health and educational activities; they can influence politicians and health authorities to address pediatric issues. Indeed, schools are the natural public agencies to take the lead in child-honoring. Schools that provide safe and nurturing environments for children can have a significant impact on commerce. By switching to organic foods, for example, schools would provide an enormous market, a huge economic incentive to the agricultural sector to go green.[9]

6. Build new health programs that provide many different kinds of support to families with children. Most parents are not aware of the harms their children are exposed to, and don't recognize the signs of environmentally induced illnesses when they see them. This leads often to long, expensive, frustrating, and demoralizing searches for diagnosis or no treatment at all. What's more, where children are diagnosed correctly and their treatment requires remedial schooling, long-term administration of nontoxic foods, pristine and chemical-free environments, special pharmaceuticals and treatments, and nutritional supplements, many families are drained well beyond their capacities to provide these supports.

7. Integrate law enforcement into the project of environmental health. Depending on the location and size of a given police force, special officers working with public health officials and government officials should regularly take on the monitoring of their jurisdictional environments for environmental crimes, support public health initiatives to stop toxic wastes or products as necessary, and assist with the full force of the law in taking whatever actions are necessary to safeguard children's environmental health.

GREENING THE WORLD

Twin Crises: Ecological Decline and Human Livelihood

The global environmental crisis and the crisis of human livelihood are two aspects of survival that must be considered together. This is one excellent reason we need another word for *economy,* a word that in common usage separates money and work from their effect on workers, communities, and nature. Perhaps Raffi Cavoukian's term *bionomy* better captures the connections.

Environmentally created illnesses are rooted in a corporate economy that still largely relies on "dirty" technologies. This corporate economy has gained in independence and nonaccountability in the last two decades, as public power—what I call prosocial government—has declined, and neoliberal policies (free trade, globalization) have grown. To understand the degree to which democratic sovereignty has given over to corporate rule, consider that nation-states are unable to stop many polluting industries or practices, or are unable to enact environmental protections, because trade law declares these to be barriers to trade.[10] Yet the life-threatening consequences of toxic technologies require a much stronger public realm than we have ever had—an unprecedented level of environmental sovereignty. Democracy is only meaningful if we can control the deployment of technologies, and the economic actors who produce them.

There is a social justice face to resource inequity and toxic pollution. The poor (poor communities in wealthy nations, and poorer nations as a whole) always suffer disproportionately: they are nearer to toxic production and dumping sites, and they have the fewest resources for treatment and remediation. Poor children in every nation carry an appalling burden of environmental harms. At the same time, people of all classes, colors, and nations are suffering at least some of the dangerous consequences of our decades-long global chemical spree.

Epidemics of learning and behavior disorders, obesity, and asthma among the middle classes in North America, for example, attest to this reality.

In recent years, we have seen a growing equity deficit. While the wealth of the super-rich—the top 5 percent of the world's population—increases every year, more and more people live in precarious economic circumstances.[11] Certainly there has been a shrinking of the middle classes globally. But there has also been a dramatic increase in numbers of the poor, the destitute, and the environmentally endangered.

This development itself, as the United Nations (among other organizations) has noted, is a major obstacle to sustainability.[12] A destitute farmer in Malaysia may have no other means to support his family than to slash and burn some hectares of forest—contributing, with many like himself, both to forest destruction and to vast clouds of toxic air pollution. A working-poor single mother in the United States may want to buy organic food for her kids and pay the premium on benign cleaning products, but she simply can't stretch her subsistence budget to do it. Communities in British Columbia or Quebec may want to throw the forest companies out rather than log threatened ancient forests and protect biodiversity, but if logging jobs are the only ones available, they may feel they have no choice. Many farmers worldwide want to shift to organic food production and to end the health risk to themselves and their families from toxic agricultural chemicals, but find they can't afford to. The Jamaican Organic Agriculture Movement, for example, lags far behind its goal of turning 10 percent of the island's production organic by 2010. Today, perhaps 1 percent of Jamaican farmers use organic methods, despite the fact that they get many requests for specialized organic products such as mango puree or ginger.[13]

It is impossible to overstate how much the world needs organic agriculture. Arguments against it based upon productivity are no longer valid. Recent reports of long-term studies at Cornell University show that organic farming not only produces healthier food and healthier farmers, but over a five-year period, surpasses the yields of chemically based farming, produces one-third less greenhouse gases, and turns organic fields into carbon sinks—actually absorbing greenhouse gases and reducing global warming threats.[14] But most farmers have no incentive and no support to make the change because it takes at least three years of fallow fields to achieve organic capacity. Just as few agribusiness corporations would want to lose three years of income, few farmers can afford to earn little or nothing for three years while their fields detoxify. They need more effective support to go organic.

A GLOBAL GREEN DEAL

Assessment—Problems and Solutions

During the years of the Great Depression, years of great suffering and crisis for the United States, President Franklin Delano Roosevelt initiated what he called the New Deal: a set of economic policies that collected and redistributed his country's wealth to simultaneously rebuild the country's infrastructure, economy, and even its culture, at the same time as giving Americans a living wage, meaningful work, and a way out of penury and starvation. The New Deal rescued the United States. It helped lay the basis of the prosocial state in that country—though American federal administrations since Ronald Reagan have greatly eroded that state, and the Bush administration seems philosophically and practically committed to finishing it off.

To bring about technological and economic changes of adequate pace and scale, *the world needs a model of political change unprecedented in scope.* We need much more than a few new regulations here, an incentive or two there. We need an overarching and comprehensive framework—a systemic and flexible strategy with myriad creative tactics—for thoroughly detoxing and greening our world from the most local to the most global level. We need a *Green Deal:* a set of coordinated policies, agencies, programs, and powers that can shift human society from environmental toxicity and economic poverty to environmental sustainability and economic viability. In my view, and in the view of many experienced and insightful people, only an initiative as comprehensive and powerful as this truly has a chance of succeeding in our race against time.[15] A Green Deal would use the collective wealth and will of humanity to create a fundamental shift in how we organize our lives; and that includes reclaiming government to represent the human majority—reviving prosocial states, not oligarchies.

The Green Deal would have three major components that can be adapted to work at virtually all levels of government, from the municipal to the international. None of these components need await action until each or all of them are in motion or complete—each can be started in local and partial ways, and be built upon so that eventually the actions and initiatives meet across levels and jurisdictions to create a vast web of connected change. For this crucial function, we need extensive public agencies with a triple mandate:

1. Identifying what's bad today: to determine accurately what harms are being done by what substances, processes, and technologies in given sectors and jurisdictions, using the vulnerability and susceptibility of children as an important benchmark in all evaluations. Some of this information is already known and simply requires codification and collection in accessible ways. But the effects of many chemicals and production technologies—especially synergistic effects—are still unknown and require urgent research. As well, these agencies should be charged with thoroughly assessing the environmental and social impacts of economic development proposals.

2. Identifying what's better in the short term: to determine what substances, processes, technologies, and organization of economic activities represent better or benign alternatives and strategic improvements. Remarkable new ways of doing almost every human activity have already been developed, and every day new and better ways of producing plastics, fibers, papers, energy, food, clean water—you name it—are being devised. In agriculture, water conservation, urban transportation, and other fields, older and better ways have been revived or rediscovered.[16] From the agricultural Navdanya movement initially begun by Vandana Shiva to public bicycle programs in Lille, France, the revitalization of existing benign technologies will be as much a part of the greening of society as the mass production of brand-new technologies.[17]

3. Identifying what is best in the long term: Here we need far-seeing, multi-faceted, and coordinated programs that look at medium and long-term directions and strategies for change. Minimizing air travel and transport, regional sufficiency in food production, long-term energy and water conservation, wholesale phasing out of toxic chemicals and oil-based plastics—these ideas involve multiple issues, multiple jurisdictions, multiple answers. They need to be organized democratically because technocratic control more often leads to errors in judgment, not to wise decisions in the public interest. (These discussions cannot be limited to scientists and technicians but must include citizens in all their capacities.) The concepts of bioregionalism and eco-urbanism suggest the co-development of economic activities and polities in ways that safeguard very specific ecological systems as well as the people within them.[18]

Funding the Transition

No green plan can be effective unless it addresses the question of transitional funding and sources for it. Governments, in their capacity of gathering and redistributing society's wealth, will be a primary source for transition funding and for creating the economic conditions necessary to widespread change. Beginning immediately, all government budgets—all levels, all departments—should be required to create green transition lines as part of their normative budgeting processes, and pools of transitional funding should be established whenever surpluses are declared. Military budgets are another obvious source for the rerouting of capital to productive ends.[19] A version of the proposed Tobin Tax[20] could also yield substantial funding for greening the global economy—or "bionomy." Without question, funding must also come from tax shifts and reverse subsidy disincentives on harmful technologies and industries, for these have a direct effect on the targeted technologies and are immediately understandable by citizens, who are also taxpayers.

Disincentives are the Big Sticks. Especially at the beginning of the Green Deal process, these are crucially important. All direct and indirect subsidies to polluting industries and technologies must be redirected to subsidize green alternatives, including helping people in sunset industries weather the ensuing transition. Disincentives will inevitably change the price of many commodities and induce consumers to turn elsewhere.

The most harmonious lasting way to effect economic change is to make it worthwhile, rewarding, and positive. Hence for producers and employers, we are speaking of a variety of forms of subsidy—the "Big Carrots"—for desired processes and products, a reversal of the disincentives. These incentives can be developed in appropriate, sensible, and sufficient ways so as to *enable* capitalizing the production and distribution of given technologies and processes. In some cases, simply banning a product, such as toxic cleaning materials by a school board, can create a large market for benign alternatives.

Sometimes, the cost of changing from a dirty to a clean production technology will require a great deal of help. For example, switching to clean hydrogen power for cars demands not just the production of such cars, but also their fuel, service stations to dispense that fuel and repair the cars, and ensuring that consumers have the incentives to buy the new technology. Moving rapidly to change the fleets of public sector agencies (post offices, utilities, municipal transport, for example) to clean hydrogen technologies, and establishing fuel distribution stations for them would immediately help the whole of society move in that direction. Serving only organic food not just in schools but in the eating facilities of all public agencies, including in restaurants licensed on limited-access highways, would push agriculture toward sustainability by leaps and bounds.

Where the transition to green is time-consuming and costly, transitional funding—to help employers and employees weather the change to new production processes, or to retrain, or to convert to benign alternatives—is the only way to ensure that we move quickly enough but avoid creating unintended socioeconomic hardships. Going green, however, will lead to extraordinary economic opportunity and should be welcomed, not feared. Retrofitting the majority of residences with solar panels, to take just one example, creates manufacturing jobs, installation jobs, and planning and public policy jobs. Going green will be good for everyone.

Enforcement

Making legislation and jurisprudence work for Nature, not against it, will be crucial for a green transition, and for making the Global Green Deal work, especially in the early years, when change is always more challenging. In many places, political bodies will need to reorient the judiciary—both personnel and jurisprudence—in order to mobilize the justice system towards environmental protection. For example, in many countries new norms that disallow the endless postponement of trials for polluting industries will be needed; governments will have to enact a variety of new laws and assert political control over wayward courts; and stiff penalties—not a license to pollute—will be needed.[21] Clearly, sending CEOs to jail for a long time (as would have been appropriate in the case of Bhopal or the Exxon *Valdez*) or setting fines that break the profitability of an intransigent company's business are two ways to make this strategy meaningful. Creating environmental crime units in police forces, from the international to the local level, will be important to ensure detection and enforcement.

To restore the sovereignty of communities and nations, we will need to instruct our governments to redraft international agreements that restrict a country's protection of its environment and citizenry. Such agreements should be replaced with override clauses stating that any trade activity likely to result in the wider distribution or use of toxic substances must be halted regardless of any previous agreements between governments or private corporations. It's a pity that we need these additional big sticks, but we do. To create them, as well as to bring about the other components of the Green Deal, we will have to enact and enforce the strictest of conflict-of-interest guidelines with respect to government and judicial personnel.

The means to keep children—all the world's children—from toxic harm while giving them an excellent quality of life already exist and, with government support, can go from good to great. From wind turbines and solar panels, to herbal anti-infectives and probiotics, to scientifically enhanced methods of organic farming, to filtration systems that use plants to produce pure drinking water without depositing one ounce of sewage in our waterways, to methods of manufacturing that take no resources from the biosphere, to plastics made of corn and soya from sustainable agriculture, to paper and everything else made without chlorine, we *can* help our biosphere to survive and protect our children and their children after them—*if* we prioritize their health, and control the deployment of technologies and the major actors who drive them.

The coalitions that made schools ban junk food, toxic cleaning products, and pesticides got political, and successfully so. To fully protect the children, concerned citizens have to extend the scope and degree of political action even further. We've got to stop separating environmental issues from economic or health issues in the belief that somehow we'll be able to "deal with those later." Everywhere, we must make a peaceful revolution that recreates government in the public and biospheric interest. We can replace the strictures of the international corporate order with a new politics: a Global Green Deal that respects children and protects environmental health. It's the most worthy and rewarding challenge of all.

Chapter 19

Tomorrow's Child

RAY ANDERSON

These thoughts are addressed to all adults, everywhere, on behalf of every child to come, not just *homo sapiens'* children, but children of all species, for all time. I shall offer my personal interpretation of four long-term trends, which, as they unfold into the future, will most likely determine the fate of humankind on the Earth. Human children obviously have a huge stake in the outcome. You should first know that I am an industrialist: some would say a radical industrialist, yet I am as competitive and as profit-minded as anyone. So, before I offer my thoughts on the future of humankind, let me tell you how I even came to have a point of view on such a lofty subject.

For a moment, step into my shoes: You are 60 years old. Interface, Inc., the industrial company you founded from scratch when you were 38, is now over 21 years old. It makes commercial carpet, carpet tiles, and textiles. You remember vividly that day in your start-up year, in the teeth of a recession, when your factory had been built and equipped, your initial work force hired and trained, raw materials bought and paid for, products developed, and there was not a single order on the books. You learned that day, indelibly, the value of the customer—the source of the next order, the next heartbeat, without which everything would be lost.

But now, in your 61st year, the business has succeeded beyond anybody's wildest dreams. Interface, at age 21, is a public company doing business in 100 countries, manufacturing on four continents. It has come through three major recessions, and is on its third leg up. Sales are approaching a billion dollars a year, successful by anybody's standard definition of success. Furthermore, you've put a succession plan into effect; the next generation of management is in place and battle-tested. Now where do your thoughts turn? To retirement in the mountains, to the seashore? To chasing a little white golf ball? (Birthing a new business had been a frightening experience; my life savings had been at risk; I had left the security of a perfectly good job to "bet the farm" on an idea. Looking back, a sense of legacy was now working away in my subconscious, if not my conscious mind, in the summer of my 61st year.)

Imagine, then, how you might have reacted if you had begun to hear through your sales force a strange, new question from your customers: "What is Interface doing for the environment?" If you had begun to hear about requests for bid quotations that asked your company to state its environmental policies when it competed for business? If a report had come to you through one of your top sales managers that an environmental consultant to a major customer had said, "Interface just doesn't get it!" Do you know what *I* said? "Interface doesn't get *what?*"—rather confirming the consultant's comment.

What *were* our environmental policies? Two of my managers approached me and insisted that our sales force was begging for answers. They suggested convening a new task force of people from our businesses around the world to assess our company's environmental practices, to begin to frame some answers. "That sounds good to me," I said. "Go for it." Then the showstopper: "We want *you* to address our new environmental task force," they replied, "give us a kick-off speech, and launch it with your environmental vision." What? What environmental vision? In my whole life, I had never given one thought to what I or my company were taking from the Earth or doing to the Earth. I did not have an environmental vision. I did not want to make that speech. I couldn't get beyond, "We obey the law. Comply." So, I dragged my feet for a while, but I finally relented and agreed to speak, and a date was set: August 31, 1994. Come the middle of August, I had not a clue as to what to say, but I knew "Comply" was not a vision. I was sweating.

EPIPHANY

At that very moment, out of the blue, a book landed on my desk: *The Ecology of Commerce,* by Paul Hawken.[1] I'd never heard of him; it was pure serendipity. I started to thumb it, and on page 19, I came to an arresting chapter heading: "The Death of Birth." I begin to read, and on page 25, I found the full meaning of the chapter heading and encountered four terms

I had never before seen in one paragraph: *carrying capacity, overshoot, collapse, and extinction*—the death of birth, species disappearing never ever to be born again. I read:

> A haunting and oft-cited case of overshoot took place on St. Matthew Island in the Bering Sea in 1944 when 29 reindeer were imported. Specialists had calculated that the island could support 13 to 18 reindeer per square mile, or a total population of between 1,600 and 2,300 animals. By 1957 [13 years], the population was 1,350; but by 1963 [six more years], with no natural controls or predators, the population had exploded to 6,000. The scientists double-checked. The original calculations had been correct; this number vastly exceeded carrying capacity, and sure enough, the population was soon decimated by disease and starvation. Such a drastic overshoot, however, did *not* lead to restablization at a lower level [with just the "extra" reindeer dying off]. Instead, the entire habitat was so damaged by the overshoot that the number of reindeer fell drastically below the original carrying capacity, and by 1966 [just three years later] there were only 42 reindeer alive on St. Matthew Island. The difference between ruminants and ourselves is that the resources used by the reindeer were grasses, trees, and shrubs and they eventually return, whereas many of the resources we are exploiting will not.[2]

Reading this for the first time in August 1994, I *knew*—in my head and in my heart—that it was a metaphor for the Earth and humankind. It was an epiphanal moment, a spear in the chest, for me. I read on and I was dumbfounded by my ignorance about how Nature was impacted by the industrial system—the very system of which I and my "successful" company were an integral part. A new definition of success stormed into my consciousness, as that lurking sense of legacy asserted itself. I got it: I was a plunderer of the Earth, and *that* was not the legacy I wanted to leave behind! I wept.

Hawken made the central point of his book in three parts:[3]

1. The living systems and the life support systems of Earth are in rapid decline; we are degrading our biosphere; if unchecked, its decline will continue and *we will lose the biosphere,* which consists of, contains, and supports all of life.
2. The biggest culprit in this decline is the industrial system—the linear, take-make-waste industrial system, driven by fossil fuel energy, wasteful and abusive.
3. The only institution on Earth large enough, powerful enough, wealthy enough, pervasive enough, and influential enough to lead humankind out of this mess is the one doing the most damage: business and industry, my institution.

CLIMBING MOUNT SUSTAINABILITY

I took Paul Hawken's message to heart and gave that speech to my task force, drawing shamelessly on his materials. I challenged my people to lead our company to sustainability, which we defined as operating our petro-intensive company (for energy and materials) in such a way as to take nothing from the Earth that is not naturally and rapidly renewable, and ultimately to do no harm to the biosphere. I stunned that little group, shocked even myself and, in the process, found a whole new purpose in life, in my 61st year. I simply said, "If Hawken is right and business must lead, who will lead business? Unless somebody leads, nobody will. Why not us?"

Since that moment in August 1994, Interface has been on a mission; we call it, "climbing Mount Sustainability," a mountain higher than Everest, to meet at that point at the top that symbolizes zero footprint—zero environmental impact. Sustainable: to me it means taking nothing that is not renewable, and doing no harm. I have told this story in detail in my book, *Mid-Course Correction*.[4] Its title represents my own personal mid-course correction, my company's, and the one I would wish for humankind—especially its industrial system, of which my company is a part. Today, I would phrase Paul Hawken's third point differently: *Unless business and industry are transformed, our descendants will inherit a hellish world.*

What started out as the right thing to do quickly became, for Interface, clearly the smart thing as well, in a hard-headed business sense. First, we are leaner; our costs are down, not up. From eliminating waste alone we have avoided costs of $262 million cumulatively in the first 10 years, dispelling a myth that going green is costly, and more than paying for the entire "mountain climbing" experience. Second, our products are better than they have ever been, because sustainability—leading us to the concept of biomimicry[5]—has proven to be an unimagined source of inspiration and innovation. Third, our people are galvanized around a higher purpose. Psychologist Abraham Maslow had it right about his "hierarchy of human needs"[6]: at the top is self-actualization, and that translates into higher personal purpose. And fourth, the goodwill of the marketplace has been astounding! No amount of advertising could have generated as much, or contributed as much, to the top line—to winning business.

The most amazing thing is, our sustainability initiative has been incredibly good for business! Between 2000 and 2004, those four advantages—costs, products, people, goodwill—were the salvation of Interface during a recession that saw our primary marketplace shrink by 38 percent! As a heavily leveraged company with over $400 million debt, we might not have made it without our new initiative and the support of our customers. This revised definition of success—this new paradigm for business—has a name: "Doing Well by Doing Good." It is a better way to bigger profits, and therein lies its power to change business.

The reader might ask, but how is Interface actually doing on the environmental side? Compare 2004, our 10-year milestone, with our baseline year 1994:

- Waste, reduced nearly 50 percent, avoiding costs of U.S. $262 million, cumulatively
- Net greenhouse gas (GHG) emissions, down 52 percent in absolute tonnage; 35 percent from efficiencies and renewables; 17 percent from off-sets
- Nonrenewable, fossil-derived energy used in carpet operations, down 43 percent relative to production
- Water usage, down 66 percent relative to production
- Smokestacks, 40 percent closed (obviated)
- Effluent pipes, 53 percent abandoned (obviated)
- Trees for Travel, more than 52,000 planted, offsetting more than 78 million airline passenger miles
- Scrap to the landfill, down 80 percent, and
- 66 million pounds of material diverted from landfills and incinerators by ReEntry®, our program for collecting and recycling used products

Our customers can now buy climate-neutral carpet, meaning no net contribution to global warming throughout its life cycle (via independent, third-party verification). We call it Cool Carpet®. Today, our reduced environmental footprint is reflected in every single product we make anywhere in the world—in varying degrees, but to a significant extent in every single one. Over the last 10 years, the entire production system was redesigned, affecting *all* our products, not just one here or one there. The target year for zero footprint, at the top of Mt. Sustainability, is 2020. I hope to live to see that view.

FOUR TRENDS

Now to the four trends I mentioned at the start.

Loss of the Biosphere

In 10 years of near-total immersion in the sustainability paradigm, I gained a deeper understanding of what Hawken was saying—that we are losing the integrity of the very biosphere that supports us and some 30 million other species! I have asked myself over and over through the years, how could a living planet—the rarest and most precious thing in the universe—lose its biosphere, its essential livability, something we take for granted and can't imagine losing? But if we really thought about it, we'd know that if Earth in the distant future *had* lost its livability, it would have happened gradually, insidiously:

One silted or polluted stream *at a time;*
One polluted river at a time;
One collapsing fish stock at a time;
One dying coral reef at a time;
One acidified or eutrophic lake at a time;
One farm with polluted groundwater at a time;
One eroded ton of topsoil at a time;
One lost wetland at a time;
One new open-pit coal mine in a pristine valley at a time;
One clear-cut old growth forest at a time;
One lost habitat at a time;
One disappearing acre of rain forest at a time;
One political payoff at a time, one regulatory rollback at a time;
One leaching landfill at a time;
One belching smokestack or exhaust pipe at a time;
One depleted or polluted aquifer at a time;
One overgrazed field at a time;
One toxic release at a time;
One oil spill at a time;
One-tenth of a degree of global warming at a time;
One lost molecule of ozone at a time;
One misplaced kilogram of plutonium at a time;
One ton of spent nuclear fuel (unsafe for 240,000 years!) at a time;
One songbird at a time;
One PCB-laced orca, one beluga, one dolphin, one trumpeter swan, one
    mountain gorilla, one polar bear, one leatherback turtle at a time;
One entire wild species at a time; *and*
One poverty-stricken, starving, diseased, or exploited human being at a time!

That is how it would have happened. And we know that it *is* happening, right now, just that way—in so many ways! We are losing one strand of the web of life at a time, inexorably, and it will not stop until either we *homo sapiens* come to our senses, or we, too, are gone and can do no more damage.

Environmental Ethics

Here is a brief (admittedly American) look at the second trend, an evolving sense of ethics. Within Western civilization, as with others, codes of behavior have developed and changed over time, and the field of ethics has emerged. Ethics is about doing the right thing, and today we know, for example, that a nobleman's power of life and death over another person is manifestly wrong; it is deeply unethical.

But what if a "nobleman" of more recent times (a wealthy property owner) owned or coveted a piece of land, say the northwestern corner of Wyoming, with the idea of developing those amazing geysers for his own profit, or to keep for his exclusive personal enjoyment? To head off such a possibility, the U.S. Congress in 1872, during the presidency of Ulysses Grant, set aside Yellowstone National Park. Later, President Theodore Roosevelt, under the urging of explorer, mountain climber, and writer John Muir, raised the public profile of Yellowstone and other natural wonders of America. And still later Woodrow Wilson created the National Park Service, to include Grand Canyon National Park, Yosemite, Grand Teton, and many others. So the notion evolved that ethics should extend to land, especially land of such breathtaking beauty.[7] The ethical thing to do, the right thing to do, was to protect this natural beauty for all people.

Years later in 1933, Aldo Leopold, writing about land ethics in a larger sense, observed that what happens to the land in terms of its plant life determines habitat. Habitat, in turn, supports animal life, and the specific habitat determines, even dictates, which species will live there.[8] Thus, the field of ecology developed, the science of studying the web of relationships among flora, fauna, and even the microbial world, that altogether form the web of life. Some very intelligent questions began to emerge, such as, "If the brown bear stops breeding above 5,000 feet elevations (as it has), what does that mean for us *homo sapiens?*" Out of such inquiry arose bigger questions, such as, "How are humans affecting the biosphere, the intricate interconnected web of life of which they are a part?"

Then, a brilliant and brave woman named Rachel Carson brought such inquiry to a new level with her exposure of the chemical industry—a human invention and a central part of the modern industrial system—in her landmark book *Silent Spring,* published in 1962.[9] Carson extended the field of ethics beyond people and land to include all the creatures that live on the land, and in the air above the land, and in the waters that cover the land. The prospect of a silent spring brought to life in our minds' eyes (and ears), and in our hearts, the chilling reality of industrial pollution; and we knew it was manifestly wrong. She gave compelling new meaning to the term *environmental ethics.* Rachel Carson was pilloried by the chemical industry, just as Copernicus, centuries before, had been pilloried by the church for saying the earth was not the center of the universe. Copernicus backed down and withheld publication—Carson did not.

By now the field of ecology was broadened to extend to *industrial ecology*, and people were asking, how bad *is* the abuse caused by the industrial system and what should we do about it? The answer was: pretty bad! And out of Rachel Carson's shock wave came practically all of the legislation of the 1960s and 1970s aimed at protecting our environment, including the creation of the American Environmental Protection Agency and its regulatory authority.

The regulatory system: Has it slowed the rate of abuse? Yes, it has. But has it turned the negative trends around? NO. My advisors and researchers—and they are among the best in this field, Paul Hawken, Janine Benyus, Amory Lovins, Bill Browning—tell me that *not one peer-reviewed scientific paper published since 1970 has said, yes, the global trends are now positive.* Though there are exceptions and occasional victories to be celebrated, the world's major ecological trends are still headed in the wrong direction. Biodiversity is plummeting—"the death of birth." The human footprint is ever growing, already well exceeding the planet's carrying capacity.[10]

The trend in environmental ethics, however, has become well established, and it dates from way back. Though religious conservatives prefer to call it "creation care," it's the same thing—a very long, apolitical evolution of our sense of the right thing to do. Ultimately, it's driven by enlightened self-interest, for not only does ecology tell us we are part of nature, not above or outside it, it also tells us that what we do to the web of life we do to ourselves. *Industrial ecology* tells us the industrial system, as it operates today, simply cannot go on and on and on, taking, making, wasting—abusing the web of life. I'm told that less than 3 percent of the material processed through the industrial system has any value whatsoever six months after its extraction from the earth. For example, 40,000 pounds of "stuff" is processed to make one 9-pound laptop computer.[11]

The industrial system developed in a world very different from the one we live in today: there were fewer people, more plentiful natural resources, simpler lifestyles. These days, industry moves, mines, extracts, shovels, burns, wastes, pumps, and disposes of four million pounds of material to provide one average, middle-class American family what it uses in a year. Realistically, with so many people aspiring to the American standard of living, this cannot go on and on and on in a finite world. The rate of material extraction and use is now *endangering* prosperity as much as enhancing it, and the toxicity of some of it *really* harms the biosphere, and thus the whole of life. The abusive industrial system is manifestly wrong. Out of a growing sense of ethics, it must and will be changed.

Clean Technologies

The third trend, growing out of the first two (the decline of the biosphere, the rise of ethics), is the means by which an ethically enlightened species will address the challenges of the slippery slope. It is the trend in clean technologies, *not* very well established as yet.

Just what are the characteristics of the problematic technologies? I suggest that those characteristics are: extractive (they take from Earth), linear (take-make-waste), fossil-fuel driven (for energy), wasteful, abusive, and intensely focused on increasing labor productivity (per person hour). For such technologies, more means worse! So, how can technology be part of the solution? When it is renewable, not extractive; when it is cyclical, not linear, and material flows are closed loops; when it is solar and hydrogen driven, not fossil-fuel driven, *when it is waste-free and benign, not wasteful and abusive,* and focused on the productivity of *all* resources, not just labor.

This trend is only in its early stage, with renewable energy technologies, with recycling technologies, with clean, lean manufacturing technologies, and with hybrid gas-electric propulsion. It must grow much more deliberately and much more quickly.

Ascendancy of Women

Here I would add my fourth trend, and say that, following progenitor Rachel Carson, the ascendancy of women in the arts, in business, the professions, in education, and in government is one of the most encouraging of all trends, as women bring their right-brained, nurturing nature to address the seemingly intractable challenges created by left-brained men and their preoccupation with bottom lines and other "practical" considerations. After all, it's left-brain pragmatism that got humankind into this mess. Surely, a different kind of thinking is needed to get us out.

We know by now that societies where women are honored, supported, and well educated are the ones with low birthrates and high indicators of a good quality of life. How long will it take all the world's cultures to learn to help themselves by rallying to the support of their women? To turn away from destructive ways and towards sustainability will require a different order of love, courage, and imagination. The female half of the population may have some answers, and may intuitively hear the call to honor our children.

ROLE OF UNIVERSITIES

Let us turn to the role of our universities—where some of you readers have, or in time will have, influence. Are universities part of the problem, or part of the solution? Where do they stand with respect to the nexus of these trends?

Are our mechanical engineers still learning about internal combustion engines or are they studying fuel cells? Are our electrical engineers still learning about coal-powered central generating stations, or are they studying wind, photovoltaic, and biomass distributed generation? Are our ceramics engineers still learning heat-beat-treat methods, or are they studying the abalone's natural nanotechnological method that makes better ceramics (than any human-made) out of readily abundant minerals in sea water at 40° F? Are our textile engineers still learning to make Kevlar® with boiling sulphuric acid, or studying how the spider makes a five times stronger, more resilient "textile fiber" out of bugs, at body temperature? Are our chemistry students learning to make the next PCB, or learning about green enzymatic chemistry in water?

Are our economics students being taught that social and environmental costs are "externalities" that don't count in the economic system, and that perverse subsidies are somehow good, even deserved; or are they learning about true, full-cost accounting that would put the cost of a barrel of oil at fully $200 per barrel (if the cost of Gulf wars were included; or if the costs of global warming to future generations were added)? Are our designers being taught to invent clever things that make a lot of money, or are they learning the principles of *ethical* design, designing for sustainability and committing to it for life? Are our law students being taught compliance, to keep the regulators at bay, and to protect their clients; or are they being taught "beyond compliance," and to encourage their clients to embrace ethical behavior and to count the externalities?

Furthermore, are our teachers being taught the present, outmoded abusive system, so they can pass it on and perpetuate destruction for another generation or two, or three; or are our universities waking up to both their opportunity and responsibility to challenge the status quo in every aspect of curricula?

All of these questions are equally applicable to our industrial development efforts, and how we develop our existing businesses. Are they focused on the obsolete, destructive past, or on a sustainable, restorative future?

MIND-SHIFT: REDESIGN

A truly sustainable society will depend totally and absolutely on *a vast redesign of the entire industrial and economic system,* triggered by an equally vast mind-shift—one mind at a time, one organization at a time, one technology at a time, one building, one company, one university curriculum, one community, one region, one industry at a time—until the entire interconnected web of which we are each a part has been transformed into a sustainable system. We must develop an ethical human system that coexists in harmony with Earth's natural systems, upon which every living thing, even civilization itself, depends. The worldview that treats Earth as if it had an infinite supply of stuff to feed a ravenous industrial system, when clearly (for one example) oil's coming peak tells us vividly that Earth is finite—is a flawed, obsolete, *short-term* view of reality—a myopic and selfish worldview. Surely, we would be wise to adopt the Native Americans' "seven generations" view of life, by which we would consider in our every deliberation, the effect on seven generations.

The flawed obsolete view holds that:

- Technology, coupled with left-brained intelligence, will see us through; ignoring its extractive, abusive aspects.
- The "invisible hand" of the market is an honest broker, when we know it can be very dishonest, because it is blind to the externalities as it establishes prices.
- Increasing labor productivity is the route to abundance for all, when in a world of diminishing Nature and increasing population it is clear that we must increase *resource* productivity through recycling and conservation, employing more people in the process.
- Happiness is to be found in material wealth—the trappings of affluence—when we know that consumerism *cannot* bring happiness, despite the pervasive advertising with which our children (and we) are bombarded.
- Business exists to make a profit, when the new paradigm holds that business makes a profit to exist, and must exist for some higher purpose.
- Our environment is a subset of the economy, you know, the pollution part. In our new enlightenment, we know that the economy is the wholly owned subsidiary of the environment, to quote the late U.S. Senator Gaylord Nelson.

Is it not plain to see? Nature is the parent. The economy is the child. It is not the other way 'round, *despite what most economists still seem to believe.* Will we shift paradigms in time and truly embrace a new vision of reality? Will we, from a new view of reality, enable the three good trends to reverse the one that is destroying life?

OPTING FOR SURVIVAL

There is no doubt in my mind, based on our experience at Interface, that there is a clear, compelling, and irrefutable case—business case—for sustainability. Still, skeptics remain. So, given their stubborn reluctance to accept my case, I have begun to challenge the skeptics to make *their* case. More precisely, I would challenge *anyone* to make the business case for:

- Double-glazing the planet with greenhouse gases; and counting only the cost of preventing global warming, while ignoring the exponential costs of ignoring it.
- Destroying habitat for countless species, whose importance and connection to humankind, in many, even most cases, are yet unknown.
- Poisoning air, water, and land.
- Disrupting pollination and photosynthesis. (That ought to be a good one!)
- Overfishing the oceans to the point of collapse.
- Destroying vast coral reefs, forests, and wetlands.
- Depleting or polluting aquifers on which food production depends.
- Destroying the life support systems of Earth.

As Paul Hawken asks, what is the business case for an economic system that says it is cheaper to destroy the earth than to take care of it? How did such a fantasy system that defies common sense even come to be? How did we—all of us—get swept up in its siren's song?

Finally, what is the business case for destroying the basic infrastructure of civilization itself, the natural systems upon which everything depends, including the economy? For, what economy can even exist without air, water, materials, energy, food, *plus* climate regulation, an ultraviolet radiation shield, pollination, seed dispersal, waste processing, nutrient cycling, water purification and distribution (through natural filtration and the hydrologic cycle), soil creation and maintenance, flood and insect control—all supplied by Nature and her natural systems?

Without Nature, there can be no economy, or anything we cherish! How can it be good business to destroy our global home? Therein lies the *inevitability* of sustainability. It's only a question of how much pain Earth and her inhabitants must endure before a growing sense of ethics gets us off our slippery slope and we opt for survival.

Coming full circle, back to my opening salutation, who is really most at risk here? In March 1996, early in my "mountain climb," a few days after my sustainability talk to our sales people in southern California, I received an e-mail from Glenn Thomas with a poem, *Tomorrow's Child,* which he wrote after hearing me. Reading it was one of the most uplifting moments of my life; I knew at least one person had really got it.

Without a name an unseen face, and knowing not your time or place,
Tomorrow's Child, though yet unborn, I met you first last Tuesday morn.

A wise friend introduced us two, and through his shining point of view
I saw a day that you would see, a day for you, but not for me.

Knowing you has changed my thinking, for I never had an inkling
That perhaps the things I do might someday, somehow, threaten you.

Tomorrow's Child, my daughter-son, I'm afraid I've just begun
To think of you and of your good, though always having known I should.

Begin I will to weigh the cost of what I squander, what is lost,
If ever I forget that you will someday come to live here too.

Since I first read this poem, it has spoken to me every day of my life with one simple but profound message: We are each and every one part of the web of life, and we have a choice to make during our brief visit to this beautiful planet—to hurt it, or to help it. Which will it be? The choice is yours: Tomorrow's child is watching.

Onward!
Making a Vow: Living the Covenant

RAFFI CAVOUKIAN

Nelson Mandela's call to "turn this world around, for the children"[1] is the plea of this century, the cry of humanity's elder on behalf of the young on every continent. And yet, never in history has there been a revolution inspired by the growing child. Child Honoring seeks to spark just that: a compassionate *reglobalization* towards a child-friendly world that would benefit everyone.

Whatever the future brings, in best-case scenarios or the worst—natural calamities, terrorist strikes, wars, rising sea waters—we have a duty to the children. How can Child Honoring, as a moral imperative, grow to be understood, shared, and engaged worldwide? It will take the whole village: parents and educators, CEOs and policy makers, grandparents and graduates, social justice and human rights activists, nongovernmental organizations and students, professors and health professionals, scientists and faith leaders.

No belief system is more vital than a child's need to believe in the love of their caregivers and community. May our love for children activate the joyful power of possibility. In a number of ways, let me play to your imagination.

SCENE 1: "BIONOMY"

In April 2020, the lead article in both the *Online Bionomist* and in the United Nations Bionomic Report reads: "The bionomy[2] shows robust signs of restorative energy, the Living Planet Index is in recovery mode, and for once, *all* indicators signal the overall turn towards sustainability that bionomists have predicted. The tax shift has been an unqualified success, sparking a reversal of decades-old destructive subsidies and practices. The Well-Being Index, established in every country, is a welcome change. . . ."

This future article touches on what *today's* business news could be reporting. It goes on to read: "The Humane Cultures indicator has been very active: A multifaith consensus on an initiative to end child beating has garnered widespread reaction and surprising levels of cooperation. After a passionate speech by the 85-year-old Dalai Lama in Vancouver, the Council of Children's Commissioners worked round the clock to reach agreement with the Young Catholics and the Muslim Youth League, and thus secure the pan-religious accord. This 2020 gathering of the World's Parliament of Religions has been named by the Global Center for Child Honoring as the recipient of its 12th annual Humane Stewardship award."

The present is the ground that shapes our futures. Sixty years—six decades—is long enough for nuclear bombs to hold us for ransom and to now threaten us again, too long to keep measuring societal progress with the wrong tools,[3] and far too long for electing "I'll grow the economy" politicians on false premises, for false promises. Forty-five years is too long to ignore Eisenhower's warning about the military-industrial complex. Fear-induced Realpolitik has bullied and pillaged the world far too long, and oil industry dominance has run its course. Two thousand years is far too long for money vendors to rule the temple, for money to have the upper hand, for children to be for sale, for human potential to falter.

May the immeasurable currencies of compassion accumulate (with interest!), actualizing and maximizing society's loving potential. This is the age of Real Magic: organic foods and fibers, smart money, hydrogen and hemp, infinite sunshine. Make room for the playful child, for love of life, to lead the way. Come feel the glory of Nature, our Creation mystery day and night, Universe of a bijillion stars. Tend the heart-mind, groom the garden. Wizards: light up the "muggle" culture! Individuate, meditate, activate. Put your soul to work.

SCENE 2: A CHILD SHALL LEAD US

> If a thing must be done, it can be.
>
> —Eleanor Roosevelt

The global human family faces a basic conflict of interest: between a child's right to breathe and a corporation's limited liability protection by which it can do unlimited harm to that child and to all children. Imagine *your* infant (or grandchild) in a heroic stand-off, your David against the multinational Goliath, with nothing more than a moral slingshot—a reasonable right to breathe, play, and grow up in a nontoxic world.

In the multinational child, the multinational corporation has met its match: the universal child, essential human of every culture. The spirit of humanity.

Your Honor:
My people come from no single country, they are in all of them;
they come from a space and time called childhood,
the place of our common origins; they have no vote,
no way to sway their fate except with the play of their eyes,
their curiosity, their songs, their dance, and their drawings;
for centuries these people have struggled for recognition, to take their
rightful place in communities, as part of the evolving intelligence of our species.
These small and impressionable members of our human family,

Your Honor, they look up to you and the parental society
and believe you love them more than anything;
they expect you to rule in their favor;
as apprenticing adults, they are acutely sensitive to example,
they need consistency and fairness,
they are easily confounded by double standards,
hurt and demoralized by grown-up cynicism.
Do you remember how it felt to be their age, Your Honor?
The children are counting on you.

In a genuinely human court, the child would prevail. The soulful corporeal being would easily prevail against the heavy-footed rootless multinational, the soulless abstract entity, the pathological habit run amok. In the court of humane ethics, "Honor the child, serve its communities and its habitat" would be the clear directive. For a theft of futures, guilty as charged, the sentence might mean revocation of corporate license, umpteen years of community service, untold forms of retribution. A time to come clean.

Throughout the world, the young of the human family—the untapped power of our species—must be seen, heard, and respected. The primacy of the early years must become the key tenet by which to redirect our societies towards peace. Addressing children's universal needs can emerge as the new standard by which compassionate cultures tilt their priorities towards families and communities. *A vibrant "first ecology" is the systems key that opens lifetimes of change towards restoring our planet's life supports and securing a viable future.*

SCENE 3: THE POWER OF PERSONAL ACTS

In this book, you've read about the emotional growth of the mind, the unique vulnerability of the first years, every infant's foundational need for respectful love and bonding. And, about the corporate assault on children's minds and bodies—the bottom-line thinking that has poisoned our planet and imperiled us—about the theft of our children's futures. No spiritual tradition or holy book condones such a culture. Ask yourself: If it's morally and ethically repugnant to exploit children and undermine families, why is it legal? And now ask: Am I complicit? Does my conscience condone this? What am I prepared to do about it?

We don't have decades in which to sue the chemical industry and other multinationals for redress. (Some systems thinkers say we have but 20–25 years to decisively set the course for humanity.) We can and we must engage every democratic forum available—to challenge, for example, political candidates to make sustainability the foundation of their platforms, and to make child-friendly profamily policies the focus of their corporate commerce agenda. There's no better way to tell wizards from muggles.

A defining moment in history is no time for paralysis or pessimism. Apartheid, the Soviet Empire, and the Berlin Wall have come and gone. So too will the global money-complex decline and fall, by will or by Nature. The obsession with money has been killing us. Maximizing capital has cost us the world. Delete the notion of maximizing capital. Let us maximize goodwill. Put money back in its place. Curb its excesses. Redefine its role. Let the children breathe.

Imagine a compassionate revolution that invites you to dance! Imagine trading the warrior archetype (spiritual or other) for *the lover,* the lover in you who loves life. The early troubadours of the twelfth and thirteenth centuries were lovers. In an age of male savagery and marriages for territory and power, the troubadours' writings of love for the sake of love were revolutionary, as were their concepts of chivalry and the gentle man.

Nelson Mandela's triumph was that of a lover: of freedom, of his people, of South Africa, of an important idea. His life has been an epic tale of ennobling love. During his confinement, he held his *captors* captive!—by his Gandhian dignity, and by his faith in the possible. In a previous century, those who achieved the unthinkable abolition of slavery in the United States knew it was time. They didn't get stuck on feasibility, thinking "Oh, it'll never work—the economy's built on slaves." They knew it was time for an untenable situation to end.

So too, the colonization of the child psyche must end.

Each person's inner nature longs to be known and to act in life's play cast as itself. Centuries apart, Socrates and Shakespeare said (respectively), "Know thyself" and, "To thine own self be true, and . . . thou canst not then be false to any man" (*Hamlet,* act 1, scene 3). We need institutions built around that fundamental psychological value—authenticity, authentic being, true authorship of ourselves. A child only wants us to be real, to be truthful (isn't that what we keep asking of the child?), to be true.[4] Isn't that what you want in whomever you meet?

The sweetest freedom is creative: freedom—not from, but *towards* something. When children can be free to be their true selves, we too are freed. Free to enable more love, more joy, and more creativity. We want to remake ourselves in the image of intelligent Nature, our loving *human* nature reclaimed and celebrated.[5]

SCENE 4: RESISTO DANCING:
AN INVITATION TO "BELUGA GRADS" (BGs)

DEAR BELUGA GRADS: YOU'RE INVITED TO DANCE!

"Resisto Dancing"[6] is my graduation song for you, a fusion of Maslow,
Goldman, Dylan, Shakespeare, and hip-hop . . . remember Abraham Maslow's
saying: "Healthy individuation *requires resisting* unhealthy enculturation,"
and Emma Goldman's, "If I can't dance, it's not my revolution."

The best dancers have a strong core,
a middle that lets them leap and turn with ease.
A child needs a strong middle too; we all do.
A sense of self as lovable and love-able, with potent conscience,
a power that's response-able—the lover, powered with a joy for life.
Resisto dancing, to keep your love alive . . .
to keep your songlines open and hummin'

* * *

You are neither alone, nor a drop in the ocean: you are the ripple, the wave, the gathering swell at a historic turn of the tide. In this age, the spirit of King and Gandhi are very much with us in the likes of Jane Goodall, Arundati Roy, Howard Zinn, Naomi Klein, Desmond Tutu, Louise Arbour, Stephen Lewis, and Wangari Matthai, and in the distinguished voices of this anthology. We must become the change we seek in the world, Gandhi said. Lead by example, as best we can.

Riane Eisler's partnership ethic begs us to *live* it in our intimate relations, to weave a loving legacy from the strands of our daily lives. David Korten's Earth Community comes alive in every acre of farmland converted to organics, every restaurant devoted to local foods, and every family devoting a portion of its food bill to buying organic; every business transformed by. . . .

We turn this world around with every call, fax, or email to an elected official praising a sustainable action or supporting change; every publisher, nongovernmental organization, and state government that switches to chlorine-free paper[7]; every material designer who opts for nontoxic threads and dyes; every municipality that votes to ban pesticides; every school greening its playground; every Roots of Empathy classroom; every mosque where a woman leads prayers (as happened in Toronto); every cop or politician who stands up to corruption, every act of personal integrity.

Calling All Grads: Choose your resisto, and dance up the hood! Shake those sillies out. Keep a clear head and make positive waves. Belugas swim in pods . . . hmm, BG pods and podcasting . . . podsinging and pod-pals . . . podpunning! Podruple your power.

SCENE 5: THE WORLD WE WANT

From 80 countries, four hundred 8-to-12-year-olds at a 2002 environmental conference in Victoria, British Columbia, joined me in singing the chorus of "Turn This World Around,"[8] my Mandela-inspired song. As I've heard repeatedly from children of many cultures, there was in these diverse young people an overwhelming desire for *all* children to live in a healthy world, a world of diversity and peace.

Towards this end, there is much that universities can and must do. Good news from my part of the world: the University of Victoria (UVic) and the University of British Columbia (UBC) are engaged in a variety of child-honoring initiatives. In the last two years, UVic has held a Colloquium on Child Honoring (which led to a Child Honoring task force), infused its teacher training program with the Covenant and Principles, held a seminar on children's rights with Irwin Cotler, Canada's justice minister, and created the World We Want Global Arts Project.[9]

The latter initiative grew from an exercise in paintbrush diplomacy: a children's art exhibit shown at UVic, with drawings from the children of Victoria and those of Iraq and Afghanistan, with the help of the Canadian military, who distributed art supplies overseas. There is immense power in these drawings, in the visual play of a child's soul and longing. Stunning use of color and composition along with a purity of heart produced a moving exhibit, as the drawings' titles might suggest: "I like to be a bride one day"; "Let peace prevail in every country" (from Iraq); "Young woman in a *burqua* is caged like a bird"; "Mothers that are educated can teach their children well"; "Land mines have caused death and dismemberment to many children" (from Afghanistan); and the one by Stephanie Chong (Grade 7, Victoria) entitled "Make Peace: Do It For the Children" went on to say: "The theme of my artwork is peace . . . because that's the way I want the world to be. I drew two doves carrying a peaceful world. I also drew a sun in my poster because I think the sun represents a new beginning . . . STOP WAR NOW!"

At UBC, the Human Early Learning Partnership (HELP) is a pioneering, interdisciplinary research partnership that is directing a world-leading contribution to new understandings and approaches to early child development. HELP director Dr Clyde Hertzman has been mapping the "early development indicators" of communities that correlate with positive outcomes in later life, and has provided useful research for Mary Gordon's Roots of Empathy program.

Centers of higher learning can inspire their own students by taking steps to become sustainable communities. A switch to using chlorine-free paper would be a significant step forward and set an example for other sectors. Multidisciplinary "Institutes for Child Honoring" could become hubs for advancing the next generation of research questions on Child Honoring's multiple facets.

SCENE 6: GNN—GOOD NEWS NETWORK

The shake-up of bottom-line values can help correct media's depressing "if it bleeds it leads" habit, in itself a distortion of news. A worldwide good news network could be an effective media engine for delving into the myriad stories on Child Honoring as embraced and practiced in diverse cultures, and could serve to broadcast the inspirational acts of both individual youths and youth groups.[10]

Breaking News: The World Youth Parliament urges the world's billionaires to make legacy gifts to the world's children. Among their proposals: green computer production and recovery, neighborhood Sunpower Hubs, energy efficiency contests, hemp newsprint and papers, and a Superfund for cleaning up toxic waste sites.

In a developing story, influential public figures are speaking out for the need to decommercialize childhood. At a press conference in New York, Larry King, Bill Gates, Oprah Winfrey, Shania Twain, and J. K. Rowling echoed the call of child development experts in urging lawmakers to ban advertising and marketing to children.

Headlines: Extra, Extra—Imagine . . .
UN Human Rights Commission recognizes the young child as MVP.[11]
China's internet youth initiative forms Global Green Youth Corps.
Bono and Nobel Laureates on hunger strike for free AIDS remedies.
Stunning gains for Progressive Party in U.S. congressional elections.
Windfall Profits Superfund powers Africa's recovery and revival.
Human Security Network oversees huge reductions in military budgets.
Children of every country singing Mother Earth anthems.
United States, India, and China pledge massive CO2 reductions to combat
    global warming.
With expanded powers, International Criminal Court targets corporate pol-
    luters.
In J. K. Rowling's new book, children rescue the real magic of the real world.
Ecopreneurs mark 10th anniversary of Fair Trade's makeover of Free Trade.

Choose your passion, invent your own headlines and work to make them come true.

A CIRCLE WHERE WE ALL BELONG

Awakening to full humanity, we dare to ask any and all questions:

Who gave money the power to poison the world? Courts, governments, voters.
Who gave money the power to poison our food? Courts, governments, voters.
Who gave money the power to exploit the children?
Who has the power to turn this around?

We need new words and ideas to help us get through our global survival drama. Left, Right, Liberal, Radical, Conservative, Environmentalist, these labels can't help us deal with interrelated issues like children's asthma and the toxic load of belugas, domestic violence and the "soul erosion" in our youth, international politics and dwindling freshwater supplies. This also has to be said: there is no such thing as "the environment," a phrase which objectifies and alienates the living community of Nature from ourselves. It keeps us from feeling directly connected to the real world that we literally eat, drink, and inhale. To pretend we don't is madness.

We are meant for glory, not for misery, for reaching to our highest dreams when basic needs are met. The faces of Armenian, Japanese, Gabonese, Tibetan, Salish, Irish, Iranian, and indeed *all* children are animated by the same emotions. In every culture human tears fall the same, and smiles look the same. Remembering this, we can truly celebrate differences in the human mosaic. Let nations compete, if they want, in acts of kindness and compassion. They have no logical or moral rationale for keeping billions of people from life's table.

Child Honoring recognizes both the real suffering and the real joys in living, and seeks to end the unnecessary suffering caused by ignorance. Isn't there enough everyday tragedy in life without blind ignorance adding more? If ignorance is our greatest sin, then we all have our share. Let it be our common enemy, our only enemy. Conscious living and spiritual growth is what we are born to learn.

The child-honoring society I imagine would show love for its children in every facet of its design and organization. It would uphold the basic human rights of every child, and corporal punishment would be a thing of the past. No child would live in neglect or lack access to health care. Kids wouldn't be alone after school with violent computer games, eating junk food, waiting for a parent to get home. You'd see family support centers in every neighborhood. Working with the young would be valued and well rewarded. Universally available child care facilities would be staffed by trained professionals. We'd have more schools and teachers, smaller class sizes, and a range of learning options for families to choose from. The arts would loom large, and from a young age we'd teach child development as a primary subject as fundamental as reading, writing, and arithmetic. Children would learn early on about the importance of empathy and the basics of nurturant parenting.

A child-honoring world would honor the central place of women in life. To address the dramatic rise in children's asthma and the body burden of toxic compounds, "mother's milk legislation" would detoxify the chemical industry. We'd breathe better thanks to strict clean air laws. Bionomics would accelerate a full-fledged renaissance in business. We'd have a triple bottom-line *bionomy* that factors social and environmental considerations into "full cost" market pricing; a quality-of-life index that measures what matters most; subsidy and tax shifts towards clean energies, sustainable practices, and innovative enterprise; and political cycles not financed by corporations or geared primarily towards reelection. We'd have a culture that rewards elected representatives for long-term wisdom rather than short-term power.

A child-friendly protocol for commerce would breathe new life into public health. Organic farmers would play a leading role in protecting the world's food security. Engineers would compete for child-friendly designs using the most benign chemical compounds and manufacturing processes. Corporate charter reforms would herald a new dawn in which CEOs and shareholders would be truly accountable to the public good. Released from the Midas curse, we could be free to work towards our highest aspirations.

Humanity must choose its future in a race against time.

The compassionate revolution needs you. Make a vow to live by Child Honoring principles in your own life, and to infuse them in our institutions. Let the transformative power of Child Honoring enrich our commons and strengthen the global civil society. Join the wave to restore our children's stolen future, to make this the world of their dreams as well as ours.

Notes

INTRODUCTION

1. This includes "beluga grads," the young adults who as children sang "Baby Beluga." I wrote this song in 1979 after seeing a beluga whale at the Vancouver Aquarium; in 1980 it became the title song of my fourth album.

2. Theo Colborn, Dianne Dumanoski, and John Peterson Myers, *Our Stolen Future* (New York: Penguin, 1996).

3. H. L. Needleman and P. J. Landrigan, *Raising Children Toxic Free* (New York: Farrar, Straus, and Giroux, 1994).

4. The old thinking was "the dose makes the poison." Recent findings show that exposure to even parts per billion or parts per trillion of some toxicants wreaks havoc on fetal development: on the endocrine system, for example.

5. Union of Concerned Scientists, "Warning to Humanity," November 1992. www.actionbioscience.org/environment/worldscientists.html.

6. United Nations Environment Programme, GEO 2000 Report, www.unep.org/geo2000/ov-e/index.htm.

7. *The New York Times* referred to the February 15, 2003, worldwide antiwar outpouring of some 15 to 30 million as a "second global power."

8. E.O. Wilson, *The Future of Life* (New York: Alfred A. Knopf, 2002).

9. BALLE, the Business Alliance of Local Living Economies, cofounded by David Korten and Judy Wicks. Please see www.livingeconomies.org for more information.

10. Greenspan, Shanker, Council of Human Development, www.councilhd.ca.

CHAPTER 1: THE EMOTIONAL ARCHITECTURE OF THE MIND

1. This chapter is adapted from *The Growth of the Mind* by Stanley I. Greenspan with Beryl L. Benderly. Its ideas are further developed in *The First Idea: How Symbols, Language and Intelligence Evolved from Our Primate Ancestors to Modern Humans* by Stanley I. Greenspan and Stuart G. Shanker.

2. T. T. Young, *Emotions in Man and Animal* (New York: Wiley, 1943).

3. S. I. Greenspan, *The Development of the Ego* (Madison, CT: International Universities Press, 1989); idem, *Developmentally Based Psychotherapy* (Madison, CT: International Universities Press, 1997); idem, *Infancy and Early Childhood* (Madison, CT: International Universities Press, 1992).

4. W. T. Greenough and J. E. Black, "Induction of Brain Structure by Experience: Substrates for Cognitive Development," *Developmental Behavioral Neurooscience* 24 (1992): 155299; I. J. Weiler, N. Hawrylak, and W. T. Greenough, "Morphogenesis in Memory Formation: Synaptic and Cellular Mechanisms," *Behavioural Brain Research* 66 (1995): 1–6.

5. M. A. Bell and N. A. Fox, "Brain Development over the First Year of Life: Relations between EEG Frequency and Coherence and Cognitive and Affective Behaviors," in *Human Behavior and the Developing Brain*, ed. G. Dawson and K. Fischer (New York: Guilford, 1994), pp. 314–15; H. T. Chugani and M. E. Phelps, "Maturational Changes in Cerebral Function in Infants Determined by 18FDG Positron Emission Tomography," *Science* 231 (1986): 84043; H. T. Chugani, M. E. Phelps, and J. C. Mazziotts, "Positron Emission Tomography Study of Human Brain Functional Development," *Annals of Neurology* 22 (1994): 487–97.

6. M. A. Hofer, "On the Nature and Function of Prenatal Behavior," in *Behavior of the Fetus*, ed. W. Somtherman and S. Robinson (Caldwell, NJ: Telford, 1995); idem, "Hidden Regulators: Implications for a New Understanding of Attachment, Separation and Loss," in *Attachment Theory: Social, Developmental, and Clinical Perspectives*, ed. S. Goldberg, R. Muir, and J. Kerr (Hillsdale, NJ: Analytic Press, 1995), pp. 203–30; P. Rakic, J. Bourgeois, and P. Goldman-Rakic, "Synaptic Development of the Cerebral Cortex: Implication for Learning, Memory, and Mental Illness," in *The Self-Brain: From Growth Cones to Functional Networks*, ed. J. Van Pelt, M. A. Corner, H.B.M. Uylngs, and F. H. Lopes da Silva (New York: Elsevier Science, 1994), pp. 227–43.

7. In an experiment, both an infant and a monkey looked longer at a trick box that had only one item in it even though they had just observed two items being put in the box. Is the conclusion that infants (and monkeys) therefore understand arithmetic warranted by this research? Perhaps, rather than an understanding of math, these observations reveal that infants can distinguish certain spatial relationships as well as provide evidence of basic perceptual motor skills and growing memory capacity.

8. See, for example, S. I. Greenspan, *The Development of the Ego: Implications for Personality Theory, Psychopathology, and the Psychotherapeutic Process* (Madison, CT: International Universities Press, 1989).

CHAPTER 2: STARTING OFF RIGHT

1. J. Bowlby, *Attachment* (London: Pelican, 1961).

2. M. Ainsworth, M. Blehar, E. Waters, and S, Wall, *Patterns of Attachment: A Psychological Study of the Strange Situation* (Hillsdale, NJ: Lawrence Erlbaum, 1978).

3. Bowlby, *Attachment.*

4. D. Stern, *The Interpersonal World of the Infant* (New York: Basic Books, 1985).

5. R. Clyman, "The Procedural Organisation of Emotions," in *Psychoanalytic Perspectives,* eds. T. Shapiro and R. Emde (Madison, CT: International Universities Press, 1991).

6. W. Bucc, P*sychoanalysis and Cognitive Science* (New York: Guilford Press, 1997).

7. Robin Karr-Morse and Meredith S. Wiley, *Ghosts from the Nursery* (New York: Atlantic Press, 1997).

8. A. Schore, *Affect Disregulation and Disorders of the Self* (New York: Norton, 2003).

9. Penelope Leach, *Children First: What Society Must Do, and Is Not Doing, for Children* (New York: Knopf, 1994).

CHAPTER 3: SELF, IDENTITY, AND GENERATIVITY

1. R. Karen, *Becoming Attached: First Relationships and How They Shape Our Capacity to Love* (New York: Oxford University Press, 1998), p. 3.

2. M. Small, "The Natural History of Children," in *Childhood Lost: How American Culture Is Failing Our Kids,* ed. S. Olfman (Westport, CT: Praeger, 2004).

3. J. Jolly Bruner and K. Sylva, eds., *Play: Its Role in Development and Evolution* (New York: Basic Books,1976); S. Olfman, ed., *All Work and No Play: How Educational Reforms are Harming Our Preschoolers* (Westport, CT: Praeger, 2003).

4. Jolly and Sylva, *Play.*

5. N. Angier, "The Purpose of Playful Frolics: Training for Adulthood," *New York Times,* October 20, 1992, sec. C.

6. S. Olfman, *All Work and No Play.*

7. L. Berk, *Awakening Children's Minds* (New York: Oxford, 2001).

8. Berk, *Awakening Children's Minds;* J. Kane and H. Carpenter, "Imagination and the Growth of the Human Mind," in *All Work and No Play: How Educational*

Reforms Are Harming Our Preschoolers, ed. S. Olfman (Westport, CT: Praeger, 2003).

9. E. Fromm, *The Sane Society* (1955; New York: First Owl Books, 1990); C. F. Monte, *Beneath the Mask: An Introduction to Theories of Personality,* 6th ed. (New York: Harcourt Brace College Publishers, 1999), pp. 677–78.

10. E. Fromm, *The Anatomy of Human Destructiveness* (New York: Holt, Rinehart and Winston, 1973).

11. E. Fromm, *On Being Human* (New York: Continuum, 1977), pp. 76–77.

12. Fromm, *The Anatomy of Human Destructiveness.*

13. H. E. Erikson, *Childhood and Society* (1950; New York: Norton, 1993).

14. H. E. Erikson, *Insight and Responsibility* (New York: Norton, 1964), p. 124.

15. Ibid.

16. Ibid., p. 155.

17. C. F. Monte, *Beneath the Mask: An Introduction to Theories of Personality,* 6th ed. (New York: Harcourt Brace College Publishers, 1999), p. 395.

CHAPTER 4: THE BENEFITS OF PARTNERSHIP

1. Portions of this article were published in *YES!* and *Conscience.*

2. Martin H.. Teicher, "Wounds That Time Won't Heal: The Neurobiology of Child Abuse," *Cerebrum* 2, no. 4 (2000): 5067; Bruce D. Perry, R. A. Pollard, T. L. Blakley, W. L. Baker, and D. Vigilante, "Childhood Trauma, the Neurobiology of Adaptation, and 'Use-dependent' Development of the Brain: How 'States' Become 'Traits,'" *Infant Mental Health Journal* 16 (1995): 27191. See also McLean Hospital, www.mcleanhospital.org; and Riane Eisler and Daniel S. Levine, "Nurture, Nature, and Caring: We Are Not Prisoners of Our Genes," *Brain and Mind* 3, no. 1 (2002): 9–52.

3. Michael Milburn and Sheree Conrad, *The Politics of Denial* (Cambridge, MA: MIT Press, 1996).

4. For a more detailed discussion, see Riane Eisler, *The Power of Partnership: Seven Relationships that Will Change Your Life* (Novato, CA: New World Library, 2002); and Riane Eisler, "Human Rights and Violence: Integrating the Private and Public Spheres," in *The Web of Violence,* eds. Lester Kurtz and Jennifer Turpin (Urbana, IL: University of Illinois Press, 1996).

5. For detailed descriptions of these models and the tension between them throughout history, see Riane Eisler, *The Chalice and The Blade: Our History, Our Future* (San Francisco: Harper & Row, 1987); *Sacred Pleasure: Sex, Myth, and the Politics of the Body* (San Francisco: HarperCollins, 1995); *Tomorrow's Children: A Blueprint for Partnership Education in the 21st Century* (Boulder, CO: Westview Press, 2000); and *The Power of Partnership: Seven Relationships that Will Change Your Life* (Novato, CA: New World Library, 2002).

6. Riane Eisler, David Loye, and Kari Norgaard, *Women, Men, and the Global Quality of Life* (Pacific Grove, CA: Center for Partnership Studies, 1995).

7. Hilkka Pietila, "Nordic Welfare Society—A Strategy to Eradicate Poverty and Build Up Equality: Finland as a Case Study," *Journal Cooperation South* 2, no. 2 (2001): 79–96.

8. See, e.g., United Nations Development Program, U*nited Nations 2000 Human Development Report* (New York: Oxford University Press, 2000).

9. For the World Competitiveness Ratings, see http://www.weforum.org. Search for Global Competitiveness Reports.

10. For more information on Natural Step, see www.naturalstep.org.

11. Peggy Reeves Sanday, *Women at the Center: Life in a Modern Matriarchy* (Ithaca, NY: Cornell University Press, 2002).

12. Stuart A. Schlegel, *Wisdom from a Rain Forest* (Athens, GA: University of Georgia Press, 1998).

13. Riane Eisler, *The Chalice and the Blade;* and *Sacred Pleasure: Sex, Myth, and the Politics of the Body;* see also Jiayin Min, ed., *The Chalice and the Blade in Chinese Culture: Gender Relations and Social Models* (Beijing: China Social Sciences Publishing House, 1995), for an account of prehistoric partnership-oriented cultures in China.

14. *The World's Women 2000: Trends and Statistics*, Statistics Division of the UN Department for Economic and Social Affairs (UN DESA).

15. *U.N. Study on the Status of Women, 2000; U.N. The World's Women 2000: Trends and Statistics.* World Health Organization (WHO).

16. *Ending Violence Against Women: Human Rights in Action, 2003.* World Health Organization (WHO).

17. *World Report on Violence and Health, 2002, WHO.*

18. *Violence Creates Huge Economic Cost for Countries, WHO Report, 2004.*

19. Conventions such as (1) the Convention on the Elimination of All Forms of Discrimination Against Women (CEDAW), adopted by the United Nations General Assembly in 1979, not ratified by the United States, and (2) the Convention on the Rights of the Child, 1990, ratified by all countries except Somalia and the United States.

CHAPTER 5: EDUCATING THE WHOLE CHILD

1. Unpublished results of a pilot study done in collaboration between the Alliance for Childhood and Olga Jarrett of Georgia State University in summer 2003.

2. National Association for the Education of Young Children, "Can You See What I See? Cultivating Self-Expression Through Art," http://www.naeyc.org/ece/1998/04.asp.

3. Statement from the alliance for childhood, May 2005. http://www.alliance-forchildhood.net/news/index.htm.

4. Carl Honoré, *In Praise of Slowness* (San Francisco: HarperCollins, 2004).

5. "Educating a Culture of Peace" excerpted from introduction reprinted by permission from *Educating for a Culture of Peace* edited by Riane Eisler and Ron Miller. Copyright © 2004 by the Center for Partnership Studies and The Foundation

for Educational Renewal. Published by Heinemann, a division of Reed Elsevier, Inc., Portsmouth, NH. All rights reserved. See also D. Oliver, J. Canniff, and J. Korhonen, *The Primal, the Modern, and the Vital Center: A Theory of Balanced Culture in a Living Place* (Brandon, VT: Foundation for Educational Renewal, 2002).

6. R. Miller, *Free Schools, Free People: Education and Democracy after the 1960s* (Albany: State University of New York Press, 2002).

7. This material first appeared in *Resurgence Magazine,* under the title "Landscapes of Learning" and is reprinted by permission.

8. Lester Brown, *Building a Sustainable Society* (New York: Norton, 1981).

CHAPTER 6: TRANSCENDENT SPIRIT

1. I am using the word *Sacred* here, knowing that it has a thousand names and faces.

2. I am using the terms *religion* and *spirituality* throughout in a somewhat interchangeable manner. While popular to say "I am spiritual but not religious," it is inadequate in my view. Religious experiences are kin to spirituality, but they need to be nurtured and sustained by religions in their complex realities. Spirituality is like playing or listening to music whereas religion is like reading the notes and understanding the musical structure. The page of musical notes does not reveal the music, nonetheless it is the structure of the music. The most profound and significant experience is to play or hear the music.

3 For example, see Scott Appleby, *The Ambivalence of the Sacred: Religion, Violence and Reconciliation* (London: Roman and Littlefield, 2000).

4. Alice Miller, *Thou Shalt Not Be Aware: Society's Betrayal of the Child,* trans. Hildegarde and Hunter Hannum (New York: New American Library, 1984).

5. Thich Nhat Hanh, http://www.wisdomquotes.com/001210.html (accessed September 18, 2005).

6. Maria Montessori, *To Educate the Human Potential* (Madras, India: Kalakshetra Publications, 1948), 10.

7. Rachel Carson, http://www.wvhighlands.org/VoiceNov99/Carson quote. htm (accessed September 18, 2005).

8. Thomas Berry, *The Great Work* (New York: Random House, 2000)

9. Donna Schaper, *Raising Interfaith Children: Spiritual Orphans or Spiritual Heirs?* (New York: Crossroads, 1999).

10. Thomas Berry, http://www.ratical.org/many_worlds/mystiqueOfE.html (accessed September 18, 2005).

11. Maria Montessori, "Montessori Wisdom: Quotes from Maria Montessori," http://members.tripod.com/~junojuno2/words.html (accessed September 18, 2005).

12. See Matthew Fox, "Honoring the Child Within—Youth and the Cosmic Christ," in Matthew Fox, *The Coming of the Cosmic Christ* (San Francisco: HarperSan Francisco, 1988), 180–98.

13. Robert Kramer, ed., *A Psychology of Difference: The American Lectures of Otto Rank* (Princeton, NJ: Princeton University Press, 1996), 271f.

14. Suzi Gablik, *Living the Magical Life: An Oracular Adventure* (Grand Rapids, MI: Phanes Press, 2002), 10–13.

15. Sue Woodrow, *Meditations with Mechtild of Magdeburg* (Santa Fe: Bear, 1982), 47.

16. John Dominic Crossan, *The Essential Jesus* (San Francisco: HarperSanFrancisco, 1994), 45.

17. Ibid., 151.

18. Kramer, *A Psychology of Difference,* 208.

19. Alice Miller, *For Your Own Good* (New York: Farrar, Straus, and Giroux, 1984), 58.

CHAPTER 8: THE GREAT TURNING

1. This article includes excerpts used with permission of Berrett-Koehler Publishers from David C. Korten, *The Great Turning: From Empire to Earth Community* scheduled for release in April 2006.

2. A complete text of the Earth Charter can be found at: www.earthcharter. org/files/charter.pdf.

3. Sharna Olfman, "Introduction," in *Childhood Lost: How American Culture Is Failing Our Kids,* ed. Sharna Olfman (Westport, CT: Praeger, 2005), pp. xi–xii.

4. "New American Dream: A Public Opinion Poll" (Washington, DC: Widmeyer Research and Polling of Washington, DC, 2004), http://www.newdream. org/about/PollResults.pdf.

5. Paul H. Ray, "The New Political Compass," April 2002, p. 29, http://www. culturalcreatives.org/Library/docs/NewPoliticalCompassV73.pdf.

6. "New American Dream," http://www.newdream.org/about/PollResults.pdf.

7. http://www.newdream.org/publications/bookrelease.php.

8. http://www.newdream.org/publications/bookrelease.php.

9. http://www.newdream.org/publications/bookrelease.php.

10. Ronald Inglehart, *Modernization and Postmodernization: Cultural, Economic, and Political Change in 43 Societies* (Princeton, NJ: Princeton University Press, 1997).

CHAPTER 9: THE ENVIRONMENTAL LIFE OF CHILDREN

1. S. Steingraber, *Having Faith: An Ecologist's Journey to Motherhood* (New York: Berkley, 2002).

2. Environmental Working Group, *Body Burden: The Pollution in Newborns* (Washington, DC: Environmental Working Group, July 2005), available at http:// www.ewg.org/reports/bodyburden2/.

3. O. Wiig et al., "Female Pseudohermaphrodite Polar Bears at Svalbard," *Journal of Wildlife Diseases* 34 (1998): 792–96.

4. See, for example, The Arctic Climate Impact Assessment, *Impacts of a Warming Arctic* (Cambridge, U.K.: Cambridge University Press, 2004). This report can be ordered or downloaded at http://www.acia.uaf.edu.

5. C. L. Curl et al., "Organophosphate Pesticide Exposures in Urban and Suburban Pre-school Children with Organic and Conventional Diets," *Environmental Health Perspectives* 111 (2003): 377–82.

6. The evolution of my children's food preferences is described in the essay "But I Am a Child Who Does," published online by the Center for Ecoliteracy as part of their "Thinking Outside the Lunchbox" series. See http://www.ecoliteracy.org/publications/rsl/sandra-steingraber.html.

7. Current advisories can be found at the U.S. FDA's Web site. See http://www.cfsan.fda.gov/~dms/admehg3.html.

8. The Mercury Policy Project tracks these debates. See http://mercurypolicy.org.

9. From the CD Raffi Radio, copyright 1995, Homeland Publishing, a division of Troubadour Music Inc.

CHAPTER 11: LILY'S CHICKENS

1. From *Small Wonder: Essays* by Barbara Kingsolver. Copyright © 2002 by Barbara Kingsolver. Reprinted with permission of HarperCollins Publishers.

CHAPTER 12: OUR MOST VULNERABLE

1. U.S. Environmental Protection Agency, Chemicals-in-Commerce Information System. Chemical Update System Database, 1998.

2. U.S. Environmental Protection Agency, *Chemical Hazard Data Availability Study: What Do We Really Know about the Safety of High Production Volume Chemicals?* (Washington, DC: U.S. EPA, Office of Pollution Prevention and Toxics, April 1998).

CHAPTER 13: THE POWER OF EMPATHY

1. T. Brazelton and S. I. Greenspan, *The Irreducible Needs of Children* (New York: Basic Books, 2000), p. 148.

2. T. E. McCullough, *Truth and Ethics in School Reform* (Washington, DC: Council for Educational Development and Research, 1992).

3. For a comprehensive description of the Roots of Empathy curriculum please visit www.rootsofempathy.org.

4. M. Gordon, *Roots of Empathy; Changing the World Child by Child* (Markham, Ontario: Thomas Allen, 2005).

5. Ibid.

CHAPTER 14: WHAT MATTERS MOST

1. All facts and statistics in "Measuring Genuine Progress" by Ronald Colman are from the Genuine Progress Index (GPI) Atlantic reports and articles, and citations contained in those reports and articles. These documents are all available free of charge on the GPI Atlantic Web site at www.gpiatlantic.org.

CHAPTER 16: KIDS AND THE CORPORATION

1. Varda Burstyn and David Fenton, "Toxic World, Troubled Minds," in *No Child Left Different,* ed. Sharna Olfman (Westport, CT: Praeger, 2006).

2. As Burstyn and Fenton, ibid., point out, child and fetal biological systems (nervous, respiratory, reproductive, immune) are underdeveloped and thus unable to defend against toxins, meaning these toxins can cause serious and irreversible harm when transmitted to the fetus through the placenta. Young children are close to the ground, where toxins are concentrated, and have a lot of hand-to-mouth exposure; they have higher metabolic rates than adults, faster multiplying cells , a higher proportionate intake of food and water, and they breathe more rapidly, all of which leads to proportionately higher amounts and absorption of toxins in their bodies.

3. Robert F. Kennedy, Jr., *Crimes Against Nature* (New York: Harper Perennial, 2005), p. 3.

4. Maggie Fox, "Unborn Babies Carry Pollutants, Study Finds," Reuter News Service, July 15, 2005, found at: http://www.planetark.com/dailynewsstory.cfm/newsid/31656/newsDate/15-Jul-2005/story.htm; see also www.ewg.org/reports/bodyburden2 and www.ewg.org/reports/mothersmilk/es.php.

5. Jennifer Armstrong, "Femmes Fatal," *Entertainment Weekly,* August 5, 2005, p. 8.

6. Stephen Eaton Hume, "YA Fiction: How Racy Is Too Racy?" *Vancouver Sun,* September 3, 2005, p. F16.

7. And HMOs, always looking to cut the costs of care, and thus raise profits, are only too happy to replace expensive counseling and psychotherapies with much cheaper drug therapies.

8. See Michael Brody, "Child Psychiatry, Drugs and the Corporation," in Olfman, *Drugging Our Children* (see note 1).

9. Michael Brody, "Child Psychiatry, Drugs and the Corporation" in *No Child Left Different,* Sharna Olfman, ed. (Westport, CT: Praeger, 2006).

10. Quoted in ConsumerAffairs.com, "A Cell Phone for Kids," March 10, 2005, at www.consumeraffairs.com/news04/2005/cell_firefly.html.

11. Roger O. Crockett and Olga Kharif, "Calling Preteens with a Barbie Phone," BusinessWeek online, February 18, 2005, at http://www.businessweek.com/technology/content/feb2005/tc20050218_4609_tc024.htm.

12. Yuki Noguchi, "Connecting with Kids, Wirelessly," Washingtonpost.com, July 7, 2005, at www.washingtonpost.com/wp-dyn/content/article/2005/07/06/AR2005070602100.html.

13. Some companies have addressed this problem by designing phones that have calling and receiving restrictions and lack Internet capacity.

14. Quoted at www.rfsafe.com/article475.html.

15. Crockett and Kharif, "Calling Preteens."

16. Though there may be room for genuine corporate social responsibility in privately owned corporations, where legal obligations to shareholders are either weaker or absent, for publicly traded corporations, social responsibility can be nothing more than a strategy for serving self-interested ends.

17. See Union Carbide: Disaster at Bhopal by Jackson B. Browning, retired vice president, Health Safety, and Environmental Programs, Union Carbide Corporation, 1993. www.bhopal.com/pdfs/browning.pdf.

18. A range of regulatory responses are available—complete bans on products or chemicals, restrictions on their uses or production, labeling requirements—and the right mix must be found to provide maximum protection for children.

CHAPTER 17: HONORING CHILDREN IN DISHONORABLE TIMES

1. D. Roberts et al., *Kids & Media @ the New Millennium* (Menlo Park: The Henry J. Kaiser Family Foundation, 1999), p. 5.

2. C. Marlow, "Verizon Adds Nick Content to Cell Phones," *Hollywood Reporter On Line,* May 6, 2005 (accessed from Factiva, August 17, 2005)

3. See S. Linn, *Consuming Kids: The Hostile Takeover of Childhood* (New York: The New Press, 2004).

4. Contact information for Campaign for a Commercial-Free Childhood: CCFC, Judge Baker Children's Center, 53 Parker Hill Avenue, Boston, MA 02120, 617–278–4172, www.commercialfreechildhood.org.

5. J. Schor, *Born to Buy: The Commercialized Child and the New Consumer Culture* (New York: Scribner, 2004), p. 21.

6. See Linn, Consuming Kids.

7. M. Shields, "Web-based Marketing to Kids on the Rise," *Media Week,* July 25, 2005, http://www.mediaweek.com/mw/news/interactive/article_display.jsp?vnu_content_id=1000990382 (accessed on August 14, 2005).

8. Federal Trade Commission, "Children's Television Programs: Report and Policy Statement," *Federal Register* 39 (1974): 396–409.

9. Nielsen Media Research, cited in *Cynthia Turner's Cynopsis: Kids!* (email newsletter) January 2, 2005–June 2, 2005; D. Foust and B. Grow, "Coke: Wooing the TiVo Generation," *Business Week,* March 1, 2004, p. 77.

10. V. Rideout, E. Vanderwater, and E. Wartella, *Electronic Media in the Lives of Infants, Toddlers and Preschoolers* (Menlo Park, CA: The Henry J. Kaiser Family Foundation, 2003), p. 28.

11. American Academy of Pediatrics, *Joint Statement on the Impact of Entertainment Violence on Children,* presented at the Congressional Public Health Summit, Washington, DC, July 26, 2000.

12. M. J. Sutton et al., "Shaking the Tree of Knowledge for Forbidden Fruit: Where Adolescents Learn about Sexuality and Contraception," in *Sexual Teens: Sexual Media: Investigating Media's Influence on Adolescent Sexuality,* eds. Jane Brown, Jean R. Steele, Kim Walsh-Elders, et al. (Mahway, NJ: Earlbaum, 2002), pp. 25–55.

13. R. L. Collins et al., "Watching Sex on Television Predicts Adolescent Initiation of Sexual Behavior," *Pediatrics* 114, no. 3 (2004): 280–289.

14. Joseph R. Zanga. "Message from the American Academy of Pediatrics: TV & Toddlers," *Healthy Kids,* August/September, 1998: p.3.

15. M. Snider, "Video Games: *Grand Theft Auto: Vice City,*" *USA Today,* December 27, 2002, p. 8D.

16. M. Manuel, "Dreams of Raising Extra-smart Tots Drive Billion-Dollar Baby Video Industry," *Atlanta Journal-Constitution*, April 15, 2005, p. 1G.

17. See S. Linn, *Consuming Kids,* pp. 41–60.

18. D. Carvajal, "A Way to Calm Fussy Baby: 'Sesame Street' by Cellphone," *International Herald-Tribune,* April 18, 2005, p. 10C.

19. F. Raucher, G. Shaw, and K. Ky, "Listening to Mozart Enhances Spatial-Temporal Reasoning: Towards a Neurophysiological Basis," *Neuroscience Letters* 185, no. 1 (1995): 44–47.

20. S. M. Jones and E. Zigler, "The Mozart Effect: Not Learning from History," *Journal of Applied Developmental Psychology* 23, no. 3 (2002): 355–72.

21. See Alliance for Childhood, *Fool's Gold: A Critical Look at Computers in Childhood* (College Park, MD: Alliance for Childhood, 2000).

22. D. Anderson and T. Pempek, "Television and Very Young Children," *American Behavioral Scientist* 48, no. 5 (2005): 505–22.

23. By spiritual, I do not necessarily mean religious, but an appreciation of and sense of wonder at the more ineffable splendors of life.

24. D. Christakis et al., "Early Television Exposure and Subsequent Attentional Problems in Children," *Pediatrics* 113, no. 4 (2004): 708–13.

25. M. Dennison et al., "Television Viewing and Television in Bedroom Associated with Overweight Risk among Low-Income Preschool Children," *Pediatrics* 109 (June 2002): 1028–35.

26. Christakis, "Early Television Exposure."

27. F. Zimmerman and D. Christakis, "Children's Television Viewing and Cognitive Outcomes: A Longitudinal Analysis of National Data," *Archives of Pediatrics & Adolescent Medicine* 159, no. 7 (2005): 619–25.

28. F. Zimmerman et al., "Early Cognitive Stimulation, Emotional Support, and Television Watching as Predictors of Subsequent Bullying among Grade School Children," *Archives of Pediatric and Adolescent Medicine* 159, no. 4 (2005): 384–88.

29. V. Rideout, *Parents, Media, and Public Policy* (Menlo Park: Kaiser Family Foundation, 2004), p. 10.

30. V. Rideout et al., *Electronic Media*, p. 5.

31. Ibid.

32. D. Roberts et al., *Kids & Media*, p. 13.

33. V. Rideout, D. Roberts, and U. Foehr, *Generation M: Media in the Lives of 8–18 Year-olds* (Menlo Park, CA: The Henry F. Kaiser Family Foundation, 2005).

34. S. Hofferth and J. Sandberg, unpublished paper. Hofferth and Sandberg published a study comparing the amount of playtime children spend in general; however, they did not delineate the data in their publication. They did delineate it in the study, however, and sent me their data.

35. J. Wallis, "The Message Thing," *New York Times,* August 4, 2004, p. A19. I first heard the notion of parenting as countercultural in a lecture given by Jim Wallis, editor of *Sojourners magazine*, at a Progressive Spiritual Activist conference in Berkeley in July 2005. The op-ed piece I cite was published a few weeks later.

36. See A. Hochschild, *Bury the Chains: Prophets and Rebels in the Fight to Free an Empire's Slaves* (Boston: Houghton-Mifflin, 2005).

37. Scholastic.com, Teacher Store, *Clifford's Kit for Personal and Social Development.* Available at: http://click.scholastic.com/techerstore/catalog/product.jhtml?sku id=sku3932910&catid=&catType (accessed September 6, 2003).

38. J. Golin, "Tickle U Is No Laughing Matter," *Mothering* (August 2005), available at http://www.mothering.com/guest_editors/kids_commercialism/kids_commercialism.html.

39. B. Briggs, "Wallace Hints at Ban on Junk Food Adverts as the Best Way to Fight Obesity Among Young," *The Herald,* February 1, 2003, p. A1.

40. N. Rivard and P. LeBlanc, "Advertising to Kids in Quebec No Picnic," *Strategy,* May 8, 2000, p. B10.

41. D. Rowan, "Hard Sell, Soft Targets," *London Times*, October 18, 2002, pp. 2, 6.

42. Ibid.

43. M. Metherwell, "EU Commission Targets Unfair Businesses Practices," *The Sydney Morning Herald*, June 19, 2003, p. 3.

44. C. Hawkes, *Marketing Food to Children: The Global Regulatory Environment* (Geneva: World Health Organization, 2003).

45. P. Taylor, "Liberty, Equality, Fraternity . . . Obesity?" *Globe and Mail,* August 6, 2004, p. A11.

46. "BBC to Limit Ties to Junk Food," *Wall Street Journal,* April 6, 2004, p. D5.

CHAPTER 18: A WORLD FIT FOR CHILDREN

I would like to acknowledge and to thank David Fenton, who has done such a wonderful job of assisting and carefully checking the research for this article.

1. The U.K. campaign was led by British chef Jamie Oliver, who launched a television series and led a huge campaign with many parents, educators, and politicians. This announcement occasioned a tremendous hue and cry from its opponents—candy and junk food manufacturers who lost a huge, captive market. C. Alphonso, "Jamie Oliver Forces British Schools to Ban Junk Food," *Globe and Mail,* September 29, 2005, p. A-1.

2. J. H. Newman, "Back-to-Greener-Schools," Environmental News Network, September 1, 2005, http://www.enn.com/today.html?=8672.

3. In California, the Los Angeles Unified School District initiated a policy called Integrated Pest Management (IPM), to use low-risk methods to eliminate pests and weeds. The policy was the first in the United States to embrace the Precautionary Principle and parents' right to know about products used in or around school sites. The success of the policy—a policy that has become the model for many school districts and communities throughout the nation—led to the California Healthy Schools Act 2000. See also the Web site for the coalition group California Safe Schools (April 12, 2005), "Children's Advocates Celebrate Six Years of Protecting Student Health: Reformed Pesticide Policy Sets National Model," http://www.calisafe.org.

4. Newman, "Back-to-Greener-Schools."

5. As a starting point for further research, see: H. Needleman and P. Landrigan, *Raising Children Toxic Free: How to Keep Your Child Safe from Lead, Asbestos, Pesticides and Other Environmental Hazards* (New York: Farrar, Straus and Giroux, 1995); T. Colborn, D. Dumanoski, and J. Peterson Myers, *Our Stolen Future* (New York: Penguin,1997); Greater Boston Physicians for Social Responsibility, *In Harm's Way: Toxic Threats to Child Development* (Cambridge, MA: Greater Boston Physicians for Social Responsibility, 2000), available at http://www.igc.org/psr; H. Hu, "Human Health and Heavy Metals Exposure," in *Life Support: The Environment and Human Health,* ed. Michael McCally (Cambridge, MA: MIT Press, 2002); and V. Burstyn and D. Fenton, "Toxic World/Troubled Minds," in *No Child Left Different,* ed. Sharna Olfman (Westport, CT: Praeger, 2005).

6. A consensus is emerging: "Climate Change More Rapid than Ever," The Max Planck Society for the Advancement of Science (Munich: Max Planck Society, September 30, 2005), available at http://www.mpg.de/english/illustrationsDocumentation/documentation/pressReleases/2005/pressRelease200509301/. See also "Climate Model Predicts Extreme Changes for US, " *Scientific American,* October 12, 2005; and "No Escape: Thaw Gains Momentum," *New York Times,* October 25, 2005; and many, many more recent articles and studies in and from every continent.

7. Best example: the Millennium Ecosystem Assessment. As reported in *New Scientist,* April 28, 2005, p. 811 (and widely reported elsewhere), in April 2005 this report, the first-ever global inventory of natural resources, was published. It cost

$24 million and took more than 1,300 scientists in 95 countries four years to complete. The report is backed by the United Nations, the World Bank, and the World Resources Institute. The assessment reached the overwhelming conclusion that we are living well beyond our environmental means. Approximately 60 percent of the planet's natural products and processes that support life, such as water purification, are being degraded or used unsustainably. The *New Scientist* editorial "Save the Humans" in the same issue (p. 5) concluded: "The most compelling reason for acting on the MA stems from one of its chief conclusions: there is a clear link between healthy ecosystems and healthy humans. Destroy those ecosystems and our economies—and our quality of life—will suffer."

8. The term *eco-citizens* appears in the work of Louise Vandelac, Université du Québec à Montréal, on eco-citizenship—still to come.

9. Schools and public health authorities are natural partners. In November 2004, for example, Dr. Sheila Basra, the Chief Medical Officer of Ontario, presented a report to the Ontario legislature that recommended banning fast and processed foods in schools, including vegetables and fruit with every meal served, and implementing portion control, along with a variety of other measures in a public war on childhood obesity. Dr. Basra has recognized that the health of school children is a public health issue par excellence.

10. Many examples are available but two will tell the tale: The packaging law Germany passed in 1991 that cut waste hugely and became a model for more than 10 other countries, one of the most enlightened and exemplary of initiatives that governments can take, was overturned in the European courts in December, 2004, because a group of British beer companies went after it as an "unfair barrier to trade": "German Drinks Packaging Deposit Draws Legal Challenge," Environmental News Service, October 21, 2003, http://www.ens-newswire.com/ens/oct2003/2003102103.asp; EurActiv.com, "Germany Drinks Packaging Deposit System Ruled Illegal," December 15, 2004, available at http://www.euractiv.com/Article?tcmuri=tcm:29-133439-16&type=News.

In several countries in Southeast Asia environmentalists have failed in their attempt to stop the destruction of mangrove groves by commercial shrimp farming because their attempts were characterized as "barriers to trade." When last winter's tsunami went through, and when Hurricane Katrina hit the coast of the Gulf of Mexico, damage was far worse because of the loss of these groves. For information on some of these cases, see, "Thailand Shrimp Farming," Case number 2263, The Trade & Environmental Database (Washington, DC: American University), http://www.american.edu/projects/ mandala/TED/thaishmp.htm); T.D.T. Lam, "Vietnam's Shrimp Industry Feeling the Heat" (Hong Kong: Asia *Times,* April 12, 2005), http://www.atimes.com/atimes/Southeast_Asia/GD12Ae01.html.

11. In 2004, a year in which both the Bush administration and Wall Street claimed that the economy boomed, economist Paul Krugman noted that the median real income of full-time year-round male workers fell more than 2 percent (P. Krug-

man, "The Big Squeeze," *New York Times,* October 17, 2005). Describing the United States, the CIA Factbook says: "Since 1975, practically all the gains in household income have gone to the top 20 percent of households" (H. Sklar, "Growing Gulf Between Rich and Rest of US," Knight Ridder/Tribune Information Services, October 3, 2005, http://www.commondreams.org/views05/100321.htm). See also S. Danziger, D. Reed, and T. Brown, "Poverty and Prosperity," Programme Paper Number 3, United Nations Research Institute for Social Development (New York: United Nations, April 23, 2002 and May 2004).

12. "Concern Voiced in Second Committee over Widening Economic Disparities" (New York: United Nations, GA/EF/2956, October 3, 2001); "Poverty to Rise Unless Economies Factor 'Nature's Capital' into National Accounts" (London: The London School of Economics and Political Science, October 10, 2005); P. Grier, (June 14, 2005)

13. D. Hemlock, "Caribbean Farmers Find Growing, Marketing Organic Crops a Tough Row to Hoe," *South Florida Sun-Sentine,* May 19, 2005. See also http://www.enn.com/biz.html?id=611.

14. S. Lang, "Organic Farms Produce Same Yields As Conventional Farms," Cornell University, Ithaca, NY, July 14, 2005, available at http://www.news.cornell.edu/stories/July05/organic.farm.vs.other.ssl.html.

15. My own inspiration for a title for the comprehensive multifaceted transitional strategy we need today comes from President Roosevelt's New Deal. But many environmental thinkers have come up with similar ideas, at least in part, going back quite a while, because it's increasingly obvious that we cannot continue simply doing business as usual and expect to move forward without changing the role of government in fundamental and assertive ways. By the same token, it's clear that we cannot solve our environmental problems unless we find effective solutions to our economic ones. A wealth of literature now exists expressing these insights. Here are some useful examples of different, but converging approaches: Michael Shallenberger and Ted Nordhaus, "The Death of Environmentalism," October 2004 (monograph available at www.grist.org/news/maindish/2005/01/13/doe-reprint). Al Gore, *Earth in the Balance,* first published in 1992, suggested a "Global Marshall Plan" to help green the world (rev. ed., New York: Houghton Mifflin, 2000, pp. 297–301). Gore was inspired by the original plan that saw the United States send billions of dollars Europe to rebuild its economies after World War II. Subsequent to what I thought was my origination of the term Green Deal, our web search on the term revealed that the American environmental author Mark Hertsgaard had used the phrase "Global Green Deal" in the last two chapters of his book: *Earth Odyssey: Around the World in Search of Our Environmental Future* (New York: Broadway, 1999), and in some articles after its publication. Hertsgaard, also inspired by Roosevelt's approach, said that the idea is "to renovate human civilization from top to bottom in environmentally sustainable ways." Thomas Friedman has started calling for a new New Deal, or a "geo-green strategy," to pull the American economy and American workforce out

of the deep hole into which they are plunging. (See T. L. Friedman, "Keeping Us in the Race," *New York Times,* October 14, 2005; and T. L. Friedman, "Geo-Greening by Example," *New York Times,* March 27, 2005.) A very integrated vision can be found in Vancouver-based environmental writer and consultant Roy Woodbridge's *The Next World War: Tribes, Cities, Nations and Ecological Decline* (Toronto: University of Toronto Press, 2004). Woodbridge presents a highly developed plan, a "Green Deal" in effect, for what he calls "the provisioning of societies" that depends on major government and intergovernmental mobilization of citizens, capital, industry, agriculture, education, NGOs—all our key sectors—at a level of intensity and coordination we have so far devoted only to making war.

16. Yes, remarkable benign technologies and industrial processes already exist that may be deployed in the immediate, the medium, and in some cases, also the long term. For many, see P. Hawken, A. Lovins, and H. Lovins, *Natural Capitalism* (New York: Little, Brown, 1999).

17. D. Reay, "Your Planet Needs You," *New Scientist,* September 10, 2005, p. 39. For Navdanya, see http://www.navdanya.org/ about/index.htm.

18. Roy Woodbridge (*The Next World War, see* n. 15) provides good summaries of these important ideas for polities rooted in environmentally based entities—the natural environment of specific geographical regions, the constructed environment of cities.

19. A trillion dollars or more every year is spent on war-related expenditures. The current Iraq War has already cost the United States more than $600 billion. Clearly, the military budgets of major powers should be diverted to saving children and doing biospherical good. But even the military budgets of small countries can be transformed into pools for green growth: Costa Rica decided in 1948 that they would dispense with a military sector and use the freed funds for prosocial purposes—and this now includes organic farming and Green University initiatives.

20. James Tobin, a Ph.D. Nobel-laureate economist at Yale University, has proposed an excise tax on cross-border currency transactions that can be enacted by national legislatures, and followed by multilateral cooperation for effective enforcement. Speculators trade over $1.8 trillion *each day* across borders. The proposal is that each trade would be taxed at 0.1 to 0.25 percent of volume (about 10 to 25 cents per hundred dollars). This miniscule percentage would generate $100–300 billion of revenue at current rates of trade. The revenue is intended to go to global priorities: basic environmental and human needs, helping to tame currency market volatility, and restoring national economic sovereignty. (For more information see http://www. ceedweb.org/iirp/.)

21. Last December the U.S. Supreme Court decided against Aviall, a company that used a longstanding clause in the Superfund legislation to collect monies from another company that had previously polluted the property bought by Aviall. In effect, the court said that the real polluter didn't have to pay. This is just one telling and important example of so many decisions in which many levels of judiciary

systems have gone in the wrong direction. If the courts are to be the final arbiters of behavior that affects the environment, they too will have to be greened.

CHAPTER 19: TOMORROW'S CHILD

1. Paul Hawken, *The Ecology of Commerce: A Declaration of Sustainability* (HarperBusiness, 1994).
2. Ibid.
3. Ibid.
4. Ray Anderson, *Mid-Course Correction: Toward a Sustainable Enterprise: The Interface Model* (The Peregrinzilla Press, 1998).
5. Janine M. Benyus, *Biomimicry, Innovation Inspired by Nature* (William Morrow Company, Inc., 1997).
6. Abraham Maslow, *Motivation and Personality* (Addison-Wesley Publishing, 1997).
7. Aldo Leopold, *A Sand County Almanac* (Oxford University Press, 1949).
8. Ibid.
9. R. Carson, *Silent Spring* (Houghton Mifflin, 1993).
10. Mathis Wackernagel, *The Ecological Footprint* (Global Footprint Netowrk, Sponsored by World Wildlife Fund).
11. Personal conversation with Paul Hawken, November 1995.

ONWARD! MAKING A VOW: LIVING THE COVENANT

1. In 2000, Mandela, Graça Machel, and UNICEF launched the *Say Yes for Children* campaign.
2. Bionomy, meaning the stewardship of the biosphere.
3. Never thus intended, according to Simon Kuznets, and (later) Robert F. Kennedy.
4. "I wish that everyone could be exactly who they really are." From the song "Whatever You Choose," lyrics by Bailey Rattray, music by Raffi, on the *Raffi Radio* compact disc, © 1995 Homeland Publishing.
5. David Loye's book *Darwin's Lost Theory of Love* (1998) reveals that survival of the fittest was a minor theme; that Darwin's main idea was what he called "the moral agency of man," humans as biologically social, relational, and loving creatures—also the view of biologist Umberto Maturana of Chile.
6. Full lyrics available at raffinews.com.
7. All books of New Society Publishers are on chlorine-free paper, as are all of Troubadour's books, and the paper used by Rounder Music (and Universal Music in Canada) for our music packaging. The Atkinson Charitable Foundation (Toronto) has made the switch. Praeger Press agreed to print this book on chlorine-free paper. Doing so reduces the dioxin output produced by chlorine bleaching of pulp. This is

one tangible way we can detox mothers' milk. Going chlorine-free is a litmus test of understanding the link between purchasing choices and public health.

8. "Turn This World Around," words and music by Raffi, Michael Creber, © 2001 Homeland Publishing.

9. http://www.digitaltao.ca/testarea/latwww2/index.html.

10. Ryan Hreljac (Ryan's Well), Roots & Shoots: international organization founded by Jane Goodall.

11. MVP: Most valuable and vulnerable players, needing priority protection.

About the Editors and Contributors

RAFFI CAVOUKIAN is the founder of Child Honoring, a children-first paradigm for global restoration. He is a renaissance man known to millions simply as Raffi, a singer/songwriter, record producer, systems thinker, author, entrepreneur, and ecology advocate, internationally renowned as "the most popular children's entertainer in the western world" (*Washington Post*). President of Troubadour Music, among the most successful independent record labels, Raffi was a pioneer in music for children and families: his CDs, tapes, videos, and DVDs have sold some 14 million copies and his books have sold more than 3 million copies in Canada and the United States. A generation saw him in concert and grew up singing "Down by the Bay" and Raffi's signature song "Baby Beluga." "Beluga grads" often tell him they're now raising their own kids with his songs.

A recipient of the Order of Canada and the United Nations' Earth Achievement Award, Raffi Cavoukian has recently been awarded two honorary degrees: Doctor of Music, from the University of Victoria, and Doctor of Letters, from the University of British Columbia. He is associated with many nongovernment organizations, including the Council of Human Development, the Darwin Project Council, the Center for Partnership Studies, the Center for Children's Health and the Environment, and the Canadian Institute for Advanced Research.

Raffi's work now is that of a global troubadour, lecturing and networking to help create a viable future: a restorative, child-friendly world on behalf of those who will inherit it. His *Covenant for Honoring Children* is widely circulated among child development and environmental health circles (available for download at Raffinews.com). Here's a brief sample of Raffi's recent advocacy:

- He has written and performed a number of songs for parents, educators, and decision makers. His November 2001 keynote address (in both word and song) before seven thousand teachers at the National Association for the Education of Young Children conference in Anaheim was a resounding success.
- In 2002 in New York, he sang *Turn This World Around,* his musical tribute to former South African president Nelson Mandela, who, at the launch of his campaign *Say Yes for Children* (with Graça Machel and UNICEF) said, "We must turn this world around—for the children."
- In October 2003, he wrote and recorded *Where We All Belong,* in support of the Earth Charter, a declaration of interdependence that was born at the 1992 Earth Summit in Rio.
- Twice he traveled to Dharamsala, India, where he sang at the Tibetan Children's Village and met with the Dalai Lama. During the Dalai Lama's visit to Vancouver in the spring of 2004, Raffi performed "Song for the Dalai Lama," his original composition based on a Tibetan sutra, accompanied by a 90-voice children's choir and the Vancouver Symphony Orchestra.
- In 2005 Raffi presented Child Honoring in word and song in Toronto's IdeaCity conference, at Boston's Berklee College of Music, at the Rethinking Development conference in Antigonish Nova Scotia, and at Pittsburgh's Point Park University.

SHARNA OLFMAN is a professor of clinical and developmental psychology at Point Park University, the founding director of the Childhood and Society Symposium and the editor of the Childhood in America book series for Praeger Press. Her books include *No Child Left Different* (2006), *Childhood Lost* (2005), and *All Work and No Play: How Educational Reforms Are Harming Our Preschoolers* (2003). Dr. Olfman is a member of the Council of Human Development, and a partner in the Alliance for Childhood. She has written and presented widely on the subjects of gender development, women's mental health, infant care, and child psychopathology.

JOAN ALMON is coordinator of the U.S. Alliance for Childhood, a partnership of educators, health professionals, and others committed to preserving childhood as a special stage of life. An internationally known consultant on early-childhood education, she was formerly a Waldorf early childhood educator, and she currently serves as co-general secretary of the Anthroposophical Society in America.

RAY ANDERSON commands the world's largest producer of commercial floor coverings, Interface Inc. Named one of America's 100 Best Companies to Work For in 1997 and 1998 by *Fortune* magazine, Interface has diversified and globalized its businesses, with sales in 110 countries and manufacturing facilities on four continents. In recent years, Ray has embarked on a mission to make Interface a sustainable corporation by leading a worldwide effort to pioneer the processes of sustainable development. Ray received the inaugural Millennium Award from Global Green, presented by Mikhail Gorbachev in 1996, and was named cochairman of the President's Council on Sustainable Development in 1997. He was also recognized in 1996 as the Ernst & Young Entrepreneur of the Year for the Southeast Region, and as the Georgia Conservancy's Conservationist of the Year in 1997.

In January 2001, the National Academy of Sciences selected Ray to receive the prestigious George and Cynthia Mitchell International Prize for Sustainable Development, the first corporate CEO to be so honored. In September of that year, the SAM-SPG Award Jury presented the Sustainability Leadership Award 2001 to him in Zurich, Switzerland. The U.S. Green Building Council honored Ray with their inaugural green business Leadership Award for the private sector in November, 2002. His book, *Mid-Course Correction* (Chelsea Green, 1998) describes his own and Interface's transformation to environmental responsibility.

MARK ANIELSKI is president of Anielski Management Inc., which specializes in measuring the well-being of communities and organizations. Mark teaches corporate social responsibility and social entrepreneurship at the University of Alberta in the School of Business and sustainability economics at the new Bainbridge Graduate Institute near Seattle. For 14 years he served as senior economic policy advisor to the Alberta Government, and developed Alberta's internationally recognized performance measurement system (Measuring Up). This model has been widely adopted across Canada and internationally. He is a pioneer of alternative measures of economic progress, including the U.S. Genuine Progress Indicator (GPI), the Alberta GPI Sustainable Well-Being measurement system, and other quality-of-life indicators. Mark has developed a new Genuine Wealth accounting model for measuring and managing the sustainable well-being of nations, communities, and businesses. He is currently advising the Chinese government on how to green their GDP by incorporating natural capital depreciation costs into their national income accounting system. Mark is the president of the Canadian Society for Ecological Economics and a Senior Fellow with the Oakland-based economic think-tank Redefining Progress.

LLOYD AXWORTHY is president and vice chancellor of the University of Winnipeg. He recently published *Navigating a New World—Canada's Global Future* (Knopf Canada, 2003), and in February 2004, U.N. Secretary General Kofi Annan appointed him as his special envoy for Ethiopia-Eritrea to assist in implementing a peace agreement between the East African countries. He lectures widely in Canada, the United States, and abroad. From 1995 to 2000, Mr. Axworthy was director and chief executive officer of the Liu Institute for Global Issues at the University of British Columbia, and Canada's Foreign Minister.

Lloyd Axworthy's political career spanned 27 years. He served for six years in the Manitoba Legislative Assembly and for 21 years in the Federal Parliament. He held several Cabinet positions, notably Minister of Employment and Immigration, Minister Responsible for the Status of Women, Minister of Transport, Minister of Human Resources Development, Minister of Western Economic Diversification, and Minister of Foreign Affairs. In the Foreign Affairs portfolio, Dr. Axworthy became internationally known for his advancement of the human security concept, in particular, the Ottawa Treaty—a landmark global treaty banning antipersonnel land mines. For his leadership on land mines, he was nominated for the Nobel Peace Prize. For his efforts in establishing the International Criminal Court and the protocol on child soldiers, he received the North-South Institute's Peace Award.

Since leaving public life in the fall of 2000, Dr. Axworthy has been the recipient of several prestigious awards and honors. The Vietnam Veterans of America Foundation presented him with the Senator Patrick J. Leahy Award in recognition of his leadership in the global effort to outlaw land mines and the use of children as soldiers and to bring war criminals to justice. Princeton University awarded him the Madison Medal for his record of outstanding public service, and he received the CARE International Humanitarian Award. He was elected Honorary Fellow of the American Academy of Arts and Sciences. He has been named to the Order of Manitoba and to the Order of Canada. He has received honorary doctorates from Queen's University, Lakehead University, University of Victoria, University of Denver, Niagara University, the University of Winnipeg, Dalhousie University, University of Manitoba, and McMaster University. Dr. Axworthy is a board member of the MacArthur Foundation, Human Rights Watch—where he chairs the Advisory Board for Americas Watch, Lester B. Pearson College, University of the Arctic, the Pacific Council on International Policy, and is on the Port of Churchill Advisory Board as well as on the Advisory Board of the Ethical Globalization Initiative.

JOEL BAKAN is professor of law at the University of British Columbia, and an internationally recognized legal scholar. A former Rhodes Scholar and law clerk to Chief Justice Brian Dickson of the Supreme Court of Canada, he has law degrees from Oxford, Dalhousie, and Harvard. His work examines the social, economic, and political dimensions of law, and he has published in leading legal and social science journals as well as in the popular press. His most recent book, *The Corporation: The Pathological Pursuit of Profit and Power*, was published in March 2004 by Penguin Canada and, in the United States, by Simon and Schuster. It has been translated into numerous languages and is the basis of the documentary film *The Corporation*, which he cocreated with Mark Achbar, and on which he is associate producer, and writer. His previous book, *Just Words: Constitutional Rights and Social Wrongs*, was published in 1997 by the University of Toronto Press. Bakan has won numerous awards for his scholarship and teaching, worked on landmark legal cases and government policy, and served frequently as a media commentator. He lives in Vancouver, Canada with his wife Rebecca Jenkins and their two children, Myim and Sadie.

VARDA BURSTYN is an award-winning author whose prescient work about the politics of science, ecology, technology, genetic engineering, reproductive technologies, democracy, public administration, and the politics of health policy and health care system reform has appeared in many popular media (magazines, film, television, and radio) and in scholarly venues. Since 1983, when she wrote and presented a two-part series, "New Ideas in Sickness and Health," for CBC Radio's award-winning documentary program *Ideas*, the intertwined themes of the environment (biospherical, social, economic) and health have formed a central strand of her work. Between 1990 and 1995 she spent most of her time as a major policy speechwriter for Ontario ministers of health and as a public health policy consultant to numerous organizations. Since the early 1990s, she has written about new reproductive and genetic technologies for national magazines (including *Saturday Night* and *Reader's Digest*) as well as for film and radio. *The Rites of Men* (University of Toronto Press, 1999*)*, her book on the politics of sport culture, won the Book of the Year Award of the North American Society for the Sociology of Sport. Her first work of fiction, *Water Inc.*, (London: Verso, 2005) an environmental thriller based in fact, has been translated into French (*H20 Inc.*), Korean, and German.

FRITJOF CAPRA, physicist and systems theorist, is a founding director of the Center for Ecoliteracy in Berkeley, California, which is dedicated to promoting ecology and systems thinking in primary and secondary education. He is on the faculty of Schumacher College, an international center for ecological studies in the United Kingdom. Dr. Capra is the author of several international bestsellers, including *The Tao of Physics, The Web of Life,* and most recently *The Hidden Connections: A Science for Sustainable Living.*

RONALD COLMAN is founder and executive director of GPI Atlantic, a nonprofit research group that is constructing an index of well-being and sustainable development for Nova Scotia. He is currently chairing a National Working Group of leading indicator practitioners to develop a new Canadian Index of Well-Being. Dr. Colman previously taught for 20 years at the university level and was a researcher and speechwriter at the United Nations. He has researched and written many reports on indicators of population health, social well-being, natural resource health, and environmental quality for the Genuine Progress Index.

Dr. Colman advises governments and communities on indicator work, and regularly presents this work to government, university, and community groups in Canada and abroad. In cooperation with three Nova Scotia communities, Dr. Colman and GPI Atlantic are also developing measures of well-being and sustainable development at the community level. He sat on the sustainable development indicators steering committee of the National Round Table on the Environment and the Economy, and is editor of a national magazine—*Reality Check: The Canadian Review of Wellbeing.* He is also the Research Director for the Canadian Index of Well-Being.

HEATHER EATON is Professor of Theology at Saint Paul University in Ottawa, author of *Introducing Ecofeminist Theologies,* and coeditor of *Ecofeminism and Globalization: Exploring Religion, Culture and Context* (with Lois Lorentzen). Professor Eaton is the founder of the *Canadian Forum on Religion and Ecology.*

RIANE EISLER is best known for her international bestsellers *The Chalice and The Blade: Our History, Our Future* and *Sacred Pleasure: Sex, Myth, and*

The Politics of The Body. Her other books include the award-winning *Tomorrow's Children: A Blueprint for Partnership Education in the 21st Century* and *The Power of Partnership,* a practical guide to personal, cultural, and spiritual transformation. Dr. Eisler is renowned for her pioneering work in human rights, integrating the rights of women and children into mainstream theory and practice. She is a pioneer in peace studies and a new economics of partnership. She is cofounder of the Spiritual Alliance to Stop Intimate Violence (SAIV—www.saiv.net), as a critical step toward peace and development, of the Institute for a Caring Economy (ICE) at Case Western Reserve University, dedicated to revisioning the economic ground rules, and president of the Center for Partnership Studies, dedicated to research and education (www.partnershipway.org).

MATTHEW FOX, a postmodern theologian, has been an ordained priest since 1967. He holds master's degrees in philosophy and theology from Aquinas Institute and a doctorate in spirituality, summa cum laude, from the Institut Catholique de Paris. Fox is founder and president emeritus of Wisdom University (formerly known as the University of Creation Spirituality) and codirector of the Naropa Oakland MLA in Oakland, California. He is author of 26 books, including the best-selling *Original Blessing; Creativity: Where the Divine and the Human Meet; One River, Many Wells; A Spirituality Named Compassion; Passion for Creation: The Earth-Honoring Spirituality of Meister Eckhart; The Reinvention of Work; Sins of the Spirit, Blessings of the Flesh;* and *Natural Grace* (with Rupert Sheldrake). His most recent books are *Creativity: Where the Divine and the Human Meet* (Jeremy Tarcher, Inc.) and *A New Reformation!* (Friends of Creation Spirituality).

Fox received the 1994 New York Open Center Tenth Anniversary Award for Achievement in Creative Spirituality. In 1995 he was presented the Courage of Conscience Award by the Peace Abbey of Sherborn, Massachusetts. Other recipients of this award include the Dalai Lama, Mother Theresa, Ernesto Cardenal, and Rosa Parks. In 1996 he received the Tikkun National Ethics Award in recognition of contributions made to the spiritual life of our society. Fox has twice received the Body Mind Spirit Award of Excellence for outstanding books in print. In May 2000 he was awarded an Honorary Doctor of Letters degree from The University College of Cape Breton, Sidney, Nova Scotia, Canada.

MARY GORDON, a member of the Order of Canada, is the founder of Roots of Empathy, a not-for-profit classroom program that raises emotional competence and empathy, and the author of *Roots of Empathy: Changing the World Child by Child* (2005). Recognized nationally and internationally as a child advocate and parenting expert, she is the recipient of several prestigious awards recognizing her contribution to innovation in education and international social entrepreneurism. Ms. Gordon has given numerous keynote addresses for groups that include the World Health Organization (WHO), the British Medical Association, and The Nelson Mandela Children's Foundation.

STANLEY I. GREENSPAN is Clinical Professor of Psychiatry and Pediatrics at George Washington University Medical School and Chairman of the Interdisciplinary Council on Developmental and Learning Disorders. The world's foremost authority on clinical work with infants and young children, he is founding president of Zero to Three: The National Center for Infants, Toddlers and Families. Dr. Greenspan, whose work guides the care of infants and children with developmental and emotional problems throughout the world, is the author of 37 influential books translated into over a dozen languages, including *The Growth of the Mind* and *Building Healthy Minds,* and *The First Idea* (with Stuart Shanker). He and Stuart Shanker cofounded the Council of Human Development.

BARBARA KINGSOLVER grew up in Kentucky and was trained as a biologist before becoming a full-time writer. Her books include collected poetry, novels, short fiction, and essay collections. *The Poisonwood Bible* was a finalist for the Pulitzer Prize in 1999, and voted the Book of the Year by American Booksellers. Kingsolver was the recipient of the National Humanities Medal in 2000. Her latest books are *Small Wonder,* a collection of essays, and *Last Stand: America's Virgin Lands,* prose poetry set alongside the photographs of Annie Griffiths Belt. Barbara contributes book reviews and articles on culture and politics to a variety of national publications; with her husband, Steven Hopp, she also cowrites articles on natural history. Kingsolver's books have been translated and published throughout the world in more than 20 languages. She lives with her husband and two daughters on a farm in southern Appalachia.

DAVID C. KORTEN is the author of the international best-seller *When Corporations Rule the World,* and *The Post-Corporate World: Life after Capitalism.* Korten is cofounder and board chair of the Positive Futures Network, which publishes *YES! A Journal of Positive Futures;* founder and president of the People-Centered Development Forum; a founding associate of the International Forum on Globalization and a major contributor to its report, *Alternatives to Economic Globalization;* a board member of the Business Alliance for Local Living Economies (BALLE); board member of the Bainbridge Graduate Institute; and a member of the Social Ventures Network and the Club of Rome.

He holds MBA and PhD degrees from the Stanford Business School, has 30 years of experience as a development professional in Asia, Africa, and Latin America, and has served as a Harvard Business School professor, a captain in the U.S. Air Force, a Ford Foundation Project Specialist, and a regional adviser to the U.S. Agency for International Development.

PHILIP J. LANDRIGAN is a pediatrician and the Ethel H. Wise Professor and Chair of the Department of Community and Preventive Medicine of the Mount Sinai School of Medicine in New York City. Dr. Landrigan obtained his medical degree from Harvard in 1967. From 1970 to 1985, Dr. Landrigan served in the United States Public Health Service as an Epidemic Intelligence Service Officer and medical epidemiologist with the Centers for Disease Control. He has been at the Mount Sinai School of Medicine since 1985.

Dr. Landrigan is a member of the Institute of Medicine of the National Academy of Sciences. He has chaired committees at the National Academy of Sciences on Environmental Neurotoxicology and on Pesticides in the Diets of Infants and Children. The report on pesticides and children's health was instrumental in securing passage of the Food Quality Protection Act of 1996, the major federal pesticide law in the United States. From 1995 to 1997, Dr. Landrigan served on the Presidential Advisory Committee on Gulf War Veteran's Illnesses. In 1997 and 1998, Dr. Landrigan served as Senior Advisor on Children's Health to the Administrator of the U.S. Environmental Protection Agency and was instrumental in helping to establish a new Office of Children's Health Protection at EPA.

PENELOPE LEACH is a psychologist, and a Fellow of the British Psychological Society. Her acclaimed book *Your Baby and Child* has sold over 3 million copies in 29 countries. Her more recent book *Children First* (A. A. Knopf, 1994) pleads for political and economic changes to bring what is offered to young families into line with what is known of the needs of both children and parents.

SUSAN LINN is a psychologist, the associate director of the Media Center of the Judge Baker Children's Center, and an instructor in psychiatry at Harvard Medical School. She has written extensively about the effects of media and commercial marketing on children and is heard as a commentator on NPR's *Marketplace.* Her book, *Consuming Kids,* was praised in publications as diverse as the *Wall Street Journal* and *Mother Jones.* She is cofounder of the national advocacy coalition, Campaign for a Commercial-Free Childhood. An award-winning ventriloquist and children's entertainer, Dr. Linn is internationally known for her innovative work using puppets in child psychotherapy. Combining her skills as a writer and performer with her role as a child therapist, Dr. Linn has written and appeared in a number of video programs designed as educational and clinical tools, including *Different and the Same: Helping Children Identify and Prevent Prejudice,* which she produced with Family Communications, Inc., the producers of *Mister Rogers' Neighborhood.*

GRAÇA MACHEL is a renowned international advocate for women and children's rights and has been a social and political activist over many decades. As Minister of Education and Culture in Mozambique (1975–1989) she was responsible for overseeing an increase in primary school enrollment from 40 percent of children in 1975 to over 90 percent of boys and 75 percent of girls by 1989. Graça Machel is President of the Foundation for Community Development, a nonprofit organization she founded in 1994. FDC makes grants to civil society organizations to strengthen communities, facilitate social and economic justice, and assist in the reconstruction and development of postwar Mozambique.

In 1994, the Secretary-General of the United Nations appointed her as an independent expert to carry out an assessment of the impact of armed conflict on children. Her groundbreaking report was presented in 1996 and established a new and innovative agenda for the comprehensive protection of children caught up in war, changing the policy and practice of governments, U.N. agencies, and international and national civil society.

Amongst her many current commitments, she is chair of the Global Alliance for Vaccines and Immunization Fund, chancellor of the University of Cape Town, South Africa, and panel member of the African Peer Review Mechanism. Over the years, Mrs. Machel has gained international recognition for her achievements. Her many awards include the Laureate of Africa Prize for Leadership for the Sustainable End of Hunger from the Hunger Project in 1992 and the Nansen Medal in recognition of her contribution to the welfare of refugee children in 1995. She has received the Inter Press Service's (IPS) International Achievement Award for her work on behalf of children internationally, the Africare Distinguished Humanitarian Service Award, and the North-South Prize of the Council of Europe, amongst others. Graca Machel has served on the boards of numerous international organizations, including the UN Foundation, the Forum of African Women Educationalists, the African Leadership Forum, and the International Crisis Group. Graça Machel's first husband, Samora Machel, inaugural president of Mozambique, was killed in a plane crash in 1986. She wed former South African President Nelson Mandela in 1998.

RON MILLER has worked in the emerging field of holistic education for 25 years, first as a Montessori teacher, and later, after completing doctoral studies on the cultural history of American education, as an activist scholar and publisher. He has written or edited eight books, founded two journals and an independent progressive school, and organized various conferences, networks, and other efforts to build a more coherent alternative education movement. He teaches at Goddard College in Vermont, where he recently designed a program for homeschooled teens.

STUART G. SHANKER is Distinguished Research Professor of Philosophy and Psychology at York University in Toronto, Canada. He is director of the Milton and Ethel Harris Research Initiative at York University, an interdisciplinary center for developmental, evolutionary, and clinical studies; director of the Council of Human Development, an international initiative whose goals are to promote the early development of children; chair for Canada of the Interdisciplinary Council of Learning and Developmental Disorders; chair of the Scientific Review Board of the Great Ape Trust of Iowa; and a member of the Steering Committee of the *Psychoanalytic Diagnostic Manual,* which will be published in early 2006. Among his recent publications are *The First Idea* (with Stanley Greenspan, 2004); *Child Development,* 2nd Canadian edition (with Laura Berk, 2005); *Apes, Language and the Human Mind* (with Sue Savage-Rumbaugh and Talbot Taylor, 1998); and *Wittgenstein's Remarks on the Foundations of AI* (1998).

SANDRA STEINGRABER is a biologist, writer, and cancer survivor. Currently a Distinguished Visiting Scholar at Ithaca College, she is the author of *Living Downstream: An Ecologist Looks at Cancer and the Environment,* and *Having Faith: An Ecologist's Journey to Motherhood.* In 2001, Steingraber was awarded the biennial Rachel Carson Leadership Award from Carson's alma mater, Chatham College. An enthusiastic public speaker, Steingraber has given presentations on children's environmental health before United Nations delegates and members of the European Union's parliament. She serves on the board of the Science and Environmental Health Network and as a contributing editor to *Orion* magazine.

PAULO WANGOOLA is the Nabyama of Mpambo at the Afrikan Multiversity. *Nabyama* in Kisoga—the language of Busoga, an ancient kingdom located in Uganda—means the one who is entrusted with the strategic secrets of the community. Wangoola studied at Makerere University in Kampala, Uganda, and the University of Southhampton in England. He has been both a Minister of State and a political exile. He served for many years as the Secretary-General of the African Association for Literacy and Adult Education based in Nairobi, Kenya. He has been a major spokesperson in organizations of African civil society and is a much-admired speaker at conferences around the world. He is devoted to the creation of Mpambo, a grassroots community-based center for the promotion and revitalization of Afrikan traditional thought. He is the author of many articles, chapters, and books on learning and community in Africa.

LORNA B. WILLIAMS is a member of the Lil'wat First Nation, Mount Currie, British Columbia, Canada. She is program director of Aboriginal Teacher Education and a Canada Research Chair in Indigenous Knowledge and Learning in the Faculty of Education and Department of Linguistics. She worked for the Ministry of Education as director of the Aboriginal Education Enhancements Branch for three years where she directed research, policy development, and implementation in all areas of education for Aboriginal students. Prior to this appointment, she worked as a First Nations Education Specialist with the Vancouver School Board.

Lorna codirected *First Nations: The Circle Unbroken,* a 23-program educational video series. She has written children's books and teachers' guides, and developed Lil'wat Language curriculum to teach people to read and write this language, which was oral until 1973. She has organized and trained teachers within and outside the public school system in applications based on Feuerstein's theory of structural cognitive modifiability and mediated learning. In recognition of her achievements she has been presented with the Outstanding Teacher Award, the Dedicated to Kids Award, and in 1992 was invested into the Order of British Columbia.

Selected Bibliography

Raffi Cavoukian

Arnold, Johann Christopher. *Endangered: Your Child in a Hostile World.* Farmington, PA: Plough, 2000.

Beland, Pierre. *Beluga: A Farewell to Whales.* New York: Lyons and Burford, 1996.

Berry, Thomas. *The Great Work: Our Way Into the Future.* New York: Bell Tower, 1999.

Berry, Wendell. *Citizenship Papers.* Washington, DC: Shoemaker and Hoard, 2003.

Bohm, David. *Wholeness and the Implicate Order.* London, Boston: Routledge and Kegan Paul, 1980.

Brown, Lester. *Plan B: Rescuing a Planet under Stress and a Civilization in Trouble.* New York: Norton, 2003.

Cavanaugh, John, and Jerry Mander, eds. *Alternatives to Economic Globalization: A Better World Is Possible.* San Francisco: Berrett-Koehler, 2004.

The Dalai Lama. *Ethics for the New Millennium.* New York: Riverhead, 1999.

——— with Fabian Ouaki. *Imagine All the People: A Conversation with the Dalai Lama.* Somerset, MA: Wisdom Publications, 1999.

Dyer, Gwynne. *Future: Tense—The Coming World Order.* Toronto: McClelland and Stewart, 2004.

Earle, Sylvia A. *Sea Change: A Message of the Oceans.* New York: Fawcett, 1995.

Goodall, Jane. *Harvest of Hope: A Guide to Mindful Eating.* Lebanon, IN: Warner Books, 2006.

Hertzman, C., and D. Keating, eds. *Developmental Health and the Wealth of Nations.* New York: Gilford, 1999.

Klein, Naomi. *No Logo: Taking Aim at the Brand Bullies.* New York: Picador, 1999.

Lewis, Stephen. *Race Against Time.* Toronto: Anansi, 2005.

Lipton, Bruce. *The Biology of Belief: Unleashing the Power of Consciousness, Matter, and Miracles.* Santa Rosa: Mountain of Love/Elite Books, 2005.

Machel, Graca. *The Impact of War on Children.* Vancouver: UBC Press, 2001.

Maslow, Abraham. *The Farther Reaches of Human Nature.* New York: Viking, 1971.

Mustard, Fraser, and Margaret Norrie McCain. *Early Years Study: Reversing the Real Brain Drain.* Toronto: The Ontario Children's Secretariat / Founders Network, 1999.

Pearce, Joseph Chilton. *The Biology of Transcendence: A Blueprint of the Human Spirit.* Rochester, VT: Park Street Press, 2002.

Postman, Neil. *The Disappearance of Childhood.* New York: Vintage Books, 1994.

———. *Amusing Ourselves to Death.* New York: Penguin, 1985.

Roszak, T., M. E. Gomes, and A. D. Kanner, eds. *Ecopsychology: Restoring the Earth, Healing the Mind.* San Francisco: Sierra Club Books, 1995.

Schlosser, Eric. *Fast Food Nation.* Boston: Houghton Mifflin, 2001.

Schor, Juliet. *Born to Buy: The Commercialized Child and the New Consumer Culture.* New York: Scribner, 2004.

Shiva, Vandana. *Water Wars: Privatization, Pollution and Profit.* Cambridge, MA: South End Press, 2002.

Talbot, Michael. *The Holographic Universe.* New York: HarperCollins, 1991.

Wright, Ronald. *A Short History of Progress.* New York: Carroll & Graf, 2005.

Zohar, Dana. *The Quantum Self.* New York: Flamingo/HarperCollins, 1991.

Index